Power, Process and Participation:

Tools for Change

Power, Process and Participation:

Tools for Change

EDITED BY

Rachel Slocum, Lori Wichhart, Dianne Rocheleau, and
Barbara Thomas-Slayter

Intermediate Technology Publications 1995

Intermediate Technology Publications Ltd
103-105 Southampton Row, London WC1B 4HH, UK

© Intermediate Technology Publications 1995

A CIP record for this book is available from
the British Library

ISBN 1 85339 303 7

Printed in the UK by SRP, Exeter

Contents

Editors:
> Rachel Slocum
> Lori Wichhart
> Dianne Rocheleau
> Barbara Thomas-Slayter

Contributors:
> Renuka Bery
> Nina Bhatt
> Florence Butegwa
> Gouri Choudhury
> Claire Cummings
> Andrea Lee Esser
> Elizabeth Fabel
> Cornelia Butler Flora
> Louise Fortmann
> Luisa Maria Rivera Izabal
> Ratna Kapur
> Sara L. Kindon
> Dieuwke Klaver
> Johannes Knapp
> David Glyn Nixon
> Katie Nye
> Mark Poffenberger
> Maria Protz
> Susan Quass
> Laurie Ross
> William Rugumamu
> Dale Shields
> Octavia Taylor
> Gwen Thomas
> Leah Wanjama
> Christel Weller-Molongua

Book design: Lori Wichhart and Mary Schmuki

Book layout: Mary Schmuki

About the editors and contributors

Dianne Rocheleau: I am a geographer and political ecologist and have worked with rural people in the United States, Dominican Republic, and Kenya to understand, document and apply knowledge, practice and policy in agriculture, forestry and land use ecology for the last twenty years. Much of my time has been spent interpreting across the boundaries of very distinct sciences of ecology in encounters between people from someplace and 'scientists' from somewhere else. More recently I have focused on the connection between knowledge, environment and difference – by gender, class, ethnicity, race and other axes of power and identity – which shape people's relations to each other and to the living systems of which they are a part. I have begun to apply participatory research and planning methods in studies of land use change, political ecology and environmental justice, both in faraway places and in my home country. I have a Ph.D. from the University of Florida and am currently Assistant Professor of Geography at Clark University.

Rachel Slocum: I am currently conducting research on women's access to land in Niger and development policy. Following the example of my mother I have worked on human rights and development issues in various contexts for several years, including policy advocacy in Washington D.C. with the Church World Service/Lutheran World Relief Office. After receiving my B.A. at McGill University I joined the Peace Corps and went to Niger to learn about 'development'. I have since returned to West Africa and have spent nearly five years in Mali and Niger. In working on the English and French versions of this book I have become interested in the cultural dimensions of social and gender analysis within West African contexts. After completing my M.A. in International Development and Social Change I will pursue a Ph.D. in Geography (both at Clark University). I intend to work as a human rights and social justice advocate within the field of development policy.

Barbara Thomas-Slayter: As a political scientist my formal training has led me to comparative politics, with a focus on local institutions in Asia and Africa, peasant–state relations, and women and public policy. However, for a number of years I have carried out research in a field which can best be described as political anthropology. I have become keenly interested in 'who gets what when and how' at the local level with attention to inequities determined by gender, class, caste, religion, ethnicity or other variables. This interest has led quite naturally to studying ways to rectify some of these injustices through both individual and community empowerment. The collaborative work on this book with scholars and practitioners both within and outside Clark has been a logical culmination of these interests. My B.A. is from Bryn Mawr College and my Ph.D. from Brandeis University. I am currently Professor and Director of the International Development Program at Clark University.

Lori Wichhart: I am currently working as Director of the American High School in Skopje,

Macedonia. I hold a B.A. in Geography from the University of Iowa, and am completing my Masters thesis for an M.A. in International Development from Clark University. I have served as publications editor and manager for the Program in International Development at Clark University, and have worked as a volunteer speaker with Planned Parenthood of Central Massachusetts, as a Development Communications Design Specialist for the Academy for Educational Development in Washington D.C., and as a Peace Corps volunteer in Lesotho.

The editors can be contacted through the International Development Program, Clark University, Worcester, Massachusetts, 01610-1477, USA.

The contributors

Renuka Bery is a project director and development video trainer with Communication for Change. She worked on family planning and adolescent health isssues with Columbia University in New York and the Association for Reproductive Health in Ibadan, Nigeria while getting her master's degree in public health. Renuka Bery has also consulted the PBS series 'Where in the World is Carmen Sandiego?', advised Apple Computer's Multimedia Lab on the Visual Almanac, developed the international network at Internews and assisted the introduction of video teleconferencing at Kaiser Permanente in Oakland, CA. She has lived, worked and travelled extensively in Asia, Africa, Europe and the United States.

Nina Bhatt is a rural sociologist with the Human Resources and Social Development Division of the World Bank's Asia Technical Department, working on participatory methodologies for micro-finance and group-based lending. Nina received an M.A. in International Development from Clark University and has worked with the Ford Foundation in New Delhi on evaluation of rural banking and micro-enterprise, and on water management projects.

Florence Butegwa (LL.B, LL.M) has had wide experience in community legal education in many African countries. She is currently the Regional Coordinator and Executive Director of Women in Law and Development in Africa (WiLDAF), a pan-African network of organizations and individuals working to promote women's rights in 18 African countries. WiLDAF, P.O. Box 4622, Harare, Zimbabwe.

Gouri Choudhury is one of a core group of five women who founded the Action India Women's Programme in 1979 which co-ordinates the grassroots network for women's empowerment, Sabla Sangh. Action India is a non-governmental organization working for social change in the slums of Delhi, India. Gouri works with Bharati, co-ordinator of the Community Health Programme. Since 1986, Bharati has spent half her time working with the women in Saharanpur in their struggle for forest rights. Gouri also works with Devi Kripa and Reshma who are community health workers and organizers of the Sabla Sangh in the 'resettlement' colonies in Delhi. A feminist consciousness and perspective in living, loving and work keeps them together in their dream for a better world. Action India 5/24 Jangpura B., New Delhi 110014.

Claire Cummings is a graduate student in the Women's Studies Ph.D. Program at Clark University, researching issues of gender and class. She has been an activist in the women's movement since 1968, and has taught Sociology, Psychology, and Gender Roles at Newbury College for twenty years. She has been co-editor of *Survival News* for eight years. Women Studies Program, Clark University, 950 Main Street, Worcester, MA 01610.

Andrea Lee Esser has her Masters in International Development from Clark University. She works as a researcher and development professional in the Philippines and Vietnam. Her areas of expertise include rural development, natural resource management and gender.

Elizabeth Fabel of Communications for Literacy and Health is an independent development media producer and trainer. She holds a B.A. in Cultural Anthropology from the University of Massachusetts at Amherst and an M.A. in International Development from Clark University. Currently, Ms Fabel is based in Dharamsala, India, and is working on a video with the Tibetan Women's Association. She has previously worked with the Institute for Development Research and consulted with NGOs in India, Nepal, the Philippines, Thailand and PVOs in the United States. c/o 620 Bay Rd., Amherst, MA 01002 USA.

Cornelia Butler Flora is director of the North Central Regional Center for Rural Development, located at Iowa State University. Previously she was head of the Sociology Department at Virginia Polytechnic Institute and State University, a University Distinguished Professor at Kansas State University and a program officer for the Ford Foundation, where, among other duties, she developed women's programs for Latin America. A past president of the Rural Sociological Society, she is author and editor of a number of books including *Rural Communities: Legacy and Change, Rural Policies for the 1990s,* and *Sustainable Agriculture in Temperate Zones*. Her B.A. is from the University of California at Berkeley, and her M.Sc. and Ph.D. degrees are from Cornell University.

Louise Fortmann is a rural sociologist in the University of California at Berkeley's Department of Environmental Science, Policy and Management. She conducts research in eastern and southern Africa and California on property, poverty, and community management of natural resources. She is very grateful to the women of Mhondoro for not laughing too hard at her inability to milk cows or headload woman-sized amounts of firewood. Department of Environmental Science, Policy and Management, Division of Conservation and Management, 145 Mulford Hall, University of California, Berkeley, CA 94720.

Luisa Maria Rivera Izabal has been involved in social work for 36 years. When she finished her studies in Social Work, she went to the countryside to work with men and women farmers. This was a turning point in her life; she discovered women's oppression and the need to work for social and economic change. She is now involved in gender and development work. Oxfam Tabasco 262, Colonia Roma, Mexico, DF.

Ratna Kapur, feminist lawyer and co-director of the Centre for Feminist Legal Research, conducts legal literacy training for women. She has also written extensively on issues of feminist legal theory; notions of equality in Indian Constitutional law; the meanings of secularism in India; and the impact of religious fundamentalism on women's rights in India. Currently she is editing an anthology on feminism and law and co-authoring a book on feminism, law and familial ideology. B-12 Maharani Bagh, New Delhi-110 065.

Sara L. Kindon is a graduate of the University of Waterloo, Canada and the University of Durham, England. She is currently a lecturer in regional and development studies at Victoria University of Wellington, focusing on community participation, gender and environmental issues in Southeast Asia and the Pacific. She has worked with communities in Costa Rica and Indonesia, and is planning future research in Vietnam. In Aoteroa, New Zealand, she is working with Maori exploring leadership and training for sustainable community resource management. Department of Geography, Victoria University of Wellington, Wellington, New Zealand.

Dieuwke Klaver holds a Masters of Science in Comparative Household Science and Home Economics from the University of Wageningen. She has conducted studies in Uruguay on the position of women in the household and workplace and in Burkina Faso on savings and loan associations and household income use. As a technical assistant with the Dutch volunteer service (SNV), she worked to strengthen women's associations in a UNIFEM grinding mill project. Currently she is Advisor on Women and Development and Peasant Organizations in the Office of the Niger, a Malian parastatal promoting rice production. She is working on reinforcing farmers' organizations and integrating the gender approach in the programmes of the Office.

Johannes Knapp studied Public Administration and Economics at the University of Constance. Since 1983 he has worked for the German Agency for Technical Cooperation (GTZ) in rural development projects in Asia and Africa and has specialized in participatory methods of planning and implementing small community projects. He is currently working in Mali as project co-ordinator in the Promotion of Local Initiatives project, which gives particular emphasis to the participation of all gender, age, economic and ethnic groups. Present address, GTZ, B.P. 100, Bamako, Mali, Fax: 223-22-5188. Federburgstrasse 59, 88214, Ravensburg, Germany.

David Glyn Nixon received his Ph.D. in Cultural Anthropology from the University of

Massachusetts at Amherst. His areas of study include rural peoples of North America and Europe, ethnicity, immigration, political anthropology and social science methodology. He is currently conducting ethnographic research among Eastern European immigrants in the Connecticut River Valley of Massachusetts.

Katie Nye is currently completing a master's degree in the International Development Program at Clark University. She is interested in partnership-based development with particular attention to the social and environmental dynamics of South–North collaboration. Katie has worked in Tanzania and Kenya for two years, focusing on gender issues and constituency-based linkage programmes. She discovered, in working with both the East African and US partners, that while the aim of these programmes is to build long-term relationships leading to sustainable and equitable action in both communities, they often do not address issues of power, conflict and dissent within and between the partner groups and therefore do not achieve lasting and just social change. c/o International Development Program, Clark University, 950 Main St., Worcester, MA 01610.

Mark Poffenberger is a social scientist specializing in natural resource management issues in the Asia region. He has spent over twenty years in Asia, as a volunteer, researcher, consultant and Ford Foundation programme officer. He is currently Director of the Asia Sustainable Forest Management Network and is affiliated with the East West Center in Honolulu and the University of California, at Berkeley. Center for Southeast Asia Studies, International and Area Studies, University of California, 2223 Fulton #617, Berkeley, CA 94720.

Maria Protz is a communications practitioner and co-director of Mekweseh ('Make We Say' in patois) – a participatory communication organization based in St. Ann's Bay, Jamaica, that operates a rural video cooperative and publishes a quarterly newsletter on rural life in Jamaica. Through Mekweseh, she is working with women farmers in a number of rural communities and using various participatory media (drama, video, newsletters, oral histories and social photography) to bring indigenous agricultural knowledge (especially women's) into the design of sustainable and appropriate agricultural technologies for soil conservation and fertility. She is also currently enrolled in the Ph.D. by Research Program in the Agricultural Extension and Rural Development (AERDD) at Reading University in England and is conducting ethnographic research on the effectiveness of participatory media for bridging the gap between local and official scientific knowledge in agricultural decision-making. c/o Mekweseh, Box 299, St. Ann's Bay, Jamaica, West Indies.

Susan Quass is a feminist political activist, organizer and researcher with experience in anti-imperialistic, social justice and women's movements in the US, Asia and the Pacific. Currently she is exploring issues related to gender and human rights, women's access to and control of resources and participation in political discourse and decision-making, and theorizing the construction of women's international alliances and solidarity around issues of identity, accountability, gender and power. Susan holds a Masters in Environmental Engineering from Cornell University and a Certificate in Feminist Liberation Theology from the Women's Theological Center in Boston. 58 Fairmont St., Cambridge, MA 02139.

Laurie Ross is a recent graduate (M.A.) of the International Development Program at Clark University. As a member of the Ecology, Community Organization, and Gender (ECOGEN) research project, she completed field work in Zambrana-Chacuey, Dominican Republic. She wrote a thesis entitled 'The Partnership Between Grassroots Social Movements and Development Organizations: Strengthening Civil Society in Zambrana-Chacuey, Domincian Republic.' She is currently employed as a bilingual social researcher in Worcester, MA, USA.

William Rugumamu is a senior lecturer at the University of Dar es Salaam, Tanzania, where he is currently researching sustainable management and conservation strategies for semi-arid land resources in Tanzania. Department of Geography, University of Dar es Salaam, P.O. Box 35049, Dar es Salaam, Tanzania.

Dale Shields has conducted research in the Philippines with the Ecology, Community Organization, and Gender (ECOGEN) project, a joint endeavour of Clark University and Virginia Polytechnic Institute and State University, established to examine the role of gender in rural livelihood systems. She was a U.S. Peace Corps volunteer on Siquijor Island in the Philippines from 1987 to 1989 and holds a Masters degree in International Development and Social Change from Clark University.

Octavia Taylor attended Vassar College in Poughkeepsie, New York and holds an M.A. from the Clark University Program for International Development in Worcester, Massachusetts. She is currently a research associate with the Ecology, Community Organization, and Gender (ECOGEN) research project of Clark University. She has worked as a community organizer in US rural communities, building coalitions and networks around the issues of health, housing, education and welfare for children and families.

Gwen Thomas works with CARE in Costa Rica on the environmental project, PACA (Projecto Ambiental para Centro America), evaluating resource and environment projects supported by CARE throughout the region. She holds a Masters degree from the Yale School of Forestry and Environmental Science.

Leah Wanjama, a lecturer in the Department of Development Studies at Kenyatta University, holds a B.A. in Geography and an M.A. in Urban and Regional Planning for the University of Nairobi. She serves as the co-ordinator of the Gender Issues Action Team for Kenyatta University and is a member of the Executive Committee of the Kenya Red Cross Society where she serves on its committee for Women in Development Disaster Preparedness. Ms Wanjama works internationally as a gender trainer with FEMNET, the African Women's Development and Communication Network.

Christel Weller-Molongua studied Geography at the University of Trier and Agricultural Development at the University of Berlin. Since 1989, she has worked for the German Agency for Technical Cooperation (GTZ) in rural organization and the promotion of women. She is currently working in Mali for the GTZ project, Promotion of Local Initiatives, which uses participatory research, planning, implementation and evaluation with an emphasis on gender analysis. Im Suhl 1, 74405 Gaildorf 2, Germany.

Acknowledgements

The shape and content of *Power, Process and Participation: Tools for Change* grew out of a series of working group meetings beginning in December 1993 and involving Katie Nye, Susan Quass, Dianne Rocheleau, William Rugumamu, Rachel Slocum, Barbara Thomas-Slayter, and Lori Wichhart. Much of this book is based on the work and insights of Clark University professors: Barbara Thomas-Slayter, Professor and Director of the International Development Program, and Dianne Rocheleau, Assistant Professor of Geography in the Graduate School of Geography. Their work has been supported by the United States Agency for International Development (AID), the Ford Foundation, the Fulbright Scholar Program, the Rockefeller Foundation, and United Nations University. We are specifically indebted to the Women in Development Office and the Office of R&D/EID at AID which have provided support for the Ecology, Community Organization and Gender (ECOGEN) project within the Systems Approach to Regional Income and Sustainable Resource Assistance (SARSA) Cooperative Agreement. The views and interpretations in this publication are, of course, those of the contributors and editors.

In writing this book, we have drawn on the ECOGEN field manual, *Tools of Gender Analysis,* by Barbara Thomas-Slayter, Dale Shields, and Andrea Esser, as well as ECOGEN case studies by colleagues including professors, students and international professionals: Isabelle Asamba, Nina Bhatt, Gladys Buenavista, Cornelia Butler Flora, Ricardo Hernandez, Indira Koirala, Njoki Mbuthi, Alison Meares, Julio Morrobel, Elizabeth Oduor-Noah, Dianne Rocheleau, Mary Rojas, Laurie Ross, Karen Schofield, Dale Shields, Laju Shrestha, Anne Marie Urban, and Leah Wanjama. We would also like to acknowledge the work on Rapid Rural Appraisal and Participatory Rural Appraisal tools of Robert Chambers and Gordon Conway, both of Sussex University, Richard Ford of Clark University, and Charity Kabutha, formerly with Kenya's National Environment Secretariat and UNICEF and currently Regional Coordinator for the African Women Leaders in Agriculture and the Environment (AWLAE) of Winrock International.

We thank Mary Schmuki for contributing to the book's design, and undertaking the format and layout of the book. We are indebted to both Mary Schmuki and Eileen Reynolds for their careful attention to many of the critical details necessary for the successful completion of the book. We also thank Genese Sodikoff at Clark and Christel Weller-Molongua and Johannes Knapp in Mali for their support, encouragement and insightful comments. Finally, our acknowledgments would not be complete without a word of thanks to Intermediate Technology Publications' Managing Editor, Neal Burton, and Kim Daniel, Senior Book Editor, to whom we are most grateful for their patience, humour, and assistance.

Preface

Powerlessness, marginality, and dispossession are found in all corners of the world as are the courageous efforts of women and men confronting these situations.[1] Our intent in this manual is to provide tools which will give voice to those who – for whatever reasons – have been excluded from decision-making processes and control of critical resources. We hope that this book will provide facilitators from inside and outside communities with ways to encourage the less powerful to translate their experiences and interests into action to transform unjust relations. We also hope that it will clarify how common action can emerge in community settings, through recognition of difference in ways which are inclusive rather than exclusive. Our work is predicated on the assumption that valid approaches to development which address issues of sustainable livelihoods as well as justice and equity must begin with the perceptions and interests of all people involved, whether in the North or South.[2]

In Nagal Gaon, India, and Zambrana-Chacuey, Dominican Republic, people are engaged in reflection and action to change their lives or to confront change in their landscapes. In Mazvihwa, Zimbabwe, and Diak Lay, Indonesia, there are organizers, researchers and facilitators trying to encourage dialogue, discern important information and benefit the people with whom they work in a variety of ways. In New York City and Sapone, Burkina Faso, there are organizations, large and small, that seek to design better, more useful programmes and methods for their work in what is usually called development, a term which we think applies to social and economic change around the world. Our book is for these people: activists, researchers, organizers, and practitioners who seek to promote a community-based development that addresses the aspirations and concerns of people in the midst of change.

Power, Process and Participation: Tools for Change offers innovative, collaborative tools that integrate applied and analytical methods for consciousness-raising, information gathering, decision-making, advocacy and action. The tools are sensitive across all social categories, with particular attention to gender, and can be used to address the practical and strategic interests of the disadvantaged and disempowered.[3]

Power, Process and Participation: Tools for Change is both a tool book and an 'issues' book. The two, in our minds, cannot be separated. The issues that we raise are those which are embedded in the development process and confront anyone using these tools, whether or not they are acknowledged. The ones we cover include the ends and means of participation, uneven relations of power among participants, temporal context, spatial scale, and the array of organizations involved.

The tools are designed with particular emphasis on gender because it is a major – but often ignored – factor that determines who participates and who benefits from development. However, other dimensions of identity such as class, ethnicity, race, caste, religion, age and status have also been overlooked. Relations across space and time in the context of resource use, access and control, and decision-making power have largely been ignored, and changing the institutions that inhibit various groups, particularly women, from controlling their lives has not been a priority. Our book reminds the reader to be sensitive to these markers of identity and the issues we raise. Much, however, rests on the users of these tools – the facilitators – and their decisions whether or not to encourage group reflection and action as well as a more just distribution of decision-making power and control of resources.

During the 1993-94 academic year, a group of colleagues at Clark University, including both faculty and graduate students, conceptualized, designed, and, in large measure, wrote this book, which grows out of our collective interests in grassroots empowerment, in participatory development, and gender analysis. Much of our work rests on years of previous work at Clark University in the Program for International Development and Social Change and the Graduate School of Geography and in other places throughout the world. Our work has conceptual roots in alternative models of development, such as those offered by David Korten or Dharam Ghai, in some of the post-modern critiques of development, such as the analyses of Arturo Escobar and Pramod Parajuli, and in feminist perspectives on development and social justice of scholars/activists such as Vandana Shiva, Bina Agarwal, and Chandra Mohanty.[4]

Many authors have contributed to this project. We have sought contributions from colleagues, both scholars and practitioners, who, like ourselves, have been involved in 'grassroots' community activism, research, and development. Contributors come from a wide range of backgrounds and, for the most part, provide examples of tools they have used in their work. Their contributions confirm that community change is occurring in many countries. By no means, however, do we claim a comprehensive view of the creativity and effort in 'development' processes, social action, and advocacy. In small and large ways, women and men confront oppression, exploitation, poverty, environmental degradation, resource deprivation, and many injustices occurring from local to global scales.

This manual has several attributes making it unusual among publications dealing with participatory methods, social analysis, and people's empowerment. First, it involves activists, practitioners, and academics with extensive research and training in the area of participatory methods and NGO activities. Second, it provides a historical context, offering a brief overview of participatory approaches to development. Third, it includes discussion of important contextual issues such as power relationships within a community and between local institutions and outsiders. Fourth, the style and approach are interactive, stimulating self-reflection by all parties – community members, NGO staff, organizational leaders, and other professionals. Fifth, it incorporates the facilitator as well as community participants or group members into the process. Sixth, it emphasizes the opportunity for using multi-media tools to strengthen local groups and promote community empowerment. Finally, it is 'user-friendly' with graphics and other visuals making it accessible to the reader.

We hope that you will find this book a valuable one. We invite you to give us your feedback, your suggestions, and your stories for future use in this process involving people – North and South – in social and economic change.

Rachel Slocum, Lori Wichhart, Dianne Rocheleau, Barbara Thomas-Slayter

PART I

Definitions, History and Issues

CHAPTER 1

Participation, empowerment, and sustainable development

Rachel Slocum and Barbara Thomas-Slayter

Popular participation in development is broadly understood as active involvement of people in making decisions about the implementation of processes, programmes and projects which affect them.[1] Participation, as it has existed in practice, has often been less than ideal, and the term has covered a wide variety of activities. Over the decades, participatory methodologies have been employed carefully by some and abused by others. Recently, participation has been rediscovered by such diverse actors as the World Bank, universities, national and international non-governmental organizations (NGOs), religious groups and bilateral development agencies.

In actuality, participation can be for purposes of transforming a present system or for simply maintaining the status quo. Much behaviour that passes for participation is in fact intended to maintain the system, giving no more than lip service to the notion of change. As noted by Dianne Rocheleau:

> Uncritiqued, participation in theory and practice can help to foster a positive image of development-as-usual, which has been somewhat less than benign with many of the world's people over the past 30 years. Participation can be a wolf in sheep's clothing – a vehicle for a new form of manipulation or intervention. It might even serve as a 'Trojan horse' to bring a new level of global cultural, ecological and economic restructuring processes directly to local communities, by-passing potential buffers and pre-empting critical review by national agencies or the communities themselves.[2]

Usually the terms participation and sustainable development are not far apart in development literature. The concept of sustainable development came from a paradigm that favours growth without attention to equity and social responsibility. The focus on sustainable development has diverted attention from the gross inequities that exist between and among the people of the South and North partly as a result of this paradigm.[3] This perspective locates the problem in the

3

South as a lack of development – 'a reminder of an undesirable and undignified condition'. [4] The concept of sustainable development, as it is typically used, does not challenge injustice in political, social and economic relations between and within the North and South, and justice and fairness are omitted from the definition. It does not analyse how and why sustainability means different things in different parts of the world.

The concept of sustainable development glosses over the disproportionate distribution of power and resource use within and between the North and South. Instead, it seems to imply, 'given the range of resources available to you poor people, we development experts will give you appropriate technology, the education we think you could use, and programmes that will help you to run your economies better'. With these projects, people will be able to sustain themselves at a particular level that is just enough to keep many of them from coming to the doorsteps of Northern countries hoping for a better life. According to Alan Fowler, this is part of the globalization of social welfare. He observes that the message from the 1993 UNDP Human Development Report is 'if the North does not wish its own quality of life to be threatened by Southern poverty, for example through migration of poor people and their illnesses, it is in its interest to attenuate the hardships faced by the world economy's functional underclass.' [5] Sustainable development theories that take the idea of sustainability seriously would recognize that much of the problem lies in unjust ideologies and practices of the North. A new concept of sustainable development would include social, economic and political justice and encourage the empowerment of disenfranchised people everywhere.

The authors of this book are concerned about both empowerment and participation. We regard empowerment as a process through which individuals, as well as local groups and communities, identify and shape their lives and the kind of society in which they live. Empowerment can be experienced on an individual level or in terms of the household, local groups, community or a larger entity. Empowerment means that people are able to organize and influence change on the basis of their access to knowledge, to political processes and to financial, social, and natural resources.

Our approach to people's empowerment focuses on ways to mobilize local resources, engage diverse social groups in decision-making, identify patterns which eliminate poverty, and build consensus and accountability. It integrates social analysis and participatory methodologies, identifies issues for both the researcher/facilitator and the community, and offers tools which are formulated, operationalized and tested in rural settings. Such an approach can assist long-term capacity-building and empowerment for development agencies, local communities, and the individuals, households and institutions within those communities.

We argue that individual and community empowerment, as well as the elements of programmes and projects, will be strengthened significantly by involving local people in the problem definition, data collection, decision-making and implementation processes. Such involvement encourages community awareness, understanding and commitment, facilitates decision-making, coalition formation, and consensus building, and promotes collaboration among outside researchers or development workers and the community, a co-operation which can assist processes of empowerment and sustainable development.

Participation as a process of empowerment can help to amplify traditionally unacknowledged voices. It can strengthen the confidence of all members of a group in the knowledge and capacity of each and may foster the ability to question and contribute to both local and international systems of knowledge. This form of participation implies 'constant readjustment and on-going information exchange, discussion, and conflict management or resolution under complex, changing and highly uncertain conditions'.[6] It involves consciousness-raising and knitting together a 'shared understanding of problems and a vision for the future that leads to commitment and ownership by the community'.[7]

The intention of a transformative approach is to move control over resources and institutions to disadvantaged groups, which have been excluded from such control. It requires an enabling environment, as well as transparency with processes of decision-making open to public view. It demands accountability, both politically and financially, and freedom of information or the 'right to know.'[8]

This book is about using field methods to analyse social relations as a means to encourage participation of all groups in dialogue and decision-making on competing and complementary needs and interests. However, participatory methods cannot guarantee socially just development. Much depends on objectives, power relations, and the nature of specific institutions, ideologies and personalities.

Currently, many participatory methodologies, such as Participatory Rural Appraisal (PRA) or Participation and Learning Methods (PALM), do not address issues of social relations, the exclusion of particular social groups, or gender. Questions about who participates in community decisions are just beginning to be asked. Rarely do these methodologies take into account gender analysis, gender-based differences in labour allocation, and gender differences in access to and control over resources and their benefits. They ignore the vital roles that women play in maintaining the social and ecological fabric of communities, overlooking their knowledge and experience. There is no single 'women's perspective'; class, ethnicity, religion and other characteristics lead to different and distinct experiences for all women. Gender is only one of many key variables defining access and control. Others vary according to the situation and may include ethnicity, race, caste, age or other locally-specific factors. In most settings there are groups which have inadequate voice in decision-making processes concerning their community.

While the book identifies ways to encourage participation across all social groups, it pays particular attention to gender. Gender shapes the opportunities and constraints that women and men face in securing viable livelihoods and building strong communities across cultural, political, economic and ecological settings. Gender influences the roles and relationships of human beings throughout all dimensions of activity. A focus on gender in community-level development activities and decision-making is long overdue.

Gender is central to positioning both men and women *vis-à-vis* institutions that determine access to land, to other resources, and to the wider economy. Conceptualizing gender is essential for disaggregating and interpreting information about the functioning of households and community organizations.[9] With the growing numbers of female-headed households throughout the world and the increasing role of women as household providers in declining rural economies, it is essential to incorporate gender into the discussion of resources and sustainable development.

Using this book

Part I, Definitions, History, and Issues, is comprised of Chapters 1 to 3. It focuses on some of the broad issues underlying the theme of this book. The first chapter offers some definitions and perspectives on North–South relations in the context of participatory community change which must be clarified before undertaking activities at the community level. Chapter 2, A brief history of participatory methodologies, puts our contribution to participatory methodologies and social analysis in a historical context. In this chapter we introduce the philosophical roots of participation, such as Paolo Freire's conscientization approach, and specific methodologies such as Participation and Learning methods (PALM), Participatory Rural Appraisal (PRA), and Training for Transformation. We also introduce our particular approach to analysing gender and social relations. Chapter 3, Participation in context: key questions, explores some important issues that are embedded in the development process but which are often overlooked. They include the facilitator's agenda, power relations within and between groups, institutional issues, sliding scales of access, use and control, and the temporal context. A grasp of these issues is critical for anyone concerned with encouraging environmental and social change locally or in the broader socio-economic and political context.

Part II, Methods and Ethics in Our Research and in Our Use of the Media, includes Chapters 4 and 5. Chapter 4, Women's renderings of rights and space: reflections on feminist research methods, explores two areas of feminist ethical concern: honouring local people's knowledge, and empowering women through recognizing their knowledge. Chapter 5, Media ethics, considers a variety of questions concerning the use of media tools in ethical ways.

Part III, Tools for Environmental and Social Change, consists of the tools themselves. Chapter 6, How to use the tools and how to facilitate, opens with an introduction which offers suggestions on using the tools and facilitating the various activities recommended. This chapter is devoted to the tools which are arranged in alphabetical order and cross-referenced according to the purposes for which each can be used. Each tool is structured to provide facilitators with a description of the purpose of the tool; materials needed for carrying out the activity; a step-by-step description of the processes involved in facilitating the activity; often there is also an illustration, such as an institutional diagram or maps, and suggested questions for interviewers. Also included is an example of the tool in use in a specific setting. Finally, each tool section contains a 'see also' note which gives the user options for constructing a series of activities using different combinations of tools.

Choosing your tools

The selection of tools for use together depends upon the purpose of the activity. Throughout, however, we recognize that the tools identified can be used in more than one way and, often, for more than one purpose. Indeed, it is essential that facilitators adapt these tools to fit the context. Tools are only a starting point and are not meant to be followed word for word, step by step.

Some of the tools are excellent for consciousness-raising. One premise of this book is that raising awareness on both an individual and a community-wide level is an important part of an empowering process. We observe that there is a need for consciousness-raising in many communities as a foundation for participation. We include a number of tools that focus on ways to bring disadvantaged or excluded groups into decision-making processes. We include tools leading to legal rights awareness and to self-confidence in dealing with authority. These tools can be adapted to raise awareness not only about gender but also about other dimensions of identity such as class, race, and ethnicity.

Another set of tools helps with identifying resources and gathering information. These tools facilitate discussion and an awareness of issues of power relations, access to, and control of available resources. The user and the participants will be able to see how these issues manifest themselves across lines of gender, ethnicity, age, class and religion. These tools help researchers and community activists, as well as policy-makers and planners, to discern the strategic interests and practical needs of a particular group or constellation of groups, and to design policies and programmes accordingly.

Some tools are particularly relevant for participatory research methods. The tools best suited for these purposes include focus group interviews, various mapping techniques and traditional tools, such as household interviews, which can be approached in new interactive, participatory ways.

Action takes place at different levels and in different contexts. Some tools can be part of the project cycle, while others are useful for recognizing, managing and resolving conflict, or for scaling up, linking up, and advocacy.

Development theatre, photography, video, radio and print are all types of media which can be used by people to present new ideas, to clarify an argument, to advocate, to raise consciousness, to educate, or to promote community development efforts. Used alone or in combination, different communication methods can stimulate discussions about issues, and raise awareness of problems and their solutions.

In sum, we are designing new tools and adapting existing methods in order to identify ways to:

- Collaborate with local groups to design action strategies and processes for social change bringing a more just future;

- Facilitate community management of resources and community capacity-building in ways that address the practical and strategic interests of the disadvantaged, in community decision-making and organization;

- Promote stronger local groups and provide them with the tools/means to direct their own 'development' process;

- Promote a process of heightened group awareness of the social variables which shape access to and control over resources within a group or community;

- Gather data within a participatory, socially-sensitive framework.

Conclusion

To ensure effective, participatory community action, approaches to development and empowerment must identify the various forms of stratification and difference and the ways in which they are translated into voice or silence in the context of common decisions and actions. They must offer ways to conceptualize and analyse the implications of these differences for people's life choices, as well as for specific programmes and projects. They should enable communities to incorporate that information into their decision-making processes and action plans. We hope that these tools will contribute to a process of strengthening individual and group capacities for common action to resolve conflicts and to address shared concerns.

CHAPTER 2

A brief history of participatory methodologies

Barbara Thomas-Slayter

This overview of participatory methodologies first offers a glimpse of the origins and nature of participation, as we have viewed it over the last half century. Second, it introduces the concept of 'people-centred' or transformative participation. Third, it reviews six approaches to participation and the models and methods characteristic of each approach. This survey is merely illustrative. Its purpose is to give the reader an idea of the range of experience and ideas available. After this, there is a discussion of our conceptualization of ways to link participatory methods with analysis of gender and other social relations.

Traditional approaches

Historically, there have been three approaches to participation: (a) people's organizations and co-operatives, (b) community development or *animation rurale,* and (c) guided participation in large-scale projects. The first category contains a wide range of people's activities including welfare agencies, membership organizations, and co-operatives.[1] Relief and welfare organizations arise out of a long history of assistance to victims of war, drought, or other disasters. The aim is to supply relief and welfare goods and activities, and the only participation required is that of the needy in receipt of benefits. Many NGOs fall into this category; others are attempting to work with membership organizations in a bridging, support or linking capacity, often without a clear idea about the nature of local empowerment and participation.

Co-operatives are found throughout much of the world as a means to pool members' economic resources for their benefit. They vary widely in structure and purpose and include such activities as marketing associations, credit unions, consumer societies, or producer co-ops. While they are formed with the intention of mobilizing the potentials of collective power, they often have strong top-down sponsorship by the state rather than local recognition of the benefits of collective action. Often they benefit larger, more prosperous farmers rather than the poorer members of the community.

Membership organizations include a wide range of local associations, and sometimes larger federations, formed around specific tasks, such as a water users' association; around the needs or interests of a particular group, such as a tenants' union or an ethnic or women's or youth association; or around multiple tasks, such as a neighbourhood association. In some cases popular social movements may give rise to associations and federations such as peasant land reform and self-help groups which also fall within this category. These groups operate largely by consensus or persuasion and are generally more oriented toward public benefits rather than private, for-profit enterprises, although some may encompass co-operative ventures within a broader array of activities.

Community development and *animation rurale* are two types of programmes in which the state has promoted participation by local residents in development activities. Emerging from colonial roots in many parts of the world, community development and the French *animation rurale* are approaches whereby local communities are organized to address problems of development with limited capital assistance and outside expertise. Usually the French *animation rurale* recruited local people as facilitators, while the British community development system organized a nationwide, professionalized extension service. Many regard community development as naive, assuming homogeneity among the various local interests, promoting government projects which have been planned by central bureaucracies, and ignoring the underlying causes of poverty.

A third general approach to participation seeks to 'include people in the planning and implementation of development projects which are usually externally initiated, funded, and ultimately controlled, creating a working relationship between development authorities and the rural population'.[2] While these efforts cover a wide range, from essentially community-centred to largely government-centred approaches to popular participation, ultimately it is the professional planners who determine levels of people's participation in these arrangements.

Over recent decades these approaches to development have been the target of serious criticism as their shortcomings have become increasingly evident. Usually such approaches to development have been top down and unsustainable. Data have been taken out of the community; planning and project design have been external to the community. Among the best-known critics of 'participation' in this top-down mode are Robert Chambers, Norman Uphoff, and David Korten.[3] Cohen and Uphoff[4] reflect an early concern to bring people into participation in development programmes and projects. They emphasize that participation includes: (a) involvement in decision-making processes about what can be done; (b) involvement in implementing programmes and decisions by contributing various resources or managing specific organizations or activities; (c) sharing in the benefits of development programmes; and (d) involvement in efforts to evaluate such programmes.

Perhaps the most obvious criticism of the traditional approaches to participation concerns the ease with which they become manipulative or even coercive. At best they may help to develop local capacities and lead to local responsibility for a project which is based on local wishes. At worst, they satisfy bureaucratic imperatives, keep local people in a passive subordinate position, and cause dissatisfaction and frustration over implementation of participatory approaches to development.

Many of the analyses of participation have limited their focus to development programmes and projects without looking at the broader issues of empowerment which underlie the immediate problem.

People-centred perspectives

The people-centred critique of these traditional methods of participation casts a broader net. It focuses on issues of power and control. It is concerned about the nature of the society in which programmes and projects are developed, rather than the technical and managerial aspects of organizations and participation in them. 'Inescapably, where development is concerned,' assert researchers from the Coady International Institute, 'participation is about power, an increase in the power of the disadvantaged.'[5]

The alternatives to traditional approaches to participation are inspired by the works of Paolo Freire, whose processes of conscientization lead to people's awareness of the structural causes of poverty and help build consensus and action based on individual creativity and knowledge.[6] E.F. Schumacher's *Small is Beautiful* and Ignacy Sachs's *The Discovery of the Third World* have also contributed to this process with their notions of alternative approaches to organizing community life and livelihoods.[7] In the United States, the Cornell Rural Development committee has pioneered both theoretical and empirical research in an effort to understand participation, local organizations and local institutional development.[8] Korten, writing in 1980, conceptualized the 'learning process approach', in which an essential component of the inductive style is to 'embrace error' and learn from one's mistakes, as an alternative to the 'blueprint' approach.[9] Korten and Klass have put forth people-centred as opposed to production-centred approaches to development, while Robert Chambers and other colleagues at the Institute for Development Studies at the University of Sussex in the UK have written over a twenty-year period on ways to put rural people first in the development process.[10] Central to these approaches is the belief that ordinary people are capable of critical reflection and analysis and that their knowledge is relevant and necessary.

11

Empowerment and transformation involving real social change inevitably lead to the possibility of conflict and confrontation. In practice, those who advocate participation make fine distinctions between transformation and amelioration. 'Short of revolution, participatory development programmes are almost always going to be vulnerable to charges of being merely reformist.'[11] For people's organizations, community organizers, and facilitators alike, the major challenges remain: to empower without being paternalistic, to enable without being top-down, to eliminate structural constraints along with patterns of passivity, to find realistic options, and to organize practical action.

Illustrative models and methods

Participatory Action Research

Participatory Action Research (PAR) involves three elements: research, education, and socio-political action. It is:

> an experiential methodology for the acquisition of serious and reliable knowledge upon which to construct power, or countervailing power, for the poor, oppressed and exploited groups and social classes – the grassroots – and for their authentic organizations and movements. Its purpose is to enable oppressed groups and classes to acquire sufficient creative and transforming leverage as expressed in specific projects, acts and struggles to achieve goals of social transformation.[12]

The techniques used in PAR involve: collective research; critical recovery of history; valuing and applying folk culture; and production and diffusion of new knowledge. It is thus hoped that a self-conscious people, those who are currently poor and oppressed, will progressively transform their environment by their own praxis. In this process others may play a catalytic and supportive role but will not dominate.[13]

A well known model for Participatory Action Research is the Community Information and Planning System (CIPS).[14] According to the CIPS model, a development intervention must be able to educate, organize, and provide for the basic socio-economic needs of the community if it is to be effective. The goal of CIPS is a well organized community which is able to do participatory research, planning, and project implementation. In this system the community carries out research, planning, implementation and management in which a local research group is trained and conducts a study of the problems suggested by the community.

Data are returned to the community for analysis, correction, and modification. This approach has been developed by the Philippine Partnership for the Development of Human Resources in Rural Areas (PhilDHRRA).

Methods for Active Participation

Along with other alternative approaches to participation, the Methods for Active Participation (MAP) methodology is predicated on the agency of rural people.[15] The MAP approach involves a two-day planning seminar in which participants consider their vision for the programme's activity, their sense of the obstacles to achieving that vision, their views about strategies and tactics which can address the obstacles, and specifics of implementation. MAP is an approach of the Institute of Cultural Affairs, a global network of affiliated, non-profit, non-governmental organizations with headquarters in Brussels.

Participatory Rural Appraisal

Participatory Rural Appraisal (PRA) is a cross-disciplinary, cross-sectoral approach to engaging communities in development through interactive and participatory processes. PRA builds on the techniques of Rapid Rural Appraisal pioneered by Gordon Conway and Robert Chambers to involve rural communities in their own needs assessment, problem identification and ranking, strategy for implementation, and community action plan.[16] It utilizes a wide range of tools, often within a focus group discussion format, to elicit spatial, time-related and social or institutional data. PRA has been widely used in Kenya by Egerton University and Clark University and has been revised and expanded by both these institutions, the Institute for Development Studies, and the International Institute for Environment and Development (IIED) in a number of countries around the world for environmentally sound development planning by rural communities.[17]

Training for Transformation

Training for Transformation (TFT) originated in Zimbabwe as a Freirean approach to enabling people to understand the structural causes of their problems.[18] A series of resource books and manuals emphasizes small group interactions and a process of self-discovery through exploration of key questions in innovative forms such as games, role play, drama, and discussions. TFT focuses on the links between development and education for liberating people from all that oppresses them. It is interested in systems which perpetuate poverty and oppression and in ways to

transform society. It starts with basic individual skills of diagnosis and analysis and the importance of team work. TFT has its roots in the DELTA training programme started in Kenya in 1974 by Anne Hope and Sally Timmel. DELTA stands for Development Education and Leadership Teams in Action. Its roots are in Freirean critical awareness, human relations training in group work, organizational development, social analysis, and a conceptualization of transformation derived from liberation theology.[19]

Productivity Systems Assessment and Planning

Productivity Systems Assessment and Planning (PSAP) is an approach formulated in the Philippines for the purpose of organizing agrarian reform among farmers who have acquired security of tenure on their land. It involves a people's organization and a community organizer working together for data-gathering and analysis, consolidation of data and analysis of problems and opportunities, through 'visioning, validation, and planning.'[20] It uses techniques of participatory rural appraisal (PRA) that involve self-critical awareness and promote confidence in villagers' capacities to generate and analyse data, across spatial, temporal and social/institutional concerns.

Participation and Learning Methods

The participatory methodology known as PALM has many similarities to PRA. It has been associated in particular with MYRADA, an Indian NGO. The PALM approach is based on the assertion that people can collect large quantities of accurate information, order it, correct it, analyse it, and start the process of development if given the opportunity to do so.[21] PALM generates data using a variety of participatory approaches, including mapping with the villagers drawing the maps, wealth ranking, transects and a number of methods from the participatory rural appraisal repertoire. PALM focuses on the learning experience and efforts to understand traditional practices and systems in rural areas and their accompanying logic and values. There is a tendency to focus on issues that can yield hard data on technology issues rather than touch upon social relationships.[22] This is an issue which MYRADA is keenly interested in addressing.

Linking social analysis and participatory methodologies

The participatory methodologies noted above have their origins in various corners of the world – Kenya, Tanzania, Zimbabwe, the Philippines, India, and the UK. In large measure, these six approaches, and others like them, have not addressed stratification issues within communities, except for poverty or class. Even in this instance, they rarely undertake analysis of tough issues such as land tenure or credit/interest arrangements. They specifically have not focused on gender, ethnicity, caste, religion or other defining characteristics which separate groups either horizontally or vertically and disadvantage some.

Social relations and gender analysis increases our understanding of the dynamics of a community, the existing structures and systems, and their supporting values. It clarifies the division of labour within a community, whether by gender, caste, or some other characteristic. It facilitates understanding of indigenous knowledge, resource access and control, and participation in community institutions. Participatory methods like those noted above cannot fully accomplish their objectives of broad community empowerment, redressing issues of poverty and oppression, or helping with the design and implementation of programmes and projects without ensuring that they employ socially-sensitive data-gathering techniques, and developing approaches and opportunities for integrating all women and men effectively into community dialogue, decision-making, organization, and action.

At the present time those who are concerned about women as a social category are engaged in a debate reflecting two schools of thought. The Gender and Development (GAD) approach to gender relations grows out of a Women in Development (WID) approach to development. In the latter, the problem is viewed as the exclusion of women from the development process and the goal is their more efficient and effective integration into this process. The GAD approach examines unequal relations of power across all categories and seeks equitable, sustainable development with women as well as men making decisions about their lives. WID is largely concerned with women's practical interests and only secondarily with strategic objectives, whereas GAD attempts to address strategic concerns in the process of addressing practical needs. Gender analysis considers the nature of women's disadvantage, the social relations (structures and institutions) which maintain their disadvantage, the historical patterns and trends in these social relations, and the relationships between local, national and international levels in creating and perpetuating poverty and other disadvantages. The discussions continue about the appropriate place to begin to address women's disadvantage. Clearly, whether a group, a community or a facilitator should adopt a WID approach or a GAD approach depends very much upon the nature of the problem, the specific setting, and the overall context in which the issue arises.[23]

Our approach, and the tools proposed in this book for use at group and community levels, suggest that social analysis is central to any process of transformation. We would argue that the experience of poverty or disadvantage is different and frequently more 'hidden' or intractable for women than for men.[24] We would also assert that social relations and gender analysis can be done more effectively with the participation of those who are affected. Hence, the importance of linking participatory methods with social relations and gender analysis is evident. While we offer a gender focus, we argue that many of the tools recommended for gender analysis can equally well untangle and clarify other forms of social conflict and injustice.

Focal points for analysing social relations in a community would include: the basis for the division of labour; the types of labour carried out by different groups, whether productive, reproductive (oriented toward family maintenance) or community labour; the differential access to and control of resources (political, social, economic and physical) as well as benefits from them; the practical needs and strategic interests identified for both women and men across all social categories; and both the condition and the position of women and men from various groups within that particular society. In addition, analysis of social relations and gender is useful for identifying problems, carrying out needs assessments, gathering baseline data, establishing benchmarks for project monitoring and evaluation, and determining constraints and opportunities which women and men from all strata encounter. These topics will help the community and the facilitator or researcher to understand the circumstances confronting any social group and to engage the members of this group in a process of critical discovery, self-awareness, organization, and action.

CHAPTER 3

Participation in context: key questions

Dianne Rocheleau and Rachel Slocum

Participation, like development, means vastly different things depending on who defines it and uses it, and to what end, where, when and how. Past experience suggests that participatory development can bring about both negative and positive change.[1] Much depends on the relations of power embedded in the broader social context as well as in the participatory process itself. We acknowledge the need for significant change in social, economic and political institutions in order to address the deep rooted problems of poverty, unequal relations of power and environmental degradation. However, we will focus here on the practice and process of participatory research, planning and governance in the context of community development. We suggest careful consideration of six sets of key questions as a checklist against some of the common pitfalls of participatory development:

- **Why** is this participatory process needed? What ends does it serve?

- What are the **relations of power** at play in the local community, in the larger social context and in the specific activities planned?

- **Who** is involved? Whose interests are at stake? Who is in control of the process?

- What is the most appropriate **time frame** for the problems to be considered, the process itself, and the plans and actions to follow?

- What are the **appropriate spatial and organizational scales** for analysis, for action, for advocacy, for policy change and for follow-up? How can participatory efforts scale up to influence regional and national policy?

- Given the answers to the first five questions, how should a participatory process proceed? What methods, in what sequence, and under whose direction will best serve the interests of the people involved?

We explore each of these points in the sections which follow.

Why a participatory process?

The importance of defining the ends served and making them explicit in collaborative work should not be underestimated. While it seems a simple question, facilitators and planners can better serve the interests of communities if they ask 'why?' at all the stages of participatory development efforts. The ends of participation include those of the planners and facilitators as well as the objectives of the participants. It is helpful to both groups to make their reasons explicit and then to attempt to reconcile differences, rather than to proceed on the assumption that all parties involved have no agenda or subscribe to a single general goal. Participatory exercises can then be tailored to the various ends which the group decides to pursue.

Participation as a means to specific ends

One possible end is the instrumental use of people and their participation by outsiders for the achievement of some implicit or intentionally concealed aim. More often than not, it is an end that the initiators believe to be the best or necessary objective. Hand in hand with instrumentalism is mobilization, which in this sense means getting certain people to do something, even if it undermines their interests. Whatever action is being taken, it is probably not on the terms of the women and men involved. A good example of instrumentalism is the promotion of widespread local participation in the design and construction of rural reforestation, water management or soil conservation structures that serve the interests of urban water supply authorities or electric power generators. When they find that participation is used in such an instrumental way by outsiders, the intended participants may withdraw, or they may welcome the opportunity to negotiate for an exchange, including benefits for their community or for individuals.

Some people targeted by development have also used externally directed and designed ends that do not suit their immediate needs or interests as a way to gain something potentially useful later. In one specific case in Burkina Faso, researchers found that people allowed themselves to be mobilized by a land management project, calculating that it would be a way to get services that they really wanted later.[2] If nothing else, making such ends explicit at the beginning opens up possibilities for more honest – and perhaps more mutually beneficial – collaborative arrangements.

Development relationships between donors and 'recipients' usually involve different ends. Outsiders often seek to help or to mobilize, while people in local communities participate or resist in order to survive, to thrive or to change something for the better. People find ingenious ways both to get what they want from outside initiatives and to protect themselves from unwanted development. In some cases, in spite of all efforts to the contrary, people are unable to re-orient or resist inappropriate interventions, and projects are perpetrated upon them rather than being designed and carried out by and for themselves. Participatory process, combined with an explicit treatment of the objectives of the process itself, can prevent such abuses.

Within local communities there may be many distinct objectives for participation, including hopes of personal profit from the resulting actions; a platform for voicing needs of marginalized groups; a means of capturing resources for the poor from local elites (or vice versa); or an attempt to control the damage from an unwanted intervention. Facilitators will rarely find all of these groups ready and willing to declare their intentions, for obvious reasons. However, they may be able to address the implicit or submerged objectives of each group, and their own. As the process unfolds, they should be attentive to signals about these unstated agendas.

Participation as an end in itself

Development agents or local participants may also value participation for its own sake. It implies that men and women are learning, organizing, deciding, planning and acting, whether quickly or slowly, easily or painfully, and with or without a specific end. In some cases the end is participation for its own sake in a first phase, so that people are in a position to define their own goals and to act on them in a second phase.

Participatory research

In the context of research, the objective of participatory approaches may be simply to extract information from people – the more common approach. On the other hand there are many participatory research efforts which place outside researchers at the service of local communities or popular social movements. Other options include collaborative efforts ranging from documentation of local experiments and innovations by professional scientists to farmer participation in outsider-designed agricultural and forestry experiments.[3] Environmental, agricultural and develop-

ment researchers who claim to engage in participatory research often mean that 'we' (the researcher) allow 'them' (local people) to participate in 'our' research. For community organizers or rural communities, it may mean that 'they' allow outsiders (us) to take part in local experiments. What we all imply, but seldom discuss, is that we propose to join together people and institutions with very distinct traditions of acquiring and testing knowledge, and often, very different needs and uses for knowledge.[4]

Participation and relations of power

It is important to recognize and address uneven relations of power in local context and in the participatory process. The workings of power pervade all of our dealings in everyday life and we ignore them at our peril. There is no reason to assume that they do not influence even the most carefully designed participatory process. To promote social change through participatory development it is essential to understand better and to address the way that power is distributed and wielded: in local communities; in the internal operations of development agencies; in their relationships with each other, the state and the local community; and in specific participatory initiatives. In order to do this facilitators need first to identify the multiple actors within communities, as well as those who work within and between communities and others whose decisions affect local development from afar.

Several critics of development (including Patricia Stamp, Wolfgang Sachs, Arturo Escobar, Sonia Alvarez, Gustavo Esteva, and Vandana Shiva) have pointed out the cultural arrogance and the everyday abuses of power within much of development practice.[5] Likewise many feminist scholars and activists have examined the workings of power not only between men and women but also those based on class, ethnicity, religion, race, nationality and ideology. It is crucial to consider the insights of both groups in the process of participatory development, in order to navigate through the complex relations of power between outside actors and local communities as well as between and within communities and between and within development organizations.

Central to any development process is an understanding of power relations embedded in the culture and social structure within local communities. Facilitators of participatory exercises need to consider carefully their choice of partners to organize and plan activities, whose interests to address and whom to include in any given event. Local authorities, political leaders and business people often present themselves as collaborators but may represent a very narrow range of experience, based on their wealth and social status (including gender, age, religion, race, caste, lineage, education and other factors).

It is often advisable to acknowledge and include official leaders along with representatives of the various social groupings which people themselves recognize in the community.[6] For example, facilitators might meet with women's groups, landless people's groups, a smallholder farmers association and a group of herders in a given community in order to identify members of each group to serve on a planning or oversight committee. These same groups could provide guidance as to what kind of format and procedure would be suitable for them to speak and discuss openly both among themselves and in combination with other groups and officials.

The relationship between outside development agents and local insiders is also framed by parameters of power. An outsider may be from a national or international NGO, a government extension service, or a bi/multilateral aid agency. The more specific identities that precede organizational affiliation – nationality, gender, race, ethnicity, religion and ideology – also influence whether someone is perceived as an insider or outsider, and further whether they are perceived as friend or foe. As noted by Ian Scoones and John Thompson,[7] there is no essential attribute that makes someone an insider or outsider. These terms are relative by their very definition and depend upon context. However, there is a general trend toward powerful outsiders wielding influence in local communities through participatory initiatives by a variety of institutions, including NGOs.

International and national NGOs, despite all intentions to the contrary, can develop a relationship with local communities that is best described as dictatorship.[8] Because of the power that comes from the simple fact of having funds, and the assumption that all participatory efforts are inherently good, the NGOs may overlook the question 'Did anyone invite us, and if so, who?' With their substantial power, outside development agents can justify their presence and dictate the ends and means of participatory development. Financial assistance made too easily available can crush local initiative and undermine existing initiatives, corrupt accountability, and ruin the viability of local organizations. Some critics, such as Lecomte, contend that 'the main enemy is the supporting institution with its keenness to assist, to provide funds, to solicit needs and convert them into projects.'[9] Outside organizations of all stripes need to be sensitive to the power that they wield and to carefully apply both their resources and their own priorities.

Whose interests, whose voices, whose actions?

Development practitioners often speak of communities as if they are undifferentiated wholes. They may assume that a project will bring equal benefits to all (and have equally shared negative or unintended side-effects). This assumption renders invisible the situation of women, whose distinct interests, perspectives, and position in society have been largely ignored or subsumed under community within even the most participatory initiatives. Class, ethnicity, race, age, religious group and caste may also become homogenized within the term 'community.'

The opposite trap consists of grouping people based on one fixed or essential category such as women vs. men, Christian vs. Muslim, poor vs. wealthy, or other easy dichotomies. None of these is a homogeneous group. Individuals may identify more or less strongly with gender, class, ethnicity or religion, depending on their own experience and the current context. These attributes also interact. For example, a poor, lower caste Hindu woman in India may define and experience gender very differently from a wealthy Muslim woman in Morocco, and African-American, Latina and Euro-American women in the United States may likewise have very different notions of gender. Women and men are also more or less powerful relative to each other depending on the culture, situation, place and time. Both genders have many dimensions and distinct sources of identity and sometimes different power relations accompany each. There is also more to gender relations than power and conflict – gender divisions of work, knowledge, and authority may include conflict, competition, co-existence, complementarity and active co-operation.[10] Other kinds of groupings are embedded in similarly complex circumstances.

The tendency to focus on identity, whether single or multiple, also fails to address the way that people group together based on more flexible criteria, such as shared interests on a specific issue, coalitions between very distinct groups with a common goal or broader affinities among groups and between individuals. This implies that groups will shift on the basis of the context and the issues at stake, which requires a highly sensitive and flexible approach by NGOs and government agencies. Facilitators need to grapple not only with difference, but with a multitude of different possible groupings and, beyond that, a shifting constellation of groups with flexible boundaries. For example, groupings such as those listed in Gendered Resource Mapping (reproduced opposite) often help to define distinct land user groups as participants in a resource management project. They are based on identity, land tenure status, occupation, and membership in various types and scales of organizational affiliation.

Not only must facilitators explicitly attempt to include the distinct perspectives and interests of diverse groups, they must also confront the question of how actively they will promote the participation and follow-up actions of the less powerful groups. For example, participatory efforts that challenge restrictions on women's or other groups' access to decision-making power often draw criticism and provoke debate over respect for cultural norms. However, culture and social relations are not static with respect to gender, class, race, caste or other dimensions of difference. Creative practitioners who care about the position of women in society have in many cases found ways to raise the awareness of men and women and to support women trying to claim the power to decide and act. In the case of Philippine land tenure reform programmes, facilitators in some districts have helped communities to register household lands in both women's and men's

Subdivision of land user groups (from Gendered Resource Mapping)

Land users by activity

Producers
    Gatherers
    Hunters
    Herders
    Farmers
        large/small
        paid/unpaid
    Farmworkers
Processors
Market vendors
Consumers

Land users by rights of access and ownership
(Applies to trees and/or land)

Owner (state, group, individual, *de jure* or *de facto*)
Tenant (rent paid)
User by permission or exchange agreement
    Continuous
    Regular
    Occasional
Squatters, 'poachers' (illegal users, occupants)

Land users by management unit/unit of analysis

Individuals or household sub-groups
    Women, men, children; age group members
Households
    Managed by men, women; small/large; young/old; rich/poor
Communities and community groups
    Families, clans, self-help groups
Companies and co-operatives
Administrative units
    States, districts, villages, neighbourhoods etc.

---

names.[11] The possibilities range from support of power relations as usual, to the demonstration of alternative options within participatory processes, to the empowerment of marginalized groups. Facilitators have a wide range of choices with respect to their own position and the degree of engagement with relations of power within and between groups of participants.

The temporal context

The time frame for analysis of problems and opportunities, for methods of research and action and for planning of new activities should reflect a careful consideration of the local context, the specific concerns to be addressed, the institutions involved in collaborative efforts, and the objectives of the local and outside actors. Participation has recently become associated with 'rapid', based on the popularity and widespread adoption of such methods as RRA and PRA. As a result, ambitious objectives for broad and sweeping changes are often paired with very rapid or one-time appraisals of the present and plans that apply over short time horizons. However, there are several ways to match the time frame of analysis with the topic, the actors and the scope of their concerns. The choices to be made include the time frames for understanding the current situations, for conducting research and planning activities and for implementing plans.

Most participatory approaches agree on the need to understand the history of the current situation in any given place and of any given group. This includes such elements as individual life histories, the history of specific groups and communities, and their relation to outside interventions and national policies. These histories encompass social, cultural, economic and environmental changes as well as the usual political and military markers of the 'march of time' through people's lives and landscapes, and are seldom written. The history of 'development' will include such items as outside interventions, local resistance and/or participation, local initiatives and innovations.

While in official parlance we may record history in terms of numbered years and global wars, people in many places 'reckon time in famines and remember them by name'.[12] In other cases people may name epochs for presidents, national milestones such as independence, political movements, heroes/heroines, or prophets, while others may refer to human and livestock epidemics, to IMF-mandated price changes, to land tenure reform, to surveys, or to road and market construction. This may well translate into many histories in single places, even more so when literacy and language as well as perspective vary dramatically by class, gender, age, ethnicity, race, religion or political affiliation and other points of identity and difference. For example, in some places men will readily speak to outsiders in English, and recount the past in terms of World Wars and national Independence dates, while older women refer almost exclusively to 'traditional' calendars based on pest outbreaks, epidemics, droughts, floods and famines, as well as popular struggles and key political moments of local import.[13] The time frame of these discussions will influence the understanding of current problems and opportunities by local residents and outside participants alike.

Many schools of participatory research favour recording of the longest time frame available to local oral history, while others may tend to use political markers (i.e. independence for African states, or founding dates of particular villages or changes in political leadership and development policy). The safe approach is probably to explore oral history and then to focus in on the time frame which people deem most appropriate to the issues at hand, given a shared sense of the larger picture.

There is a clear need to think about the future as well as the present and the past. Depending on the scope of the work planned, collaborative efforts may be limited to specific actions for the immediate future (three years) or they might take in much longer time frames for planning and action (10 to 20 years). In either case it may be equally important to envision the options and to 'try them on' in the form of possible futures in landscape drawings or stories, in order to 'picture' the likely effects of any interventions on the future of the groups involved. This allows people to use imagination of possible futures as a sounding board for choices that must be taken in the present.

Issues of time also relate to institutional concerns and the array of actors in the process. Even groups with similar conditions and concerns in the present may be on divergent trend lines that will take them to very distinct futures. Contemporary commonality of interests may indicate long historical alliances and strong identification across groups. It might also be an ephemeral coalition based on specific shared interests at the moment, readily subject to reversal. In either case, the basis for alliance could change and interests could diverge or converge in the future.

In summary, we need to situate the origin of problems and opportunities in time, as well as the groups involved, and the nature of our interventions/partnerships, in order to choose the time horizon of participatory research, planning and action agendas. Participation need not be associated with either one-time appraisals or a life-time residential commitment, but should reflect an honest search for the most appropriate time frames suited to the context of the place, the people, the partnerships and the scope of changes contemplated.

Where to focus participation

Participation has increasingly been associated with community level meetings in many recent publications and in professional development circles. Perhaps the epitome of the newly popular participation is a large public meeting attended by all members of a given community, where 'local people' and officials engage in planning discussions about local problems and proposed development solutions. However, participation can take place in national policy discussions and legislative process as well as in small, quiet meetings between family members, neighbours, or members of particular groups based on occupation, class, race, ethnicity, gender, religion, or other bases of identity and difference. In fact, close attention to the appropriate scale of problem definition, analysis and action can make a major difference in the quality of participation, the rate of participation, and the representation of all groups involved in a given process. The scale of these participatory efforts can also dramatically influence the outcome, both overall and for particular groups.

Nested, sliding scales of access, use, control and management

Scale matters because problems that manifest at one level may be caused at another and may contribute to additional problems at a smaller or larger scale. To address the problems of one community group at a given time and place may require a much broader look at the regional and national context, as well as a closer look at the daily lives and landscapes of individuals and particular groups. For example, the actions of three large-scale farmers and two groups of herders in one upland location may affect the availability and quality of water in nearby downstream water points as well as the sedimentation of a hydro-electric dam further downstream. In the case of the nearby downstream water points, a participatory planning and problem-solving exercise might focus on a specific kind of degradation to be addressed locally by the individuals directly involved as causal agents, and/or as consumers and resource users. A community level organization or a local government agency might also act to address the problem at the community or village scale. However, in the case of dam sedimentation, there would be a need for the co-ordination of responses by a number of actors across communities if this problem were repeated elsewhere. The local actions might be quite distinct for upstream and downstream communities, while a single policy at district or river basin level would be needed to guide these diverse actions toward a just and viable conclusion for all the land and water users in the area. Participation in such a case would need to begin with multiple scale analyses of the problems and potential solutions and would need to occur at several levels. While many activities could feasibly take place at community and small group level, others would be best conducted at household, individual or regional level.

We suggest careful attention to scale in three specific areas of participatory research, planning and action. The first is the exploration of problems and opportunities at multiple scales, always looking at larger and smaller-scale processes that influence or are influenced by any given problem. The second is the process, with special attention to the size and nature of the social unit of resource users and stakeholders and the size of the landscape units involved in various stages of participatory initiatives. Third, the size and nature of the landscape area and the social units for follow-up action will vary with the type of problem and the context. Careful attention to the scale of both social organization and ecological units can improve the quality and outcome of each of these stages of participatory activity.

Multiple scales and multiple interests

Facilitators need to pay careful attention to choice of size, composition and format of groups for research and planning activities and to the choice of the scale of organization to act on decisions and plans. It should be noted that these will often not be the same. Even though the problem affects a group at one scale, the analysis may need to involve larger and smaller groups and the solution may need to be addressed by national or regional as well as local agencies.

Most people participate in resource use and environmental practices from a number of distinct but overlapping perspectives. They use and manage resources as individuals, as members of a group (based on criteria ranging from clan to caste to church affiliation, from political party to gender-specific self-help organization to social movements) and as legal residents of a given administrative unit such as a village, town or district. That is, as land users or stakeholders, they may be members of several different groupings, as illustrated in the partial list on page 23.

Regardless of the number and size of stakeholder groups, facilitators will also need to consider the appropriate scale of participant groups for various activities. Participation extends well beyond group meetings, whether to learn, to plan, to make decisions, or to discuss points of conflict and to search for consensus. Every activity, in a given geographical and historical context, has a particular set of opportunities and limits with respect to the nature, size and number of groups that can readily take part. These activities may include everything from research planning to detailed documentation of local history to work parties to act on specific solutions already identified. The appropriate size and nature of participatory groups will vary with the outsiders and local residents involved and their respective facilities/preferences for working in small or large group settings, with men or women, with homogeneous or diverse groups or with individuals. There is also the issue of whether always to work with groups as they are already organized and defined on their own terms or whether to convene special meetings to work with other groups that suit the topic and situation at hand. Good reasons for doing this might include allowing the poor, minority racial and ethnic groups, or women to voice concerns not readily raised in a larger, more diverse forum controlled by members of more powerful groups.

Nested and multiple land units and ecosystems

Most environment and development issues are enmeshed in a web of political, social, cultural, economic and ecological relations that encompass two or more scales of organization, and which often include problems which are caused at one level and expressed at another. For example, a local scarcity of a particular fodder grass might be linked to national policies affecting the grazing practice of a transhumant pastoral group that moves over a broad savannah region. Likewise, the crop-raiding behaviour of a particular form of wildlife may be related to the eviction of that species from a forest or park site some distance away. The original habitat and migration routes of the animal would be relevant spatial units for wildlife management, while the individual farm holdings would be appropriate units for design of protective measures.

Some problems have multiple causes originating at many different scales, with distinct expressions and consequences of the problem appearing at yet other scales. The case of a watershed is one which is most clear with respect to the need to look at nested watershed units of different scales to address the causes and effects of, and solutions to, water quality and availability problems. For example, a watershed with serious erosion problems could include farm level causes of hillslope erosion in croplands and farm level problems such as crop yield decline. Overgrazing and subsequent compaction of hillslope grazing lands at community scale could lead to farm level problems such as malnutrition of livestock as well as watershed problems such as rapid and excessive drainage of rainfall into local streams. National land use and agricultural marketing policies would also influence farmers' decisions to use particular cropping methods or to keep more or less livestock. The net result of all this could create a serious national watershed management crisis with respect to water supply and hydroelectric power generation. Such a problem would require a network of participatory efforts across many communities and a regional or national co-ordinating body, to negotiate settlement of differences within and between various communities as well as between local and national interests in watershed management.

What are your means?

The overall approach and the particular process employed often reflect the predisposition of the outside organizations and the individual facilitators who initiate such a process. This is not entirely wrong, since the ability to carry out such activities rests partly on past experience and acquired skill. However, the five previous points can guide the choice of both approach and techniques to better fit a given situation and the preferences and needs of the participants. Planners and facilitators can find a variety of activities to suit the objectives of organizers and participants; the spatial and time scale of problems, opportunities and potential actions; the diverse groups in the place; the relations of power and affinity within and between them; and the situation of the facilitators with respect to a given community.

If a group is interested in consciousness-raising or becoming organizationally stronger, a facilitator will use tools in ways that are different from those used if the goal is mobilization. If a problem exists at one scale but an institution is able to address it only at another, that may influence the choice of methods for both discussion and analysis. An understanding of group power relations may suggest bypassing some people and listening to others, or gathering information in different ways to get all sides of a story. This might also lead facilitators to air and resolve conflicts, or to negotiate a settlement where resolution proves impossible. One would employ different means for a group beginning to think about doing something and one that has already joined together, chosen leaders, and (to use a Southern US social action expression) 'wrestled with the alligators.'

It is also important to reach a consensus among the people involved about the role of the facilitator. They can point out problems at a conceptual or procedural level and suggest what kind of process, formats and activities may work best. For example, many peoples have a strong oral tradition. Histories and other knowledge have been passed through generations in this way. Opting for visual tools because people cannot read or write may overlook the strength of the oral tradition and the value of detailed narration or lively discussion. People may have other methods that planners and facilitators have not yet imagined. It may also be interesting to mix methods, such as drawings by both participants and researchers based on narratives by skilled oral historians. This is simply a note of caution to suggest that we examine participation fads and our own preferred means and that we explore those of participating communities.

This book does not try to set up a list of good and bad methods, or to identify and promote the 'best' approach and methods. In some circles, visual is in and verbal is out, qualitative is in and quantitative out, and informal is in while formal is out. It may be more useful to realize the limits and potential of what facilitators know how to do, to tailor the process to the local context and to respect the needs, preferences and knowledge of the participants.

Conclusion

Tools can empower or disempower. If they are adaptable to different contexts and easily used by people of any class, gender, or culture, they can enable women and men to take greater control of their lives. We need to think about what we are doing in development and why we are doing it. We need to reflect on these questions in the midst of everyday practice as well as in the context of policy, planning, and administrative procedure. A careful review and consideration of the six issues presented here provides a sounding board for the choice and application of the tools in Part III.

PART II

Methods and Ethics in our Research and in our Use of Media

CHAPTER 4

Women's rendering of rights and space: reflections on feminist research methods

Louise Fortmann

Participatory research across boundaries of race, class, and culture is not an entirely simple and innocent matter. As a university professor I recently found myself face to face with the contradictions of research ethics, methods and, above all, posture, in international versus 'domestic' contexts. During the course of a class on the management of a southern California water basin[1] I asked a student who had lived in the area what she knew about the region in general and that town in particular. 'Oh,' she said, 'I only lived there a few years, so I really don't know very much about it.' 'In international development,' I said, 'a few years would make you an "expert".'

     In development circles, including the arena of women and environment, who is an 'expert' and whose expertise 'counts' is often shaped by the unsavoury forces of elitism, racism, and neocolonialism. Expertise, in short, is problematic. Feminist research and research on women is no exception.

     This chapter is about generating and sharing knowledge and expertise on women's knowledge, use, control and management of trees in a rural community in Zimbabwe. It both presents research findings and describes how the knowledge generated and revealed through a research project came to be 'owned' by the study village through the use of participatory methods and the deliberate and systematic empowerment of both the village research team and other villagers. Because the story concerns a personal intellectual journey as well as more traditionally scholarly matters, I tell it in my own voice and include my own reflection on the process.

     In 1991 I undertook field research exploring the intersection of tree tenure, gender, and tree planting and use in two villages located in two different ecological zones within 200 kilometres of Harare, the capital of Zimbabwe. Residents of both sites depend on rain-fed agriculture and jobs in town for their livelihood. Trees play a crucial role in the livelihood strategies in the two study sites. They provide domestic and commercial sources of food, medicine, browse, poles, fuel, mulch, and wood carving, as well as serving ecological and religious functions. The research took three complementary forms – a standard random sample survey, participant observation, and a series of participatory methods.

Having been trained as a rural sociologist, one of the ways I approached this question was through the use of a survey of a stratified random sample of households. Since my Shona never progressed beyond the me-go-store-now variety, I hired a team of seven villagers to help with the administration of the survey. There were four women in this research team, three of them between the ages of 36 and 52, middle-aged women like me. They were wonderful beyond belief and also provided a way into the situated knowledge of middle-aged and elderly women, their own knowledge and that of their friends.

I have always been adamant about returning data to the village, both making sure the village gets copies of any written reports, and going back to discuss my findings with villagers. That is what I originally intended to do in this case. But perhaps because of the obvious excellence of the team and the equally obvious need for the villagers to be able to do their own research, I realized that I had to give them my own skills.

How do we leave our skills behind? Obviously, formal survey methods which require paper, duplication facilities, and statistical analysis are of little use to the average village. In contrast, participatory methods not only got me useful data, but they are skills and techniques that villagers could learn and replicate whenever they needed similar sorts of information.

To develop a participatory research process, I returned to the lessons I had learned at Cornell University in the 1970s from Ivette Puerta, a Puerto Rican doctoral student working with Latinas. Wanting to find a way of building community through the research process, Ivette [2] developed the strategy of using community members as a research team. The idea was that as community members gathered information through a survey, three things would happen. First, people would develop a consciousness about their problems as they talked about them in the interview. Second, the research team would become experts on community problems and could become community spokespeople. Third, they would, through their interviews, develop a network which could be mobilized later on.

I had used Ivette's methodology in my dissertation. At the end of the survey, the five women (all welfare mothers, none with even a high school education) who worked with me took the Dean of the College of Agriculture on a rural poverty tour of the county with articulate and pointed commentary throughout. He was in shock for quite some time.

So, rather like Rip Van Winkle, I had returned to my methodological roots after two decades. I decided to adapt my methods so that the villagers would really 'own' this research. And I wanted to empower the women at the same time I was learning from and with them. This took four basic forms: Foxfire books, resource mapping, wealth ranking, and public presentation of the research by the research team.

Foxfire books

As I began rethinking my methods, I ran into Dianne Rocheleau, a feminist geographer, who reminded me about the Foxfire books. So I explained to the headmaster of the village primary school about these books – they are books written by schoolchildren about their own culture and their own environment. They can interview their parents or grandparents or describe something they know themselves. But since I wanted this to be their book, not my book, I stayed out of the process.

The first batch of essays I received were a terrible shock. Most of them had been copied (two sets were identical) or paraphrased from a book on trees. Each said at the bottom: 'Warning: District Council Prosecutes Illegal Tree Cutters'. This is the persisting legacy of British colonialism in which education is based on memorization and regurgitation. The notion that people's own knowledge in their children's own words could have any value is quite inconceivable in that system. I went to the headmaster and said, 'There are a few problems with these essays.' And he, fortunately, said, 'Yes, I thought you would say that.' So I wrote some titles: 'How My Grandmother Uses Trees', 'My Favourite Tree' and so on. And we started again.

The final book consisted of all the second set of essays plus salvaged ones from the first round if the author hadn't written in the second round. They were typed and bound and every child who wrote – plus a bunch of village dignitaries – got a copy of the book at the farewell ceremony described below. The headmaster of the secondary school where some of the children were now enrolled came to pick up their copies. A few children read their essays aloud. Everyone was incredibly proud! They had written their own book which they could use in school. They could read it to themselves and to others. It captured their own knowledge and information. The headmaster thought perhaps it could be published and distributed all over Zimbabwe.

I did not use the Foxfire books as a data source, although with more careful planning I might have. But that makes them no less valuable. It is important to remember that not everything in our research needs to be for us.

Resource mapping

Mapping is just what it sounds like. You ask people to draw a map. You can have them map anything you need to know about – the village, the wealthy, water, markets and so on; I asked people to map where they obtained tree products. For this they need a long stick and a lot of twigs: the stick is for drawing the map on the ground, and the little twigs represent trees. Rocks and other props are also useful. For example, one group of men filled a cup with water for a dam. A group of women fashioned a wonderful windmill out of cornstalks. In another group we were sitting under a mango tree which kept bombarding us with hard green mangoes. Finally one woman put a twig in the map and announced it was the tree that was attacking us. Drawing on the ground with a stick (or many sticks as people get into it) avoids any school and learning connotations that pen, pencil and paper carry, although there is a certain vulnerability involved. For example, the agricultural extension agent drove his motorcycle right through the village research team's practice map.

After people had done their maps, I asked them what it looked like in 1970, in 1980 and what they would like it to look like. Not surprisingly, everyone said there used to be more trees and they wished that there were more once again.

It is very important to do this sort of thing separately for women and men. For starters, women and men map things differently, putting different elements in their maps in different order, with different degrees of detail. Both began their maps with the two rivers which bound the village. Women then drew a very detailed map of social space – household by household, sometimes with details of particular houses, extra windows, tin roofs, and so on. Men, in contrast, concentrated on production spaces – roads, the grazing areas, the shops.

But in order to tease out these different spatial perceptions, you must allow women their own arena for mapping. On two occasions women were included in the same group as men. Perhaps the most striking example of gender hierarchy occurred in the village research team. They had insisted on doing a 'proper' map with pencils instead of the 'childish' map in the dirt, so I bought a large piece of poster board and they did a second map. Each researcher had an individual pencil and eraser, so everyone could draw. In the group that day were the three middle-aged women, a 20-year-old woman and a 19-year-old man. Who drew the map? The young man, of course! In this case, the older women were far above the young man in the age hierarchy and were confident and assertive, at least in the research arena, so they were quite vocal about what should go on the map and made the young man erase things and redraw them to their specifications.

Other women were less able to make their voices heard in a mixed group. Women who participated in the grazing committee mapping exercise primarily muttered only an acquiescent *'ndidzodzo'* (it's OK) as the men drew the map. In response to a direct question, one woman indicated specific termite mounds that were good places for collecting fuel wood. But, on the whole, the shy silence of these women was a striking contrast to the assertive laughter of women of the single gender groups.

The maps provided a useful visual indication of resource clusters. They were also the most accurate check on elite myths, in particular the myth of the community woodlot. The Chairman of the Grazing Scheme proudly took visitors around the village woodlots: an area of substantial eucalyptus and an area of regenerating indigenous woodland. This, the story went, was where villagers came for their wood. But, with the exception of the elite grazing committee, when villagers drew their maps of where they obtained tree products, the village woodlots were conspicuous by their absence. Survey data confirmed that only the rich used these woodlots. Their absence from the maps tells an even more powerful story – most villagers do not even think of the woodlots as an available resource. No survey can tell you that quite so clearly.

Wealth ranking

Participatory methods for wealth ranking involving card sorting are pretty standard. I sat down with my research team and said, 'Tell me what rich people have, tell me what poor people have.' I wanted a five point scale. They pushed me to six. Their scale included the usual cast of variables – cattle, house type, and employment. But also included among their variables was one I had never thought of – secondary education, where (in the village or in town), and how continuous. They laid out categories of people who were dependent on other people for livelihoods. There was a huge argument over the importance of owning a means of production (ploughs, cattle, fields) against owning consumer durables (fancy house, radio).

Then I asked each village researcher to rank all our respondents, leaving blank anyone they could not or did not want to rank. What I found particularly interesting in these rankings was that they ranked a number of widows much lower than I would have ranked them. Why? They ranked widows on what they themselves personally controlled/owned as opposed to what their children were able to give them. Since their children might withdraw their favours or be run over by a bus, their largesse did not count. There was a very strong sense of vulnerability in these rankings.

These rankings were eventually used in statistical analysis. They correlated highly with the traditional measures (cattle ownership, tin roof) of wealth. But they reflected the nuances of local reality far better, and the research team got practice for future use in thinking through categories of people and how they were affected differently by various things happening in the village.

Reports by the village research team

If the villagers are to own research, they ought to be able to use it right from the start. So I asked the team if they wanted to present the results to the village. They were enthusiastic. Each one picked a topic. I ran the data for them. They wrote a speech in English. I checked it. They translated it into Shona. My colleague,

Nontokozo Nabane, checked it. I gave them tips on public speaking. And then every Tuesday at 10 a.m. for ten weeks we practised. At the beginning I was a little worried. These were youth and middle-aged women – people whose role in meetings is generally to listen respectfully to older men. We had gigglers. We had 'clutchers'. Who knew what would happen on that day!

The day came. The meeting began with a very long and eloquent prayer about trees. The school choir sang about trees. And then the research team gave their speeches. The gigglers and the clutchers had turned into seven confident, polished, authoritative speakers. They were dynamite! They were proud! And everyone listened. 'We never thought,' said the chairman of the Grazing Scheme in his concluding speech, 'that we would learn something from a woman, but we have.'

This sort of thing is the best way I know of that will enable villagers to 'own' the research.[3] Whenever someone wants to know something, they can just pop round and ask their neighbour. The community can replay that meeting or parts of it any time they want to. There are now women who can speak for them-selves, for women, and for their village. And, of course, they could also do some research for themselves.

Paying in our own currency

Our own currency has nothing to do with foreign exchange. It has to do with credit for ideas and knowledge. A classic example can be found in another twenty-year detour to an acknowledgement I read in the mid 1970s in a development book. It went something like this:

> I would like to thank my wife who accompanied me in the field, assisted in the interviews, typed my field notes every day, coded the questionnaires, helped with my data analysis, read and commented on all my drafts, and typed and proofread the final manuscript.

'And why is she not the co-author?' I muttered for the next week (and indeed for the next twenty years). I have long forgotten what the book said or even who wrote it. I have never forgotten that acknowledgement.

In my survey, I asked what trees people used and for what. We ended up with a list of 122 indigenous trees. (There were also a large number of exotics.) The next task was to gather physical specimens since the same tree has different names and different trees have the same name in Shona. And people sometimes made up names; for example, around the school grounds grew clumps of Banket Hedge, named for the town of Banket where the headmaster got cuttings and brought it back to the village.

So, one very hot day, the research team and I sat down under a mango tree and went through the list. They quickly grouped the trees by habitat: trees that grow in rocky places, trees that grow in fields, trees that grow by the river. One 'tree' that grew in the river turned out to be a water lily – another reason for doing this exercise. Then we set out and in four hours we had collected specimens of 95 different species of indigenous trees. Not only did my team know the habitat for each species, they knew the location of individual trees. It was an absolutely staggering exhibition of expertise.

There were, of course, duplicates. Some, like the water lily, were not trees at all. And some trees turned out to be located in distant places where people had worked so we could not collect them. In the end we had a list of 114 different tree species, 99 identified in the Herbarium by botanist Robert Drummond.[4]

Of course, all this brought to mind the acknowledgement that has been irritating me for so long. That acknowledgement reminded me of the acknowledgements I see in so many works utilizing local knowledge. And it came to me that if local knowledge really is so important and not just something we pay lip service to, then we should pay for it in our own currency – not with an off-hand acknowledgement, but with full-blown academic credit.[5] If we have really relied on their knowledge, then they should be co-authors. And so Chidari et al. 'The Use of Indigenous Trees in Mhondoro District' was born. The villagers are the senior authors.

This booklet was also presented at the farewell ceremony. Every member of the research team, every headman, the headmaster, the chair of the grazing scheme, the Forestry Commission representatives, and the District Officials all received individual copies. Everyone was proud. This was their knowledge, and it had the potential to be used in future development efforts.

Subsequent thought and conversations and correspondence with people from all over the globe have convinced me that paying in our own currency *must* be a model for the way we publish our research whenever that research depends on local people's knowledge. We would not use our colleagues' ideas without ac-knowledgment. The same principle applies here. To do anything other than paying with academic credit is probably unethical and certainly colonial.

Concluding thoughts

The ability to articulate needs for and rights to natural resources to government agencies and NGOs is an increasingly important skill for villagers as pressure on these resources rises and government and NGO penetration of rural areas in-creases. In this context the need to use participatory research methods is obvious. For one thing, these methods are empowering if they are done right. They provide a forum in which people learn and share knowledge together. This in turn provides a common basis for certain kinds of planning and decision-making. In particular, it means that right from the start you are plunged into people's own categories and language and this is essential for getting things done. In short, they serve both the researcher and the researched.

The message from this chapter is that researchers have ethical responsibilities to ensure that not just they – but also villagers – benefit from and own any village-based research.

CHAPTER 5

Media ethics: no magic solutions

Renuka Bery

Ethical issues abound when introducing technology into a society for the first time. Technology is not neutral; it brings complexities and raises numerous ethical questions which defy past experience and present new challenges. This chapter raises some of the questions and issues I have encountered in my experiences with and knowledge of social change organizations in the South [1] using communication tools. The discussion here is far from exhaustive. There are no magic answers. Ethical questions are extremely subjective. Finding solutions to ethical dilemmas depends on the situation, the cultural context and the participants involved.

Participatory communication

Many terms are used to discuss participatory communication at the local level. Terms such as 'community media', 'process video', and 'alternative communication', to name a few, might be defined differently from one group to another. In my work at Communication for Change, a not-for-profit video training organization based in New York, we define participatory communication as a process which allows people to speak for themselves about themselves and about their own issues. Community members, who would otherwise have limited access to media, can control the tools, not outsiders who mediate information and representation. Individuals, organizations and communities learn to *use* media, in particular video, rather than *be used by* media. The process is an exchange among individuals that values each person's perspective and voice. Community members produce tapes to meet their own needs, but the process continues long after a tape is completed. Playback sessions, at which members of the community gather to watch and discuss tapes, are critical to participatory video. Facilitators engage viewers in discussions about the tapes they have just seen. Through these exchanges participants can relate what they have seen and heard to their own experiences and lives.

Who has access and control?

The role of participatory video or media in a community must be considered carefully. Some ethical issues related to communication technology seem evident. What will it mean to introduce this technology into the community? What is its purpose? Will this technology introduce a new system of values? Who will control these new tools?

When introducing costly electronic technologies into economically disadvantaged societies, the issue of appropriateness if often raised. Should a community have a video camera or computer access in an area where there is no potable water or where people in the community are starving? This is a valid question that needs to be asked. But who should answer it?

If video is being introduced to raise awareness about health and hygiene issues, it may be able to reach a wide range of people, some of whom might not be literate. If it is being used to document programme activities, however, a written report may be more effective. If it is being used to record a marriage ceremony, there may be a local entrepreneur who should be contacted instead. If an organization wishes to document the marriage ceremony because it is a rarely performed ritual and they wish to preserve cultural traditions, however, perhaps video is the most appropriate medium.

A village in Mali asked a group of literacy teachers trained in video to make a tape about sanitation and hygiene. One year later, a cholera epidemic swept the region but the villages where people had seen the tape did not suffer as many casualties as other villages. They felt that the hygiene practices that they had learned from the tape had prevented the cholera from spreading. This outcome could not have been predicted.

Each organization or individual should assess carefully which medium is best for the task. The question remains, who decides what is an appropriate medium? It would seem that in a participatory environment, the organization or community involved should decide. When members of a community work together to define their goals and priorities, they have vested interests in the outcomes. Determining how to fulfil these goals is the next step. Usually there are numerous ways to achieve them. If video is considered a viable tool, the community involved must assess carefully how video would assist them and whether it is the most suitable medium for their purposes. These are suggestions for questions to ask when considering media options for communication:

- What is the best medium to communicate the message?

- Is the chosen style (drama, interview, group meeting, lecture, music, etc.) the best way to communicate this message?

- How much time will it take to produce?

- Are there resources and time available to do it?

- Can something else be produced more efficiently with fewer resources and still be as effective?

- What are the advantages/disadvantages of choosing one way or another?

- What are the long-term implications of the choices?

Many people believe that access to information and technology is the key to empowerment. For example, with computers to open doors to the world's vast information data banks, people's lives can change dramatically. But one should also ask whether, in fact, just having access does lead to changes in knowledge or attitudes. While communications and access to technology can strengthen individuals and communities, the existing power bases will not crumble just because more people in the South can log on. The structure of control might shift as more people gain access, but ownership will remain in the hands of a few.

Who controls the tools is a critical element in the access debate. It determines the perspective, style and content of any message that is created. Putting communication technologies directly in the hands of people at the grass roots, especially women, challenges existing power structures. But, like all tools, media are as powerful as the people who use them. A village communicator will construct a message about economic self-sufficiency very differently from someone from outside the community. In turn, the slant would again be different if a foreigner went into that community and told the story.

Allocating resources

An organization considering any communication technology as a tool to strengthen its work should determine whether it has the organizational resources necessary to accommodate the desired medium. Most media cannot be used in isolation. It takes time, training, commitment, and lots of practice to gain the proper skills. A key consideration when introducing media activities is obtaining equipment and training simultaneously. Although anyone can learn to operate equipment, telling a convincing story and facilitating discussions after playbacks are equally important and more difficult to master. Thus training is important. In addition, training without regular access to equipment can be a trap as well. Learning a new skill is a powerful experience which, if not nurtured and supported, will be forgotten – and

the strength and confidence people gained by learning to voice their issues will be undermined.

It is very easy for outsiders to enter a community and tell its members what is needed. These outsiders are often accorded elevated status. They are the experts; they know the 'right' way. This acknowledgement of experience can be a trap, especially for trainers using participatory methodologies. It is a top-down, often patronizing approach which clearly suppresses or distorts participation. The presence of outside advisers poses a number of challenging questions. Should outsiders be invited to share their ideas and knowledge at all? Should people from outside the culture introduce non-traditional communication methods which are infused with ideas and values that are new and perhaps not compatible with the existing social mores? Should any communication technology be introduced across cultures? But if the world is moving toward instantaneous communication and globalization, should not everyone have the option to join?

Sustainability

There is constant tension in participatory video groups about the issue of sustainability. Making video requires an upfront investment in equipment, training, and tape supply. While some costs are one-time and finite, others such as tape stock, are ongoing. In addition, equipment can break, so repair and/or replacement costs need to be factored into the larger sustainability picture. Funding is often available for start-up and training, but what happens after the initial funding has finished? If an organization has successfully integrated video activities into its core programme, tape and repair will be funded through the general or programme budgets. If video remains a separate entity, specific funds need to be raised to continue supporting the video activities. To address the issue of long-term sustainability, organizations often contemplate making tapes about popular issues to sell, or hiring out their production services to clients. Working for clients is very different from working as a participatory team. The introduction of money into the production equation changes a producer's relationship with the work. The decision to produce for money raises a new set of ethical questions to be addressed:

- Can the organizational goals for video be met if the video teams hire out their services?

- If tapes are made for sale, will the issues focused on pre-empt organizational priorities?

- Does the video unit have enough resources to produce for clients?

- Is the compensation (financial or otherwise) enough to justify the time and resources spent on the production?

- Who will have control over content, direction and product? Is control important?

The issue of professionalization extends beyond production values to organizational dynamics. Careful consideration should be given to questions such as: What are the potential consequences (positive and negative) in professionalizing a participatory video producer or team? How will the relationships change both within and outside the organization? Will the organization value a professional team differently from a participatory team? If so, how and with what effects?

Ownership

Ownership is clear when producing for hire; the client pays for a production and owns the rights. If ownership is not specified, it can be questioned when a production gains recognition and status. Although these issues may seem improbable, they can occur unexpectedly. A producer in a village in Bangladesh made a tape about her neighbour. The production is a strong and honest interview with a woman who had been abandoned by her husband when she was not able to pay him more dowry[2]. She survived many hardships, eventually became financially solvent and educated her daughter despite the odds against her. This tape powerfully illustrates the injustices of the dowry system as well as an individual woman's strength in overcoming adverse situations. It has been shown and discussed in villages all over Bangladesh.

This tape was subtitled in English to make the content more accessible to outside audiences and funders. As a result, it was submitted to an international Women in Video competition; it was one of eight winning tapes from 76 submissions from 23 countries. The prize was either cash or a trip to Britain to receive the award.

The prize introduced the participatory video teams to issues of ownership for the first time. The organization arranged a celebration in Dhaka to honour and recognize the value of participatory video to the organization and the communities. In addition, the producer attended an awards ceremony in New Delhi for the Asian winners. But she thought she should have gone to Britain. To whom did the prize belong? The organization? The production team? The producer? The interviewee? Each thought he or she should benefit from this prize. The video teams asked why the producer was singled out when it was a team effort – and all the teams were making interesting tapes. The interviewee accused the organization of profiting from her story. Other video team members subsequently reported that

some people were reluctant to speak on camera because they did not want their story exploited, or because they wanted payment.

Another issue of ownership relates to the rights of footage. Some organizations in the North have given Southern organizations communications equipment in exchange for footage. What does an organization do if offered video equipment in exchange for raw footage documenting human rights or environmental abuses without any control or knowledge over how it will be used? Does an image taken out of its larger context change its meaning? To answer that, one needs only to think of a sound bite that is separated from a conversation. There are questions both donor and recipient organizations need to consider and explore:

- Will this technology assist the community in meeting its goals?

- Does the recipient organization need more than the equipment? If so, what other technical support is necessary and how will it be secured?

- Why does this donor want these images? How will the images be used?

- Will the footage, taken out of context, add to the stereotypes, or negative images that most Northerners see of the South or can the organizations ensure that positive examples of life, culture and development are presented?

- If people around the world see these images, do they have a right to interfere in the issues? Would the recipient organization want them to? How? Why?

With video, as with other forms of media, respecting copyright is important. It is very tempting to duplicate a tape without permission rather than to buy it; but it is not ethical. Every organization needs to find ways to maintain its video activities, and users and producers need to support each other's efforts. Some organizations try to spread social change ideas and messages and encourage others to copy their materials. Yet if an organization wishes to market tapes to support its video activities, unauthorized duplication of these tapes would undermine that organization's sustainability.

Propaganda or information?

Propaganda is the spread of particular ideas to further a cause. The term has evolved with a negative connotation. But is propaganda necessarily bad? There is no such thing as objectivity. Technology is not neutral and neither is communication. Everyone is influenced by his or her background, knowledge, experiences, context, and frame of reference. Everyone has a bias – a unique point of view. A video producer can try to make a balanced programme showing many different opinions, but she or he still has an opinion to convey.

Information is powerful. The person sending the information determines the way the information is communicated. The communicator controls the message, the tone, the perspective, the style, and the mode of communication according to the audience he or she wishes to reach. A video programme on teenage sexuality for government officials would look different from a programme for the teenagers themselves. Who is communicating to whom is important in determining how the message will be framed. For example, a radio programme to encourage rural women to become more involved in family planning decisions might be most effective as a serial drama rather than as an academic programme of statistical facts gathered from extensive research findings.

A programme about the successes of a woman who joined an organization, learned to save money and became economically solvent might influence viewers to join the organization. Is this propaganda, as one villager accused? Would showing this tape to villagers at night after they returned from a full day working in the fields be considered coercive? Is this any different from television networks deciding which programmes to air during prime time and giving the advertising slots to those who pay the most? Who judges whether propaganda is good or bad?

Seeing is believing – or is it?

Participatory video producers in Bangladesh, excited about the power of video in their communities, commented that 'Seeing is believing' and 'Video cannot be bribed'. Their enthusiasm was infectious; their statements were, at once, distressing and encouraging. Video had been successfully introduced into a large Bangladeshi NGO. They had used it, decentralized it and redefined participatory video to fit their needs. Yet these statements illustrated both a naivety and a true understanding of video's power as a medium of communication. Video is not objective; a producer constructs a production to communicate a specific look and feel as well as a certain perspective.

While the communicator controls the way the information is conveyed, the person receiving the information has a responsibility to be aware of who is communicating and why. This is critical thinking. The issue of critical viewing is important when introducing video technology into a community. Video is created to communicate what the producer wishes. Viewers need to learn that although 'seeing' is powerful, one should not automatically 'believe'. Learning to view media with a critical eye is an important skill. When people develop critical skills they begin to understand where information comes from and why. It is particularly important as one learns more about media production. Critical viewing or listening is learning to ask questions about what one is seeing or hearing. Communicators create messages so the viewer will believe them.

On the other hand, video can be like a mirror. Another village producer remarked that each time someone tells a story, it is recounted in a different way. However, on video, the story and facts can be preserved. So, for example, a government official making promises on video could be held to those promises later.

Watching video or listening to the radio can be a passive experience in which the audience becomes a vessel to be filled with information. Communication for Change believes it is important to animate the process, to engage the viewers in the issues they see on the screen and to encourage them to explore these issues as they relate to their own lives. By thinking actively and discussing the issues they see, people learn to be critical viewers.

Some questions critical viewers should ask themselves while receiving any messages are as follows.

- Who is communicating?

- What message is being communicated?

- For whom is the message?

- Why is the message being communicated?

- Whose values are presented? Are they the same as mine?

As people develop critical viewing skills, more sophisticated questions can be explored. Questions about how messages are constructed, style, perspective, image choice and sequence should all be considered. Is one particular sequence of images more powerful than a different sequence? Why? How does the producer use the viewers' emotional response to engage them? Is it ethical?

Consent

Consent is important. Producers must be honest about the goals for their productions. If people do not wish to appear in a production, they should not be coerced, tricked or bribed into being on the tape – even if they have important information to share. Otherwise the producer's integrity (and consequently the organization's) will most likely be questioned. Obtaining consent from people appearing in a production is a critical issue in the United States. If any chance exists for a production to be broadcast, shown publicly or sold, producers obtain written consent from the people appearing in their production and the rights to use footage or music they do not own. In other parts of the world the protocol for obtaining permission is not always so clear.

Another issue which arises is payment for telling one's story. Perhaps someone should be paid for his or her time; however, paying for a story seems suspect because if economic gain is the motive, a convincing storyteller could easily invent a more dramatic story. It is important in video to be clear about what is real and what is fabricated.

Video and audio tape do not have to be developed. This immediacy makes it possible to replay the tape to the production participants immediately. A playback can be a way of acknowledging people's participation and the time they have taken to be involved, especially when the producer explains how the tape will be used and encourages them to give feedback.

Bulu, a village woman in Bangladesh, made a tape about her neighbour, Nasima, a victim of domestic violence who had since been abandoned by her husband. Bulu risked discomfort and crowd control problems to make the production in Nasima's village rather than in the quiet environs of the organization's facility. She wanted Nasima's husband to find out about the tape so he would be worried. In playing back the tape to Nasima and her neighbours, she asked for their comments and their permission to show the tape to other women as a way of encouraging them to seek legal aid counselling.

Conclusion

Participatory media will evolve and be used differently in every organization. Everyone has a voice and the right to be heard. But no prescriptions exist for instituting media activities. In some organizations, the media unit is centralized and services many different programmes. In other groups, media are decentralized and have developed to serve the local needs of each one's constituency. Some use video as a cultural preservation tool, others for self-expression and empowerment. Still other organizations have multiple goals – providing information about the organization to outsiders while involving media in internal training, organizing and documentation activities.

At the Self-Employed Women's Association in India, video is an organizing tool. In China after the massacre in Tiananmen Square, fax machines were used to tell uncensored stories to the rest of the world. Media are used to document activities and events, to negotiate with policymakers, to advocate for change or to communicate to large constituencies. They have been widely incorporated in training environments and as icebreakers to start discussions about difficult topics.

A leprosy clinic in India used an entertainment film to draw crowds in several slum areas. Once a group had gathered, clinic volunteers showed a film about leprosy. After the screening, the presenters led a discussion about the disease to raise awareness and to encourage people with symptoms to visit the clinic. Is this presentation technique ethical? In some cultural environments, this strategy might be considered coercive and unethical. In other environments, the same strategies might be vital to motivate change in a community.

Ethical issues cannot be prejudged because each cultural context draws on its own set of relationships and traditions. However, the most burning questions of all remain. Who raises the ethical questions in the first place? Then, once these questions have surfaced, who possesses the authority or right to answer them? Ethical issues require open, questioning minds willing to explore the concerns expressed. But whose minds? And who decides?

PART III

Tools for Environmental and Social Change

CHAPTER 6

How to use the tools and how to facilitate

Purpose

The purpose explains the value and utility of each tool. Tools are a means to start a process; they need not be an end in themselves. It is essential to understand that all the tools can and should be adapted to fit a particular context or need.

Materials

These tools can be used with literate or non-literate participants. Many of the tools suggest markers and paper; however, other methods, both local and foreign, exist for recording and passing on information. Those methods range from using local orators and artists, drawing on the ground, using locally found materials, drama, song and story-telling to tape recorders, cameras and video cameras.

Time box

We have estimated the amount of time each tool requires. For some we have suggested an hour, even though these tools can be part of a much longer process. An hour is a reasonable amount of time to ask from people who, like anyone any-where, are very busy with multiple aspects of their lives. Tools sensitive to gender, class, ethnicity and other identities require that facilitators and organizations allow more time both to collect disaggregated information and to involve people in a process of reflection and action toward more equitable relations. A variety of techniques such as focus groups, household interviews, and key informant interviews may be necessary to understand the full range of views and interests, but using multiple methods takes time. Season is also a factor. Usually, planting, weeding and harvesting seasons are the busiest times for rural people. Gender and age also

> **Time**
> The amount of time required is an estimate.

define the time people have available; young women in many countries, because of their multiple tasks, may even have greater difficulty than most to find even an hour to talk. And, as always, the right time for you may not be the right time for participants.

Process

There is no 'right' way of using each tool that will, if followed, yield perfect results. The Process section is a suggestion, often based on how others have used the tool. Facilitators should guard against the tendency to become too involved in the details of using the tool. Many of these tools are most useful as a means to encourage discussion and whether the steps are followed to the letter is often not important. The tools are arranged in alphabetical order to discourage any tendencies towards seeking a blueprint model and to encourage the use of any tool at the appropriate point according to the participants' context.

Remember

Many of the tools assume literacy, whereas many rural people are not literate. Substitute icons or symbols as appropriate. Summarize frequently. Draw on people's skills. You will probably find they have excellent memories and are verbally articulate and persuasive.

See also

The tools are cross-referenced with others that complement them.

Examples

Many of these tools have been field-tested. The examples describe some combination of the following: how the tool has been used; difficulties and rewarding experiences; insights and information gained from using them; and how the tool could be useful to the people with whom one is working. There may be examples of maps, diagrams or sample questions that make the tool easier to use.

How to facilitate

Much has been written about the art of facilitating and many workshops have been designed to teach it. The following points do not pretend to capture all the wealth of information generated. Instead, they offer a few important guidelines. One aspect missing in many books on facilitating is how to ensure that the views, interests and needs of those often ignored are not silenced by the more powerful. Most often, techniques suggest ways to hear different perspectives, but they do not offer advice on what to do when a group is trying to decide on an action and the views of women, for example, are not allowed to enter into the decision-making process. It is difficult, but still possible, for a facilitator to make a difference at this point.

Facilitating for change

Gouri Choudhury

The notion of facilitation is undergoing radical changes. It once implied that the facilitator/trainer was the knowledgeable one who had something to teach, and the participant was the learner. This one-way process does not take us toward equality.

The workshop method can break this one-way, up-down, unequal relationship between teacher and learner. The workshop process involves sharing ideas and information. Workshop activities create opportunities for learning by doing. The trainer facilitates the process by leading the discussion and dialogue towards a conceptual goal which could be open-ended or specific and finite.

Whatever the specific content of the workshop may be, its intention is to set off new ways of looking at life and new ways of thinking which lead to a change in perception, understanding and behaviour. A well-planned dynamic workshop allows the maximum freedom for every participant to express him or herself without fear of failure or ridicule, releasing the creative potential in individuals at each one's own pace. Encouraging the silent or less articulate, and subduing the aggressive, over-assertive to make space for others, starts off a process of levelling which the facilitator(s) must handle with sensitivity and care. Learning is more likely to be internalized when every participant is involved in the collective process which seeks to build understanding from shared experience.

In our endeavours to bring about social change, we do not presume that the poor, the non-literate, and the inarticulate do not know that they are exploited victims of oppression. Of course they know – they live it – but they may not know why. Setting off an analytical chain of thoughts to motivate questioning is an attempt to break the acceptance of one's lot and move from the reliance on fate, destiny and God's will towards self-reliance.

The ultimate outcome of the workshop must be a sense of self-worth. We

see ourselves in relation to others. Our image and opinion of ourselves is a reflection of how our family sees us, how our group perceives us, and how well we meet the standards and norms set by the society in which we live. A workshop for women (and men) can be deemed successful when we create our own image and come home with a sense of positive self-worth. (See Mapping the Body.)

Ethics for facilitators[1]

- Demystify your role so as not be perceived as the authority and reach a consensus with the group on the scope of your work.
- Ensure that the group understands your role.
- Be explicit about your ends.
- Encourage the group to take responsibility.
- Do not use facilitating techniques to control the group.
- Facilitate to help a group work together.

The qualities of good facilitators[2]

- Good listening skills;
- Respect for the participants;
- Interest in what people have to offer;
- Assertiveness that is not overbearing – knowing when to intervene decisively;
- Clear thinking and observation of the whole group;
- An understanding of the overall objectives of the group.

Factors creating a participatory environment

- Choose a space that accommodates all.
- Avoid classroom-style seating with people in rows and the facilitator at the front.
- Plan meetings with an awareness of the schedules of women and men.
- Arrive on time even if you have to wait for the group to come.
- Divide large groups into small teams.
- Use humour without belittling people.
- Celebrate the group's work.
- A tangible product of the discussion such as charts, a video recording, a song or speech committed to memory by a local orator, maps, drawings, or a written report are ways to keep the discussion and its outcome in the minds of the participants.
- Distribute maps and charts to all participants before concluding the discussion.
- Honour individual and group contributions.
- Assume that some wisdom lies behind every contribution.
- Pay attention.

- Intervene and mediate when some people are dominating and call such behaviour into question for the sake of the group.
- Avoid being a visiting important person (taking the best chair or place).
- Avoid over- and underdressing.
- Mix freely with participants.
- Avoid positioning yourself with one group (gender, age, ethnic, etc.).
- Demonstrate some form of identification with the participants.

Discussion techniques [3]

- 30-minute discussions are often well received. If the topic requires more time, break it down into smaller discussions.
- Prepare good questions – questions that cannot be answered by yes or no and that are not vague.
- Explain the purpose and importance of the discussion.
- Try asking everyone in the group to answer a question to accustom people to participating, or divide the group so one part answers one question and another the second question.
- Be prepared to rephrase questions in several different ways or provide an example.
- If the discussion is straying from the topic, restate the last question and acknowledge the other issues raised as important enough to come back to later.
- In disagreements, make sure each understands the other's point of view and summarize the disagreement.
- Help participants clarify vague ideas by asking them for an example.
- Be firm with those who have spoken too much or who are answering questions for others by turning the discussion to other people in the group.
- Ask someone to remember or take notes on the points raised and ask note takers or local orators to summarize at certain stages.[4]
- Use every opportunity to encourage people to reflect on what they are saying or proposing rather than reflecting yourself and telling them what you think.

Checklist for researchers and practitioners

Factors affecting the ways in which the residents of a locality and various types of outsiders interact:[5]

1. Length of time and ways in which the locality has been linked to other regions and exposed to the state, missionaries or development agencies;

2. A history of conflict;

3. A history of patron-client relationships;

4. The class structure of the locality;

5. Attitudes of various types of people within the community towards representatives of the state and other authority figures and whether the outsider is perceived as representing a particular group or institution;

6. Typical attitudes of men and women, members of different ethnic groups, social classes and age groups towards someone of the researcher's or development facilitator's gender, age, marital status and social class;

7. If the organization is working on a development project, the nature, scope, and purpose of the project and the history of that organization with the community;

8. If it is a research project, its specific nature, funding, purpose, and organizational affiliation;

9. The ways in which the facilitator or researcher are introduced into the community, perhaps through an outside agency or through a group or individual within the community, and the way in which the 'gatekeeper' is regarded within the community;

10. The conduct, lifestyle, and involvement of the outsider with the community and its activities.

Activities, Resources and Benefits Analysis

Adapted by the editors from *Tools of Gender Analysis*[6]

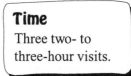

Time
Three two- to
three-hour visits.

Purpose

Using this tool, a facilitator can generate detailed information about the livelihood strategies of households. It reveals the connections among activities, resources and benefits. The tool can be a starting point for more detailed focus-group discussions on a variety of topics: the relationship of a household with the larger community, the closest town, the region, the nation or the world economy; transparency within household financial management; gender differences and inequalities in work, benefits, and resource control and access.

Materials

Cards or slips of paper, larger pieces of paper for mapping and diagrams, and coloured pens.

Process

Step 1: Determine the categories of households to interview. Use Wealth Ranking or a similar method to determine socio-economic categories.

Step 2: Arrange for three visits to each household. Try to involve as many family members as possible. Clarify that each part will be time consuming.

First visit – activities analysis

Step 1: Ask the family to draw a seasonal activities calendar representing the labour of all members of the family and non-family labourers who are hired or work in exchange for something. (See Seasonal Activities Calendar, Tubod, The Philippines, p. 184.)

Second visit – resources analysis

Step 1: Give the men and the women of the family each a sketch map of the community. Ask them to work in groups and ask each group to draw the household and the resources on which it depends. (See p. 62, Resource map of Ghusel, Lalitpur District, Nepal.)

Step 2: Ask each group to draw how the household contributes to other households, to the community, or to the larger economic, natural, or human environment.

Step 3: Ask the family members to use arrows to draw in networks, kinship, and other social relations on which the household depends or that are dependent on the household. Use arrows to draw the flow of resources to and from the household. People who have used this tool have found that families enjoyed it when it was treated like a game.

Step 4: Some questions to accompany the diagramming include:

- Who has access to the particular resource? Why?
- What are the terms of access?
- Who owns or controls it?
- Who uses it or works with it?
- What are the family's formal and informal credit sources?
- Who has access to credit? Why? How much?
- What are the primary sources of income?
- Who is responsible for which household expenses?
- Where are products sold?
- Who produces them and who sells them?
- What inputs are used?
- What are the sources of these inputs?
- Who exchanges what with whom?
- On whom do the households/communities rely for support? What support?
- Who in the community is not part of any exchange networks? Why?

Draw the answers on the map if possible.

Third visit – benefits analysis

Step 1: Analyse the seasonal calendar and resource analysis to generate cards with products of the family's labour. Put the name or a picture of the product on each card or, in lieu of cards, something representative of a product. For example, the

Benefits Analysis Chart from Agbanga, Leyte, The Philippines[7]

BY-PRODUCTS	HOW USED	WHO DECIDES ON USE	WHO DOES IT	HOW CASH IS USED	WHO DECIDES CASH USE
Leaves	Sun or rain umbrella	anyone	anyone		
	Dish or platter				
	Food wrapper	♀	♀		
Fruit	Sold at markets	♀	♀ ♀♂	for home needs (food, basics)	♀
	Gifts to friends	♀♂	♀♂		
	Home use (boiled, fried, raw)	♀	♀		
	Sold at local social events	♀	♀ ♀♂		
Flower	Home use (salads and vegetables)	♀	♀		
	Given to friends	♀♂	♀♂		
Trunk	Shaved into pig feed	♀	♂ (cuts down) ♀ (processes)		
Sprouts	Transplanted to household plots	♀♂	♀♂		
	Given to friends	♀♂	♀♂		

Resource Map from Ghusel, VDC, Lalitpur District, Nepal[8]

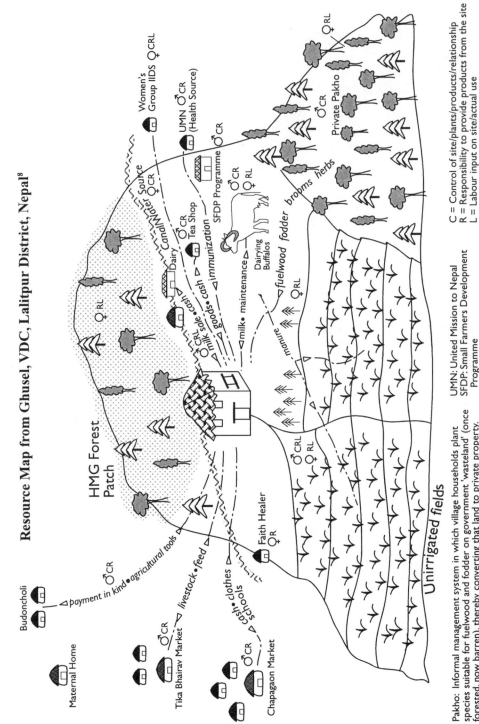

HMG Forest
Patch

Budoncholi

Maternal Home

△ payment in kind ● agricultural tools

♂CR

Tika Bhairav Market — livestock ● feed

♂CR

cash ● clothes
cash ● schools

Chapagaon Market

♂CR

Faith Healer
♀R

♀RL

Canal/Water Source
♂CR

Dairy
♂CR
Tea Shop

♂CR
♀RL
milk ● sale ● cash
goods ● cash
△ immunization

SFDP Programme

△ milk ● maintenance △

Dairing
Buffalos
♀RL
△ manure

fuelwood fodder brooms herbs

Unirrigated fields

Women's
Group IIDS ♀CRL

UMN ♂CR
(Health Source)

♂CR

♂CR
♀RL

♀RL

Private Pakho
♂CR

C = Control of site/plants/products/relationship
R = Responsibility to provide products from the site
L = Labour input on site/actual use

UMN: United Mission to Nepal
SFDP: Small Farmers Development
Programme
HMG: His Majesty's Government

Pakho: Informal management system in which village households plant
species suitable for fuelwood and fodder on government 'wasteland' (once
forested, now barren), thereby converting that land to private property.
Access to Pakho land varies widely by class, caste, and ethnicity.

various products and by-products of a tree might be fruit, fodder, fuelwood, timber, bark, medicine, poles, and shade.

Step 2: Alternatively, give each adult a card and ask them to discuss who has access to the products of the family's labour (including goods, services, and cash) and who decides how products should be used.   (See the Benefits Analysis Chart from Agbanga, Leyte, The Philippines, p. 61.)

Step 3: Ask each person with a card to describe:

- Who in the family uses the product or service?
- How is it used?
- Who decides how it should be used?
- Who controls the money if it is sold?
- Who decides how to spend the money?

If the person with the card does not know the answers to these questions, ask her/him to pass it to someone else in the family who does. Ask other household members if they agree and if the answers are complete.

Remember
You many need to combine or separate family members into sub-groups to allow members to participate freely, depending upon cultural and individual preferences and practices.

See also
Wealth Ranking
Gendered Resource Mapping
Seasonal Activities Calendar
Social Network Mapping
Focus Groups
Household Interviews
Division of Labour
Who Decides?

Advocacy Planning

Susan Quass

> **Time**
> Three two-hour sessions with additional time
> as needed for reassessment and resolutions.

Purpose

Advocacy assumes that all groups in society can have some impact on the wider
social, political and economic environment on a local, national or international
level. The target of the advocacy action may be within the organization if it is
large, or it may be outside the group. Advocacy may be as simple as using a public
forum to express a position on an issue or as complex as seeking to preserve,
change, or establish laws, institutions or organizational structures. Sometimes a
group forms for the sole purpose of advocacy; more often, advocacy actions tend
to be one component of a broader programme that focuses, for example, on
education, working conditions, wages or land tenure.

Materials

Pen and paper.

Process

Social analysis

Step 1: Identify the social, economic, cultural and political constraints on the
work of your group. As you think about the different constraints, consider how they
relate to each other. Does one seem to be the driving force or the most powerful
barrier? For example, if the goal is to have increased access to land for food
production, then the barriers may include large landowners, economic policies that
give incentives for large-scale or export production, laws against communal
ownership, laws against women owning land, or cultural attitudes honouring the
wealthy. Analyse how these social, political, economic and cultural factors support
one another.

Step 2: Prioritize these problems, and decide which one to address now. Priorities
may be based on importance or what is most readily resolved. Try to clarify both

the current social order and the goals to be achieved in transforming these conditions.

Step 3: Assess how advocacy might fit in with the other actions/programmes of the group (e.g. ongoing or periodic education or social organization of technical assistance programmes). Does the group have extra time and resources to put into advocacy? Are there other groups doing advocacy around similar issues? Perhaps you will want to connect with another group's advocacy efforts.

Strategies

Step 1: Review the interrelated political, social, economic and cultural elements that are hindrances to your goal. Restate the social analysis of the current social order and the prioritized goals for change.

Step 2: Identify your allies (see Network Formation, p. 155). Which individuals and groups may be interested in the same goals? How can you get their co-operation and support? What resources (social, political, economic, cultural) are available within your group and among your potential allies? (See also Personal and Household Resources.)

Step 3: Identify your opponents. What are the specific structures, policies and individuals involved in maintaining the social order as it is? Assess the interests, resources, and current strategy of these opponents. Who are the potential allies of your opponents?

Step 4: Identify observers. What groups and individuals may feel they have no stake in the goal you are advocating? Can these neutral parties have an effect on the outcome of the programme? Will they support the status quo or can they be organized in support of your cause?

Step 5: At this point you should have an outline of the groups and resources in support of your goal and of those likely to oppose your goal. Identify your strategy using specific objectives. Include plans for contingency, responsiveness and manoeuvrability with each objective. The strategies may be primarily social, political, economic or cultural, or may combine several or all areas. The strategic plan may need to include elements such as building and educating a constituency, training and mobilizing for action(s), organizational or movement structure and leadership, and possible resolution scenarios.

Methods and tactics

Step 1: Review the interrelated political, social, economic and cultural elements

that are hindrances to your goal. Restate the social analysis of the current social order and the prioritized goals you seek to change. Then review your strategic plan.

Step 2: Identify methods. What methods of action could be effective (and safe) against this opponent? What resources are available to be used? Some resources might include: the media, public opinion, elections, or petitions.

Step 3: Implement tactics: Who does what and when? Choose your initial method, plan and implement it.

Reassessment, resolution

Step 1: Constant review and revision of a strategy is very important. After every action of your group there will be a reaction by the opposition, and the stakes and positions (but not necessarily the interests) will have changed on both sides. You may need to review and refine your strategic plan and to reassess the choice of methods or tactics for the next step.

Step 2: You may want to go to Conflict Resolution (see pp. 75-87) when ready to end this particular advocacy action. Also, with a broad advocacy campaign, negotiation efforts may be happening simultaneously with advocacy actions on different fronts.

> **Remember**
> To make appropriate choices of strategy and method, you will need to balance effectiveness with potential risk to yourself, the participants and the larger community. Many tools described in this book can be used in Advocacy Planning.

The following tools may be used as part of advocacy planning, awareness-building, and strategizing:

- **Communicating with Officials and Outsiders**
  to build confidence and plan strategies for confronting outsiders

- **Community Drama**
  to communicate interests and to suggest alternatives

- **Conflict Resolution I-III**
  taking the step of admitting conflict and negotiating its resolution can be a form of advocacy

- **Focus Groups**
  useful for reflection and strategizing on the above points

- **Division of Labour, Seasonal Activities Calendar**
  can be used to demonstrate an inequitable division of labour as part of an effort to change this division of labour

- **Gender Myths**
  useful as part of a campaign against specific cultural practices or discrimination

- **Gendered Resource Mapping, Landscape/Lifescape, Land Use Feltboard**
  graphically present land use relationships and potential consequences of outsider and insider actions

- **Legal Rights I and II**
  the first step in a process to confront laws unfavourable to women, the poor, or a racial, ethnic or religious group or practices that continue in spite of laws

- **Mapping the Body**
  a starting point for discussion and action concerning sexual double standards, sexual violence and reproductive rights

- **Network Formation**
  to link up and, as necessary, scale up or down

- **Photography, Video I and II**
  a means to document, witness, collect testimony, state interests and promote change; cassette recorders may also be used

- **Oral Life Histories**
  to document and interpret social and environmental change in local terms

- **Study Trips**
  to collect evidence

- **Transects**
  useful as a graphic portrayal of environmental changes over time in conjunction with advocacy to promote different practices

- **Who Am I?**
  part of a reflection process prior to action

- **Who Decides?**
  to confront lack of transparency and clarify relations of power

Communicating With Officials and Outsiders

Adapted by Rachel Slocum from *Navamaga: Training Activities for Group Building, Health, and Income Generation*[9]

Time

Two hours, possibly to be repeated over a few days or weeks if preparing for a meeting.

Purpose

The ability to communicate with officials and outsiders is an important skill for groups or individuals trying to change or maintain some aspect of their lives. Often people are wary of authorities and not inclined to approach them, and some cultural norms make it more difficult for women to do so. This tool can be used as part of a confidence-building process in which people recognize the value of their own knowledge and learn to communicate with outsiders. It is particularly useful in cases where a facilitator can help a group to prepare for a specific meeting with officials.

Materials

Paper and markers (cassette recorder and/or video camera optional). Props for role play can include information the group wants to present, such as maps, diagrams or speeches. Someone representing the authority figure could dress the part for the role play.

Process

Step 1: Encourage the participants to discuss their experiences with officials and other outsiders (health officials, government extension officers, the police, NGO staff, local authorities, bank officials). Some questions to ask include:

- What did you accomplish in this exchange with an official?
- How did this experience make you feel?
- Are there both positive and negative examples of these interactions, and what specifically about them was positive or negative?

- If you had the chance to meet the official again, how would you want it to be different?

Step 2: Set up a series of role plays, such as a woman asking a local bank for a loan; a group of informants interviewing a researcher on the use of her/his research; a meeting with representatives of various donor agencies interested in doing projects in the community; a group participating in a study trip or people asking a livestock extension officer to vaccinate their animals. Discuss what information they would like to know, questions they need to ask, problems they might encounter and how they would like such a meeting to proceed. Ask them to suggest guidelines for dealing with outsiders. Questions for discussion include:

- Are the interests of the group (in the context of the meeting with authorities) one or many?
- Can you speak as a group?
- What useful knowledge do you have that the officials do not?
- What authority do you (the group) have?
- How can you use your authority as residents of this community, as users of these resources, as managers of this ecosystem, as crop experts, to your advantage in this meeting?
- What questions do you have for the officials?
- What points do you want to ensure are clear to them?
- What are some ways you would behave toward authorities?
- Is some behaviour more useful than others?
- What do you think the officials want? What are their interests?
- How do you think they might respond to your ideas?
- What can you do if you cannot proceed with your work because a government official is blocking progress?
- How can you gain support from authority figures who are initially opposed to an idea or action?
- What can you do if authorities doubt your ability to carry out a specific action?
- How can you help each other to deal more effectively with outsiders?

Remember

Know the context of the problem as thoroughly as possible to be able to help the group prepare.

If your group is mixed (by gender, ethnicity or class) be sure that the spokespeople are representative of each or acceptable to all.

Example
Survival News: Creating a dialogue between welfare mothers and welfare workers in the United States

Claire Cummings

Survival News' 'Jericho Project' is a good illustration of low/no income women and their allies working together for change in the social welfare system in the United States. *Survival News* is a publication whose purpose is to provide information about benefits and rights to welfare recipients, to provide a forum for the voices of low/no income people and their allies to be heard, and to educate people and develop theory about social welfare issues, as well as to help build a national network of people who work for change in the social welfare system. The publication is funded through small grant proposals written by the board members who are low/no income women and their middle-class allies. Skills and knowledge are shared and policy is determined equally. Twenty-five dollars is paid to low/no income persons for each article, poem, graphic or photo accepted for publication. Funding proposals are written collectively for empowerment projects such as the Jericho Project.

The Jericho Project was designed to bring welfare consumers, Department of Welfare workers and Department of Social Services workers together for five months to talk about issues that affect them when dealing with or working in the system. The participants – welfare mothers, welfare workers, and social workers – worked with a facilitator and a writing specialist to produce a special section in the current issue of *Survival News*. Grant moneys provided stipends for computer training, child care, transportation, facilitation and publication costs. In addition to discussing and writing powerful articles addressing their personal experiences, the participants produced a set of recommendations for the training of social workers, designed a pamphlet of information for new welfare clients, including rights, responsibilities, advice, and explanations, and developed policy recommendations dealing with issues of personal treatment, communication, co-ordination and quality of services which reflect the mutual concerns of clients and social workers. Thus *Survival News'* Jericho Project served as a tool to help 'break down the walls' between recipients of public aid and its official administrators; offered guidelines for communication based on respect for the dignity of recipients and social service workers on their own terms; and finally, provided a lasting tool for future recipients and workers.

Community Drama

Adapted by Lori Wichhart from *When People Play People*[10]

> **Time**
>
> Variable, depending on the type of
> drama and the context of presentation,
> but we suggest a minimum of two hours.

Purpose

Theatre can challenge conventional thinking and introduce new ideas. It can be a means to raise awareness, motivate people, enhance understanding or advocate change.

Materials

Markers and large sheets of paper, simple props from local materials (cassette recorder and video camera optional).

Process

Many areas have theatre groups which travel the country acting out dramas dealing with a variety of social issues. If there is one in the area, ask members to come and stage a production to introduce your topic. An alternative is for group participants to take on the roles of hypothetical community members to portray their concerns.

Method 1: Professional theatre groups

Using this method the actors and actresses travel with 'pre-packaged' productions which they create through a five-step process: information gathering in the community, information analysis, story improvisation, rehearsal, and, finally, community performances. The only community participation is by the audience during the discussion sessions that follow.

Method 2: Catalysts

Using actors as catalysts is another way to engage people in community drama. Improvise plays around locally suggested themes with community members themselves as performers. Actors can improvise throughout the play. They perform a short scene suggested by a local person, halt the action at a crisis point, and ask the audience to offer solutions. The actors become like puppets and perform the actions strictly on the spectators' orders. The 'best' solution is arrived at by trial, error, discussion, and then audience approval.

Method 3: Improvisation

A third way is to have participants from the audience tell a story with some social problem, then improvise, rehearse and present it to the rest of the group as a skit. The audience members are asked if they agree with the solution. Any spectator is invited to replace any actor and lead the action in the direction that seems most appropriate to him or her.

Remember

Theatrical presentations play on emotions and may elicit a wide range of responses including support for development action, anger, laughter, or hurt feelings. It is essential to follow up a performance with further discussion. Preparatory studies of the audience and its context help to ensure willing participation and effective presentation.

See also

Video I and II
Advocacy Planning

Example
Marotholi Travelling Theatre from Lesotho

Adapted by Lori Wichhart from *When People Play People*[11]

In 1986 Marotholi Travelling Theatre was approached by the Rural Sanitation Project of the Ministry of Health to create a play to reinforce the Ministry's campaign for the Ventilated Improved Pit (VIP) Latrine. The Theatre was invited to produce a play that dealt with a number of issues supplied by the Ministry of Health.

Theatre members went to the village to gather data on the villagers' own views of rural sanitation and local perceptions of the causes of the periodic outbreaks of diarrhoea that plagued that region. When the company put on the play in the first village the cast received a rousing welcome from the villagers. There was a lot of smooth audience interaction with the actors. Even village dogs which strayed onto the stage were incorporated into the play. The members of the audience had strong, conflicting views on the subject of the play but felt that the story-line was appropriate to their village. Six registered their names for the construction of toilets in their yards.

For the second performance, in a nearby village, the drama was received by a very passive and reserved audience. It seemed as though the concept of a *pitso* (village meeting) where participants were asked to participate in analysing the problems of sanitation, rather than just being instructed to build VIP toilets, was not comfortable for them. Audience members did not even sing very much.

In the third village the theatre members were welcomed by their most enthusiastic audience. Audience members loved the performance and were incorporated into the play. The nurse clinician in charge of the village clinic, 'Me Ntsoaki, was very popular. Some members of the audience were more interested in getting her attention than in the play. One elderly man stood up and addressed her directly about a toothache; another boasted that his own daughter-in-law had a VIP toilet. However, the reaction, even in this enthusiastic setting, was mixed. Some villagers felt that the play was mocking them because there had recently been an outbreak of diarrhoea there. One audience member proclaimed, 'Why don't you tell us to build toilets instead of going round in circles with plays!'

The most important outcome in all three cases was the public presentation of the issues and, in the first and third performances, the provocation of discussion and action.

Conflict Resolution I: Definition

Adapted by Katie Nye from *A Manual for Group Facilitators*[12] and *Beyond Machiavelli: Tools for Coping with Conflict*[13]

Time
One hour.

Purpose

The process allows conflicting parties to define the cause of a conflict and the dynamics of the relationship before devising solutions. This can help the parties involved to clarify the conflict together and to avoid becoming entrenched in opposing positions. This discussion will not only lead people to a better understanding of why they are acting or feeling the way they do about the issue, but will enable them to present a clear picture of their interests and needs. Negotiations often focus on positions (how much the parties want) rather than on interests (the underlying reasons why they want it). By focusing on their own interests, people will be better able to develop creative and collaborative options for resolution.

Materials

Pen, large sheets of paper (cassette recorder optional).

Process

Step 1: Explain that the purpose of the exercise is to form a group definition of the conflict at hand, not to think about solutions to the problem.

Step 2: If the group is large, break it up into smaller groups. Ask for volunteer(s) to record information for the group(s) and to ask questions such as:

- What is the issue that is causing the conflict?
- Who are the main parties involved?
- Why are they involved in this conflict? What are their goals?
- What are the underlying interests in support of this goal?
- How did the parties in conflict relate to each other before this issue arose?
- How have these parties dealt with conflict in the past?
- How have you dealt with this conflict thus far?

- Are your traditions, beliefs, and/or values embodied in this issue? If so, which ones?
- What effect would 'winning' or 'losing' the conflict have on you?

Step 3: Bring the group together to document the major points which may be used later, along with information gathered from other conflict analysis exercises, to formulate an analysis and solutions.

Remember
In some cultures people do not like to admit there is a conflict. In a gender-based conflict women and men may admit separately to a conflict but not in a mixed group.

See also
Conflict Resolution II and III
Time Line Variations
Advocacy Planning
Who Decides?
Problem Solving: Trees, Ranking, Assessment

Example
Conflict on Siquijor: Tubod Residents versus the San Juan Beach Corporation

Barbara Thomas-Slayter

Tubod is a small community (*barangay*) in San Juan municipality on Siquijor Island in the Philippines Central Visayas. In 1990, an Australian venture capitalist acquired seven hectares of shorefront for a tourist lodge and related activities. The land is adjacent to the village and although owned by several Tubod households had long been widely used by residents of the village for launching fishing boats and for gleaning. The Australian and several Filipino friends from a nearby island formed the San Juan Beach Corporation to begin the process of developing tourism on the island of Siquijor and specifically in San Juan municipality. They were being encouraged by the Congressman from Siquijor who was Chairman of Tourism in the Congress. However, many people feared that the loss of access to this shorefront would be harmful to the local residents.

In several focus group discussions with residents of Tubod, the ECOGEN research team used the approach and questions offered in the exercise on conflict definition. This approach helped to clarify the issues not only for the team but also for the residents, some of whom favoured building the local capacity for tourism and others of whom opposed it. Discussions helped to define the conflict, the underlying interests, and the options for action.

First, the exercise brought out the range of perspectives on the issue. For example, the 81-year-old mayor of San Juan, Mr Mamhot, greatly favoured the tourist resort being proposed by the San Juan Corporation. He hoped tourism would help the people of his municipality. Mr Mamhot was clearly associated with the prevailing ideology of the national government, as represented by the Congressman, and the thrust toward seizing opportunities to earn foreign exchange. He saw tourism as a way to bring additional resources/jobs/opportunities into his municipality.

On the other hand, the mayor's grandson, Richard Mamhot, disagreed. He asserted that the *barangay* had no resources except fishing and that it was critical that this source of livelihood not be damaged. Richard Mamhot was instrumental in the effort to keep the San Juan Corporation in check. He objected to tourism coming to the island and feared it would cause immorality and a deterioration of local values. He argued that Tubod and other communities like it needed business and industry but only those which would benefit Filipinos, not foreigners.

Thus, the mayor was a key figure behind the policy promoting tourism for San Juan and a key supporter of the San Juan Corporation while his grandson, Richard, was a strong opponent. Richard and his grandfather had many debates – both privately and in public – about the value of tourism to the people of San Juan and Tubod. Richard Mamhot did not doubt his grandfather's good intentions on behalf of the San Juan municipality, but he completely disagreed with his judgement about the best approach for improving livelihoods for the people of this community.

Over the months, the Tubod Barangay Council became disturbed about the plans of the San Juan Beach Corporation and specifically about its efforts to acquire other land in the municipality. There is much pressure on the land, and the lowlands are the best for cultivation. Ultimately, reflecting widespread concern among residents of the community, the Council prepared a resolution limiting the land the Corporation could acquire to the existing seven hectares. All the *barangay* captains and councillors from all 15 *barangays* in San Juan municipality shared their concern. They supported the resolution which was presented to the Provincial Government.

Conflict Resolution II – Walking in Others' Shoes

Adapted by Katie Nye from *In the Tiger's Mouth: An Empowerment Guide for Social Action*[14]

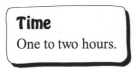

Time
One to two hours.

Purpose

Part of building a collaborative approach to conflict resolution is to develop empathy for and understanding of another's situation. It is also important to know how others perceive your interests, needs, threats, demands and offers.

Materials

List of questions, pens and paper or poster paper and markers.

Process

Step 1: Divide the group into pairs. Ask questions such as those listed below of volunteers from each of the groups in conflict or address them to the entire group. Design questions ahead of time that encourage participants to think about the issue from the perspective of the other party.

Step 2: Explain that each person should try to imagine him or herself in the position of the other. Use the following questions pertaining to the issue or conflict and to the other party's context to help each understand the other's situation.

- Who are you?
- What is your situation?
- What pressures operate in your life?
- What expectations do you have?
- What are your needs?
- What are your constraints?
- What are your interests?
- Why are you in conflict with X?
- Who is responsible for the conflict?
- Are you all in it or just some people?

- Are you afraid of giving up something?
- What position have you taken or what demands have you made?
- What does the position the other side has taken mean to you?
- How do you perceive the other group?
- What could you do to help resolve this conflict?
- Is there a way to satisfy the interests of both groups?
- What has the other group demanded from you?
- Why are their demands unreasonable?
- What does the other group offer?

Step 3: After finishing this role play so that all participants have had an opportunity to be in the 'other party's shoes', reconvene the group to discuss the insights they gained from the exercise such as:

- How did it feel to be the other party?
- What common ground exists between the groups?
- What behaviour or strategy may be helpful in gaining their respect and co-operation?
- How can the parties work together?[15]

Example
Learning from a PRA with Somali Pastoralists

Adapted by Barbara Thomas-Slayter from *PRA with Somali Pastoralists*[16]

Jeded is a village of nomadic households located in north-eastern Somalia. Founded in the early 1950s because of a new well and good grazing, Jeded is an important watering point and provisioning station for a large nomadic community. In 1994, with support from GTZ and in collaboration with the Bari Regional Council and several Somali NGOs, the people of Jeded determined to undertake a planning exercise in the form of a participatory rural appraisal (PRA) and to develop a Community Action Plan (CAP).

During the course of the PRA, a dispute began to simmer as a result of the ranking exercise. By previous agreement, about 100 men and women sat together to work out the details of the ranking of village problems. Yet some of the older men felt uneasy, perhaps even annoyed, that women were participating on equal terms with the men to make decisions about Jeded's future. Three men even walked out of the ranking session as a protest against women participating in village decision-making. The PRA team had a problem. It was becoming increasingly clear that ignoring the tension would lead to a total collapse of the PRA process and principles. Yet to take on the dispute could lead to unfortunate and perhaps

Steering Committee and Task Forces: Jeded Village[15]

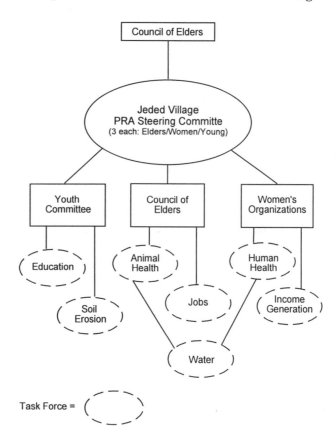

even disastrous confrontations between and among men, women, and the PRA team. No one would emerge as beneficiary from such a dispute.

On one hand, the team wanted to respect traditions and procedures within the village. There was no government, which meant that the elders were the only formal structure through which to work. Thus, respect for the elders' position was quite important. On the other hand, the PRA team had been meeting regularly with Jeded's women and had gathered fundamentally important information about their views of problems, causes, and possible solutions. Further, the very basis of PRA's rationale is that one of the necessary prerequisites for sustainable resource use is equity in resource access.

The PRA team leaders chose a third option, namely to begin a process of enabling each group to 'walk in the others' shoes.' In meetings with small numbers of elders and also with key women leaders of the village, they launched a process of reflection on the viewpoints of others involved in the PRA and on ways to facilitate working arrangements among members of the community and the PRA team. The PRA team raised questions about needs, interests, and perceptions of all parties and proposed a series of task forces as well as a PRA Steering Committee. Task forces would focus on specific project activities and include interested people from different groups in the village. The steering Committee would include three members each from Jeded's three major groupings: elders, women, and the young adults (youth). The cluster of task forces would replicate the problems identified in the ranking with some very sensitive sorting out of responsibilities. Their duties would parallel, as closely as possible, the priorities which each village group had identified.

The chart shows the steering committee and task force structure which emerged. Once these clarifications and divisions of labour were assigned, tensions began to dissolve. The men felt comfortable that they had been consulted and that the structure of the Steering Committee was consistent with village traditions. The women were pleased as the arrangement gave them a formal role in the Steering committee and specific responsibilities in human health, income generation, and shared duties in water. Even before the formal village meeting to discuss the proposed structure, elders, women, and youth were all indicating broad satisfaction with the arrangements.

Conflict Resolution III: Negotiation

Adapted by Susan Quass and Katie Nye from *Creating Peaceable Classrooms: Conflict Resolution in Schools*[18] and *Getting to Yes*[19]

Time
Three hours.

Purpose

Conflict is a natural, inevitable and even useful part of human activity. It is an opportunity to learn more about the underlying values and assumptions of people and it offers the chance for greater clarity, creativity and growth in relationships. Conflict can lead to substantial personal and social change, but it can also damage or destroy positive relationships. The process of resolving conflict can be used to generate specific solutions and to strengthen relationships between the people in conflict. Recognizing when one form of conflict resolution will work better than another helps people to devise the best possible solutions to specific instances of conflict.

Materials

Pens, paper.

Process

Before initiating a conflict resolution process, both parties must recognize that there is a conflict and must be willing to enter into the process of negotiation. Bringing the conflict into the open at an appropriate time is also important.

Step 1: Identify the group's own formal and informal methods of conflict resolution by asking them to describe how a conflict was resolved in the past.

Step 2: Identify and separate interests and positions. Positions are the concrete things you want. Interests are the reasons you want what you want. Ask each party to describe its positions and interests while the others listen. Ask them to be as specific as possible and not to attack the others personally – separate the people from the problem. After each group has spoken, encourage questions to clarify the interests of each.

Step 3: Ask the group to brainstorm for solutions to the conflict. Ask people to express their ideas and not to criticize others. The goal is not to come up with the 'perfect' idea, but to get as many ideas as possible. Encourage participants to consider carefully the ideas suggested by others. Identify as many solutions as possible that would fulfil any of the interests described by the participants. Record all suggestions without evaluating them.

Step 4: Evaluate the proposed solutions. Present all possible solutions and eliminate any that are objectionable to either party based on its interests. Jointly develop a set of questions to evaluate the remaining possible solutions. Some questions include:

- Which interests does the solution satisfy? Which interests does it not satisfy?
- What does the implementation of a particular solution involve?
- What are the potential outcomes of each course of action?
- Is the solution acceptable to those who must live with it?

Step 5: Choose a solution. Decide what steps are necessary to ensure its implementation. Decide who will do what, when, where and how. Determine methods to review and evaluate.

> **See also**
> Who Decides?
> Conflict Resolution I and II: Definition
> and Walking in Others' Shoes
> Group Definition
> Advocacy Planning
> Problem Solving: Trees, Ranking, Assessment

Conflict analysis summary[20]

Parties

- Who are the main parties and their key spokespersons?
- Who are the secondary parties?
- Are the parties well-defined?
- Do the parties want to work towards a solution?
- Are the parties capable of working with each other?

Substance of the problem

- How do you characterize the conflict?

- Different interests? Different values? (strongly held?)
- Perceived differences that do not really exist?
- Most constructive way to define the problem? Central issues? Secondary issues?
- Are the issues negotiable?
- Key interests of each party? Interests the parties have in common?
- Positions that have been taken? Options for resolution?

Procedures
Ask for suggestions by the parties about forms of conflict resolution or management.

- Does a consensus process serve the parties' interests?
- What constraints might affect the structure of a conflict resolution process (timing, legal activities, resources)?
- What other obstacles must be overcome?
- Are the parties (or other groups) experienced in using dispute resolution procedures?
- What are the chances for success?

Conflict facilitation – rules for fighting fair

- Identify that conflict is happening.
- Disagree with ideas, not people. Do not accuse or blame.
- State an issue or a problem as a shared one: 'We do not agree about X', instead of 'You are wrong about X'.
- Identify and focus on the central issues to the conflict. Do not digress into general discussion.
- Do not compromise too quickly. Quick compromise may mean that you have not adequately explored the problem or solutions. The ideal solution gives everyone what they need and meets their interests.
- Those not directly involved in the conflict can be invited to pay close attention to both sides and add perspectives on the process as well as the content.
- Be aware of your own opinions and feelings. People tend to think their wants and needs are logically justifiable, so often they focus on rational arguments even though their feelings may be the driving force.
- Use quiet time. If the discussion becomes too heated, a few minutes break or a schedule that permits meeting over several days or weeks may facilitate the decision.

Checklist of steps for successful conflict resolution[21]

- Allow enough time to deal with conflict.
- Define the problem in terms clear and acceptable to all parties in the conflict.
- Deal with negative feelings in positive ways.
- Help participants identify in concrete terms what makes them unhappy with the situation – to distinguish between feelings and reality.
- Encourage each participant in the conflict to identify his or her own real needs and values.

Example
Rural communities, environmentalists and the timber industry in Guatemala[22]

Gwen Thomas

The Fundacion de Defensa del Medio Ambiente de Baja Verapaz (FUNDEMABV) is a non-profit, non-governmental organization based in Salama in the Department of Baja Verapaz in Guatemala. Its mission is to improve the quality of life for the residents of Baja Verapaz by protecting and conserving the natural resource base and by promoting sustainable resource development.

FUNDEMABV is one of ten local counterparts of the Environmental Project for Central America (PACA), an integrated conservation and development project implemented by CARE and The Nature Conservancy. FUNDEMABV operates in and around the Biosphere Reserve Sierra de las Minas in Guatemala, collaborating with PACA in the implementation of buffer zone management and environmental education activities.

Deforestation has been a chronic problem in Baja Verapaz for about 30 years. Many families are dependent on fuelwood for household energy needs and for sale as a source of income. Loggers, sawmill operators, and forest owners are directly dependent on the forest resource to sustain their livelihood. Ambiguous forestry laws and land tenure regimes exacerbate the problem.

FUNDEMABV activities lead to conflict

FUNDEMABV has carried out activities in the forestry sector since 1985. Its initial strategy was to protect the region's resource base and the quality of life for its residents through the public denunciation of illegal and corrupt forestry activities, tracking and inspecting both legal and illegal logging sites, photographing and recording forest abuses, and reporting names and logging sites to the authorities. The approach provoked hostility and anger among members of the timber industry, as well as some small-scale forest users and forestry officials who fell victim to FUNDEMABV's denunciations. Resentment towards FUNDEMABV and its staff members began to escalate to the point where, by 1991, several members had received death threats. What had been created was a confrontational environment with conservationists and preservationists at one extreme and resource users at the other.

Identifying new approaches and strategies

FUNDEMABV's activities in the forestry sector had reached a crisis point and staff members realized that their approach was dangerous and a strategic change was in order. Firmly committed to the environmental field and to natural resource conservation and education, FUNDEMABV staff and Board of Directors sought alternative strategies for fostering dialogue, negotiation, education, and policy change. They decided to hold a preliminary seminar for the local people involved with timber to discuss problems and constraints and to seek ideas for a constructive approach for the future.

The first seminar was attended by several loggers, sawmill operators, and vendors in addition to local government and NGOs. People were wary and hesitant, but the seminar accomplished the task of breaking the stand-off and starting the process of constructive dialogue.

A follow-up seminar, funded by PACA and the World Wildlife Fund, was held to address issues of concern generated during the first meeting, including the economic aspects of the forest resource, social and ecological degradation, forestry laws, the environmental improvement laws, and protected areas laws. This seminar provided an open forum for all concerned to put their ideas and problems on the table and to initiate the process of identifying feasible solutions. It reflected a changed ambience which favoured open discussion and exchange, the identification of common ground, and strengthened opportunities for communication.

As a result of the initial two seminars, a follow-up workshop was proposed for further discussion of forest management and legal issues. Since then, two workshops have been held to address the difficult questions regarding the region's resource base, and forestry resource users and the environmental community are meeting together on equal ground to resolve longstanding conflicts over forest activities and environmental degradation.

New role for FUNDEMABV

Throughout this process FUNDEMABV has balanced two roles: (1) the convening party bringing together a variety of interest groups to discuss problems and potential solutions, and facilitating the creation of formal and informal linkages and alliances between interest groups and (2) the educator concerned with raising environmental awareness and promoting behavioural change. As a grassroots movement, FUNDEMABV's ability to influence decisions and actions lies in community support and citizen participation. By mobilizing diverse community interest groups and encouraging dialogue, FUNDEMABV seeks to establish alliances and informal agreements. Over the long run these agreements will serve as the foundation for formal policy change. Ultimately, however, the responsibility for monitoring and compliance of these agreements will rest with the community.

Strategic approaches: lessons learned from Baja Verapaz

- Identify opportunities to resolve conflict through dialogue.
- Respect individual ideas and opinions.
- Encourage participation of multiple parties.
- Seek common ground among diverse groups.
- Foster education as the foundation of the policy process. Improving citizen awareness frequently results in behavioural change and increases citizen responsibility.

Methodological recommendations

- Seminars and workshops provide a forum for allowing participants to present personal opinions and discuss ideas.
- Follow through with your intentions.
- When facilitating and moderating policy dialogue, remain neutral. Promoting a non-partisan approach will enhance confidence and credibility.
- Understand your audience. The technical language of presentations must be simple and practical. The physical location of meetings must encourage participant confidence and open discussion.

Division of Labour

Adapted by Rachel Slocum from *Participatory Rural Appraisal/ Rapid Rural Appraisal*[23]

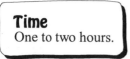

Time
One to two hours.

Purpose

This tool can provide detailed information about the division of labour by gender and its consequences for a household. It can clarify why women and men have certain tasks and not others and preferred time use. It can also be a starting point for a more general discussion of gender relations and the position of women.

Materials

Large sheets of paper and markers. Use appropriate symbols to represent time and different types of work unless written descriptions are possible.

Process

Step 1: Ask the women to indicate how they spend an average day from the time they get up in the morning to the time they go to sleep. Ask the same of the men.

Step 2: If the group is literate, write the hours of the day and, next to the appropriate times, fill in women's and men's tasks side by side. If not, use symbols that the group chooses to represent dawn, midday and evening. One variation is to ask groups of men and women not only what activities fill their day, but who helps them. (See work schedule in the Dominican Republic, p. 91.) It may also prove useful to ask men and women to outline each other's daily tasks (see p. 90).

Another way to get the same information is to draw pie charts on paper or the ground. Ask each group to divide a circle into specific activities. Working on the ground, participants can use twigs, a piece of millet stalk, an article of clothing, and a water sack to represent gathering wood, working in the fields, washing clothes, and hauling water.

Some discussion questions include:

• What is the most difficult or burdensome task of the day?

- What would you prefer to do with your time if you did not have to do X task?
- What steps have you taken to lighten your workload? If your family has helped you to do so, how?
- What do you hope your daughter or son's daily work will consist of? Why?
- Do you think what you receive as compensation is adequate for the work you do? Why/Why not?
- What task do you wish your wife/husband would help you with?

Remember

Activities may differ not only by gender, but also by age, ethnic group, class and other social divisions. Use Wealth Ranking and variations on that method to determine socio-economic categories.

Do not spend too much time getting an elaborate diagram or trying to be too precise as the discussion is more important.

Note that people often do many tasks simultaneously, such as child care and harvesting, cooking and cleaning, herding and water collection, or water and fuelwood collection. Be sure to include all of these multiple tasks.

See also

Seasonal Activities Calendar
Time Line Variations
Who Am I?
Activities, Resources and Benefits Analysis
Gender Analysis Activity Profile
Gender Myths
Wealth Ranking

Examples

Gender Division of Labour in Dingiraay, The Gambia[24]

Adapted by the editors from *Sustaining Development through Community Mobilization*

In a PRA case study in Dingiraay, The Gambia, the Daily Activity Calendar revealed that women perform the bulk of the work in the village. It also showed that women are in different places more often throughout the day than men. The facilitator recorded the information shown in Table 1.

Several men agreed that there might be more equitable ways to divide the workload and tried to think of ways that they could help their wives. Later, when the community ranked its problems, excessive labour demand on women was listed fourth. The most important of Dingiraay's problems, however, was lack of water. One villager remarked to the group that women were responsible for water collection and the community owed it to them to find solutions to make their lives easier. The PRA team noted that women wanted a borehole which would facilitate getting water. The men wanted to use the borehole and pump for growing cash crops. However, men, by selling vegetables, would have a means to pay for pump maintenance and fuel whereas the women would not. This difference raises the issue of why women do not have similar opportunities for income generation that would enable them to pay for the pump.

Table 1 Daily activity calendar, Dingiraay, The Gambia

Time	Women	Men
6:00-6:30	Wake up, bathe, and pray	Wake up, bathe and pray
6:30-8:00	Domestic services	Farm work
8:00-8:30	(breakfast, housework,	"
	collect water, sweep)	"
8:30-9:00	Food/Coos preparation	"
9:00-11:30	Water collection	
11:30-1:00	Farm work	Rest and pray
1:00-2:00	Lunch preparation	
2:00-3:30	Eat lunch, rest and pray	Eat lunch
3:30-5:30	Water and fuelwood	Farm work
	collection	
5:30-6:00	Farm work	
6:00-7:30	Leaves and vegetable	
	collection	
7:30-8:30	Dinner preparation	Rest, pray, read the Quran
8:30	Bathe, eat dinner and pray	Bathe, eat dinner, pray
10:30	Go to bed	

Women's work in the Dominican Republic

Cornelia Butler Flora

Cornelia Butler Flora, working with Plan Sierra in the Dominican Republic, used this tool as part of a needs assessment process. She began a 'dialogue of exploration' in which the 'women were clearly the experts'. After the women had finished detailing what they did and who helped, the facilitator asked the women

Table 2 Assistance women receive from other members of the household[25]

Task	Husbands	Female children	Male children	Small children left at home
Prepare fire	*	*		
Make coffee	*	*		
Feed chickens	*	*	*	
Collect Guano	*	*	*	*
Milk cow				
Get water		*	*	*
Boil plantains or yucca for breakfast		*		
Clean, sweep, dust, mop, make beds, pound the dirt		*		
Shop		*	*	*
Cook the rice		*		
Wash clothes: take clothes to the river, make the fire, boil the clothes, wash		*		*
Eat, take lunch to husbands in the fields				*
Wash pots, clean kitchen				
Make coffee				
Iron: make fire, heat iron		*		
Weave palm fibre baskets		*		
Get mud for making pots		*		
Gather firewood		*	*	*
Hull and prepare coffee beans				*
Prepare dinner		*		
Wash dishes		*		
Bathe the children		*		

what they thought about the activity. By listing and discussing all their tasks and activities, the women's contribution became visible. The women 'were thrilled to know how much they were worth and all that they contribute to the household. They asked that their husbands come to a similar session to see all that the women did.' Plan Sierra and Flora used the chart to plan activities for women, both to lighten their burden and to plan new programmes according to the time that the women had available.

Entering women's world through men's eyes in Ahmedabad, India[26]

Meena Bilgi, working with Aga Khan Rural Support, used a variation of this tool to sensitize men to women's workload. She asked a group of men to document the work that the women in their families do throughout the day. The men became very involved in remembering all that women did in an average day and finished with a very high number of hours worked (17-19 hours per day). Surprised at the figure they had calculated, they did the exercise again to see if they had made a mistake but came up with the same number of hours. Seeing that they were becoming defensive, Meena asked them to share information on what was involved in fuelwood collection and cooking. They came up with a number of problems women face including: walking long distances in the heat, snake bites, harassment by the forest guard, lack of drinking water and smoke inhalation.

Outsider vs. insider perceptions: animal husbandry, Egypt[27]

The Women in Development Office of German Technical Co-operation (GTZ) in Egypt originally developed this tool for training purposes but it can also be used by project staff and researchers to check their own perceptions against those of the people actually carrying out the tasks. The GTZ staff asked men agricultural agents and women farmers to identify the tasks associated with water buffalo care and who (men, women, girls and boys) was responsible for each. The results speak for themselves. Not only did the two groups differ with respect to gender division of labour; they also chose different categories to describe buffalo care.

Table 3 How women farmers and male agricultural extensionists described the division of labour for buffalo raising

Women farmers' view	Male agricultural extensionist view
Animal care	**Animal care** place preparation(M, F) spreading dust(F) transport dust (bedding) (M) warming(M)
Animal health bringing to veterinarian(F,M)	**Animal health** during illness(F,M) vaccination campaign(M)
Calf rearing feeding animal(F) outing(F,fc,mc) sewing of covering cloth(F) assisting during birth(F,M)	**Calf rearing** feeding animal(F) transport berseem(M) supporting nursing(F) place preparation(F,M) watering(F) outing(F,fc) assisting during birth(F,M) warming(M)
Feeding feeding in the field(M,F,mc,fc) feeding at home(F)	**Feeding** purchasing fodder(M) feeding animal(F,M) land preparation(M) sowing seeds(M) irrigation(M) fertilizing(M) cutting berseem(F, 80%) transporting berseem(F,M)
Watering carrying water home (F) watering animal at home (F) watering animal in field(F,M,fc,mc) bathing animal (M,mc,fc)	**Watering** carrying water home (F, M) watering animal at home (F, M) pumping water (F,M)

Key:

F= Female
M= Male
mc= male child
fc= female child

Women farmers' view	Male agricultural extensionist view
Reproduction detecting desire of animal (F) leading animal to mate (M,F)	**Reproduction** detecting desire of animal (F) leading animal to mate (M)
Fodder cultivation transport home(F) cutting berseem (F) sowing seeds(M)	**Fodder cultivation**
Ownership benefit(M,F) control over animal(M) access to animal(F)	**Ownership**
Production and marketing of dairy products(F)	**Production and marketing of dairy products**

Focus Groups

Adapted by the editors from *Tools of Gender Analysis* and *Focus Groups as Qualitative Research*[28]

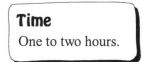

Time

One to two hours.

Purpose

Focus groups are fairly small discussion groups (10 to 15 people) led by a researcher or facilitator. They enable outsiders to understand and describe better the range of perspectives in a community or local organization through small group discussions. Focus groups can be single or mixed gender. They are very useful as single gender groups in cultures where women are not comfortable speaking in large assemblies or with men. Even when women do participate in mixed gender groups, they may speak more freely or cover more risky topics in groups of only women. The same is true for members of some class, age, caste, religious, and ethnic groups who may hesitate to speak out in a mixed group.

Focus groups can be used for any number of purposes – consciousness-raising, information gathering, analysis, and, in general, any step in a development process. In the US and Europe these group sessions are now used along with public opinion polls for everything from elections to product development and marketing. They have also been used to generate community time lines and trend lines on resource use, to explore sexuality and reproductive rights issues, and in research/ action to encourage analysis of oppression. Focus group discussions can be useful to show:

- Priorities for community action based on gender, class, ethnicity and other markers of identity;
- The level and nature of resource awareness and environmental interests of both men and women;
- Women's and men's perceptions of institutional effectiveness.

The objectives of a focus group are to:

- Cover a maximum range of relevant topics;
- Provide information that is as specific as possible so as to direct the discussion towards concrete and detailed accounts of the participants' experiences;

- Foster interaction that explores the participants' feelings and opinions in some depth;
- Take into account the personal context that participants use in generating responses.

Materials

Prepare the questions you want to ask ahead of time. Paper and markers (cassette recorder or video camera optional).

Process

Step 1: Plan and write questions before the meeting. For an unstructured discussion, two broadly stated topic questions will usually suffice. For a structured discussion, facilitators often use four or five topic questions with more specific points under each major topic.

Step 2: In some focus groups, each participant makes an individual, uninterrupted statement about her or himself at the start of the session.

Suggestions for low facilitator involvement[29]

- Present initial topic followed by unstructured group discussion.
- Introduce second topic, based largely on points that have already been raised.
- Allow discussion to come to an end on its own, perhaps with a subtle cue from the facilitator.

Suggestions for high facilitator involvement

- Apply an outline throughout the discussion; maintain clear and consistent order.
- Begin the structured discussion with a general question not intending to get a full answer, but to set up an agenda of topics within the limits of the outline.
- Hold off comments that do not quite fit in a particular stage of the discussion, but reintroduce them at a logical point, i.e. 'I recall that some of you mentioned something a little different earlier and I wonder how that fits into what we are discussing now.'
- End session with final summary statements from participants.

Some ideas for questions for a focus group meeting with a fishermen's association

Types of organizational questions which can be adapted for any group:

- What is the purpose of the Fishermen's Association (FA)?
- What financial resources does it have? Who supports it?

- How does it recruit/organize people on behalf of the organization?
- How do men's and women's responsibilities in the FA vary?
- How does the community view the FA?
- How does the FA make decisions?

Some specific activity questions:

- How has access to fishing changed in this area over the past ten years?
- Are there government policies which affect fishing techniques, where you fish, marketing, or other elements of this work?
- How much is erosion affecting your fishing?
- How does fishing fit into your other livelihood responsibilities?
- How do you think fishing in this area will be different five years from now? Ten years from now?

Remember

Include all people in the discussion.

Divisions still exist within single gender focus groups (by class, religion, age, race, and ethnicity).

Avoid closed questions.

See also

Household Interviews
Activities Resources and Benefits Analysis
Advocacy Planning
Study Trips

Example
A focus group meeting with the Fishermen's Association of Tubod, Siquijor Island, the Philippines

Barbara Thomas-Slayter

For the people living in the coastal village of Tubod, on Siquijor Island in the Philippines, fishing constitutes a major livelihood activity. In 1991, researchers from Clark University and the Visayas State College of Agriculture investigated the relationships among gender-based responsibilities, livelihoods, community action, and environmental degradation. The research team was eager to talk with the Fishermen's Association (FA) to obtain the views of members on a range of topics related to the declining fishery resources, and their strategies for addressing the changes. A meeting with the FA was scheduled for an evening at a public site in the village, at both a time and a place convenient to the community. Approximately 20 fishermen attended, along with 10 or 15 observers, some of them wives of fishermen who came on behalf of their husbands, thus assuming an important 'representational' function often designated as women's responsibility.

Researchers led the meeting informally with a series of questions leading to a discussion of a particular topic. The discussion was free-flowing with light direction on the part of one of the team members while another took notes. The meeting lasted about two hours and there was vigorous discussion of the organization, the issues which the community faced in regard to fishing, and the ways in which the Fishermen's Association was trying to address these problems. Some of the topics explored during the meeting were later investigated in more detail through household or key informant interviews.

Two categories of topics were covered in the focus group discussion with the Fishermen's Association:

(1) Organizational or institutional topics with a series of questions about the purpose of the organization, its membership, decision-making processes, resources, interactions with the broader community, range of activities, gender-based differences in responsibilities, the broad provincial and national context in which the group functions, and leadership issues.

2) Detailed information about and perceptions of fishing, including:
- Observations on changes in levels of fish catch over time and members' explanations for these changes;
- Attitudes toward the creation of a local fish sanctuary;
- Views of government actions and responsibilities in regard to fishing;
- Seaweed culturing;

- Changes in fishing techniques;
- Competition from outsiders for island fishing areas;
- Ways in which fishing fits into other livelihood options;
- Marketing arrangements;
- The impact of erosion and siltation on fishing;
- Dynamite fishing;
- The different roles of men and women in the fishing business;
- Fish pots and other equipment;
- The changing relations among government, fishermen, traders, and non-Filipino fishermen.

Gender Analysis Activity Profile

Adapted by the editors from *Tools of Gender Analysis* and *Tool Book: Gender Analysis and Training*[30]

> **Time**
> One hour.

Purpose

The Gender Analysis Activity Profile is a means to raise awareness about who is responsible for what activities in the community and why, through focus group or community-wide discussions. It can help to clarify the underlying reasons for gender-based division of labour and control over resources.

Materials

Markers and paper (cassette recorder optional).

Process

Step 1: Ask the group to make a list of community activities such as:

- School maintenance
- School fundraising
- Public works (for the government)
- Community work
- Village meetings
- Health clinic work/maintenance
- Tree planting (for the government or the whole community)
- Fixing the church/mosque
- Meeting with outsiders
- Involvement in NGO projects
- Political activity
- Preparation for community celebrations
- Leadership in community-level decision-making
- Leadership in community organizations
- Membership in community organizations

Step 2: After the participants identify activities, ask them who of the following is responsible for carrying out these activities:

- Female/male children
- Female/male adults
- Female/male elders

They might also be asked what ethnic group or class is responsible for which activities. After identifying who does the work, ask why – for legal, religious, cultural, education, economic, political or other reasons. Some questions for discussion include:

- Why does one gender (or race or class) do X activities and not others?
- What are the implications of one gender doing one activity and not another?
- Is this work paid?
- How much does the community value the work?
- Do the people who do the work benefit? In what way?
- Have these roles changed over time? How?

Step 3: Repeat the same exercise for reproductive and productive activities, which include:

Reproductive
Child bearing and rearing
Caring for the sick
Caring for the elderly
Bringing water
Collecting firewood
Cooking
Cleaning

Productive
Agricultural or pastoral work (self employed)
Work for wage, kind or salary
- industrial
- trade
- agricultural
- services
Food processing and preparation for sale
Crafts for home use and sale

Table 4 Participation in household decision-making[31]

Decision on Activity	Who makes decisions				
	Woman only	Man only	Woman usually	Man usually	Both
Use of revenue Education Time use Family planning Resource use and management Travel Savings and investment Work schedule on cash crops or subsistence crops					

Who does it?						Why? (Determinants)					
Activity	FC	MC	FA	MA	FE	ME	Legal	Cultural	Education	Economic	Political	Religious

FC/MC - Female/Male Child
FA/MA - Female/Male Adult
FE/ME - Female/Male Elder

The above table can be used as a monitoring and evaluation tool to determine who is doing what and why these activities have been allocated to women or men. When designing and implementing a project, it is important to ask whether the project takes into consideration women's triple role and to determine whether the project maintains, strengthens or questions existing gender roles, relations and levels of access and control.

> **Remember**
> Women often have three roles: domestic, 'productive' and community/ habitat management. Men often have two roles: 'productive' and community politics.[32]

See also
Gendered Resource Mapping
Division of Labour
Time Line Variations
Who Decides?
Household Interviews
Seasonal Activities Calendar

Example
Gender Analysis Activity Profile of the CARE Kenya, Siaya Health, Water, and Sanitation Project (SHEWAS)

Leah Wanjama

The purpose of using the gender analysis activity profile in this case was to examine the division of labour in the community and to assess the extent to which the project has helped to reduce or increase the workload of women. First, guided by an artist, we brainstormed on the images the community has of adult male, adult female, male elder, female elder, male child, and female child. These images were then illustrated by the artist. Next, we thought of all the activities carried on in productive, household, and community activities. Productive activities are those done for the production of goods and services. Household activities are those which concern the reproduction and maintenance of human resources. Finally, community activities are all those performed for the social reproduction and maintenance of the community.

When we had completed the list of activities, it was translated into Dholuo, the language of the community. Each activity was written on a card. The group then proceeded to inform the community about what they had discussed and explained the purpose of the exercise. Participants were asked to add to the list of activities if they perceived any that were missing.

The community members were then divided into five groups and each group was given a set of illustrations and the cards on which the activities were written. Each group was asked to form six columns according to the illustrations and to line up the activities behind the gender that most likely performs the activity. When the groups had completed this task they were asked to look at the other groups' charts to see if they had come up with similar responses. After the groups had done this they were asked to come together and comment on the gender analysis activity profile.

103

In general, the exercise was very revealing to the group members. Their principal observations were that the lines of the female adult and female child were long compared to those of the male adult and male child. The group realized that women and female children bore a heavier workload, and they commented that this was a problem considering that these tasks were vital. They did not identify any alternatives.

Gender Myths

Adapted by Rachel Slocum and Sara L. Kindon from *From Tea Makers to Decision Makers: Applying Participatory Rural Appraisal to Gender and Development in Rural Bali, Indonesia*[33]

Time

One hour for separate groups of men and women followed by one hour, at a later stage, with women and men together or with community members and government officials, NGO staff or others.

Purpose

A discussion of perceptions about women and men can help to reveal gender myths. A gender myth can be a legend pertaining to a characteristic of men or women. It can also be an idea or perception that has gained currency in the culture. Myths or stereotypes often enforce gender roles and responsibilities as well as unequal relations between women and men. In addition, they can also prevent men and women from being involved in certain activities, rising to positions of authority or gaining access to and control over resources and information. Raising awareness about gender myths and their impacts on both women and men can help to challenge and perhaps change some of these stereotypes. Discussing gender stereotypes with government officials, the staff of non-government organizations and members of other organizations is also useful given that these groups design and implement policies and programmes that maintain certain cultural values.

Materials

Paper and markers.

Process

Step 1: Prior to group discussions, prepare examples of stereotypical perceptions (gender myths) of women and men in case the group is unsure of what you mean. Some examples of popular perceptions include:

- Men are farmers; women are housewives.
- Women are emotional; men are rational.

- Women are weak; men are strong.
- Men provide most of the household income.
- Women are shy, lack knowledge and are difficult to reach; men are easier to talk to and know more.
- Men spend money and drink; women care for the family.

Step 2: Meet separately with groups of women and men. Involve participants of varying age, education, social class, caste, wealth, and ethnicity to ensure discussion of a wide variety of perceptions. Ask the group to describe its cultural perceptions about men and women.

One way to elicit these ideas is by asking participants to tell proverbs or stories or sing local songs about women and men. Another method is to ask the participants to use pictures or symbols to represent their gender perceptions. For example, an agricultural tool could represent greater agricultural knowledge or a star could be leadership. Symbols are one way to ensure that illiterate people are included and a means to share all the information with the group. They can also help to focus and keep track of group discussion. Symbols do not need to convey literally a key element of the myth, but can instead represent a concept. Ask the group to identify symbols that correspond to gender perceptions. Questions to encourage this discussion include:

- What activities are women and men expected to do? Why?
- What activities should be avoided by respectable men and women?
- Who has more leisure time? Why?
- What makes a good husband/wife? daughter/son? father/mother?
- What are women and men most valued for?
- Who make better leaders? Why?
- When do women and men lead? Who follows?
- Who is better at solving problems? Why?
- Who is more active in groups?
- Who is more intelligent? Why?
- Who knows more about agriculture, health, community practices, medicine?
- What are the strengths and weaknesses of men and women?
- What problems do women and men face today?
- What do women and men need most to improve their lives?

Some questions to ask government officials to elicit their perceptions of women and men and how those perceptions are incorporated into policy include:

- What roles do women and men play in village development?
- What skills do men and women have that contribute to village development?
- What are the strengths and weaknesses (personal qualities) of women and men?
- What are the difficulties and benefits of working with men? With women? With men and women together?

106

- What are the most important needs of women and men in village development?

Step 3: In separate and/or mixed groups, refer to the perceptions and gender stereotypes identified by the group(s) and, using questions, show how many perceptions are actually myths. Some questions to ask might be:

- Are these perceptions universal truths and/or valid representations of real life?
- Do you know of women and men (in your village or elsewhere) who do not match the stereotypes? How do they differ? Why?
- How do women's and men's perceptions differ? Why?
- What role do these perceptions play in the culture?
- What (and whose) values or interests do these myths represent?
- How do these myths both empower and disempower individuals and groups?
- Who benefits and who loses from particular myths? Why?
- Where did the myths come from?
- Are these perceptions of women and men changing? If so, how and why?
- What gender stereotypes are promoted by certain institutions (religious institutions, the government, aid agencies)? Why?
- What impacts have these myths had on the lives of women and men, and their role in community development?

Remember

Elders might be particularly helpful in demonstrating the changes in perceptions of men and women over time. Separate and joint discussions with people from different age sets can also provide examples of changing gender ideology and daily practice.

See also

Who Am I?
Time Line Variations
Advocacy Planning
Household Interviews
Division of Labour

Example

Gender myths in Bali

Sara L. Kindon

As part of my research on gender relations and village development needs supported by the Bali Sustainable Development Project (1991-92),[34] I discussed perceptions of gender characteristics with village women and men and government officials. In conjunction with these discussions, I used picture stories/life histories told by villagers in addition to Participatory Rural Appraisal (PRA) activities.

The tool worked well and elicited useful, and often previously undocumented, information about gender perceptions and myths. Reasons for its success lay in its application. For example, a wide range of participants of varying ages, education, social class, wealth and ability were involved; women and men met separately in their local village meeting hall; all information was shared visually to include illiterate people; use was made of the humour associated with many of the perceptions; and general perceptions were discussed before personal examples from people's lives were explored.

Women and men found cultural gender stereotypes easy to identify and discussion was generally relaxed, humorous and insightful. Older people helped explore the changes in gender perceptions over time and younger people reflected current perceptions and provided some insight into future change. In particular, women expressed delight and relief about being able to share their (sometimes negative) experiences resulting from cultural gender stereotypes. In addition, using this tool in a participatory and visual way with women and men in separate groups facilitated women's active participation which itself challenged the widespread perception that women are shy and lack knowledge. Where difficulties did arise in group dynamics, they usually occurred when people of higher social status or education dominated the discussion, or in mixed groups when men undermined women's perceptions and experiences. In these situations, I divided the participants into smaller groups who then reported back to the whole.

In Bali, most gender perceptions are rooted in a culturally-defined acceptance of biological determinism combined with the religious ideology of Balinese Hinduism. Together, they create a dichotomy of gender perceptions and values that identify women and men with largely opposing characteristics and qualities. Those I interviewed perceive women as being hardworking, anxious to learn, efficient and patient. Men are positively regarded as organized, active, rational and creative. In addition, women are considered to be shy, weak, emotional, associated with family and informal activities, while men are seen as being confident, strong, rational and linked to the community and formal decision-making activities. Generally, gender perceptions give men more status, rights and opportunities than women.

The gender perceptions of government officials (who are usually male) relate to stereotypes found in urban, middle-class Java where most of them were raised. They promote the central government's Panca Dharma Wanita or Five Duties of Women (i.e. loyal companion of the husband, manager of the household, educator and guide of the children, supplementary wage earner for the family, and useful member of the community) as appropriate gender roles for Balinese women. Furthermore, they emphasize the perceived legal and economic equality among women and men as a result of national legislation and government development initiatives aimed at village women. However, in Bali, where women have a long tradition of being economically autonomous (as market traders, for example) such an emphasis disguises women's inequality and subordination in religious ideology and practice, and in their political segregation into lower status development initiatives.

Balinese and central government gender myths thus tend to sustain hierarchical gender relations and the subordination of women. They also act to inhibit women's involvement in decision-making and planning for community development. However, as more women gain an education and move into positions of responsibility and authority, and as government's interest in gender analysis and gender-aware planning increases, gender myths are being challenged.

Tools that focus on the gender myths associated with women's and men's roles, relations and needs can help to raise awareness, stimulate discussion and challenge misconceptions and gender stereotypes. For example, Balinese women involved in the activities above received government training in water systems repair and maintenance after identifying their need for the technical skills normally only imparted to men. Such training for women was the first of its kind in Bali and marks a transition away from old myths around gender roles and knowledge into a more flexible approach to meet women's and men's needs to improve their lives.

Gendered Resource Mapping

Dianne Rocheleau

> **Time**
> Two to three hours.

Purpose

Maps and notes from gendered resource mapping provide a practical focus for future discussions with the community and help outsiders to understand how women and men see their own resources and how that differs from outsiders' perceptions or the results of formal surveys. This may be critical for developing mutual understanding in continuing discussions between local land users, researchers and development workers. The information should assist fieldworkers as they discuss local knowledge and practices and the choice of species, places, and combinations of plants in land use systems whether in research, development, environmental planning, land tenure reform, land use change or community organization contexts.

Gendered resource mapping can identify and present gender differences in resource use and control. The tool is useful at different scales – household, community, regional and national. It is an especially dramatic way to convey issues of gender differences in land use, responsibilities and labour, the impact of technology on women and men, and the gender distribution of access and control. This tool can help to set administrative procedure or to change land tenure codes, and water allocation protocols. It is also useful for forest codes, technology design, land use planning and technology evaluation.

Materials

Several large sheets of paper and markers.

Process

Information for drawing maps and sketches can be obtained from key informants, household interviews and/or focus group interviews. An inventory of landscape features, land uses and land users provides the basis for gendered resource maps.

Step 1: List the major classes of vegetation, land use and tenure. For example, one might select from the list below the relevant land use and land cover categories to include in a landscape sketch.

Forest	Conservation reserves
Woodland	Gathering/collecting areas
Savannah (trees over grassland)	Grazing and browsing lands
Open grassland	Croplands
Perennial crops	Gardens
Annual crops	Homesteads
Fallows	Fences
Bare soil	Property boundaries
River banks	Public markets and meeting places
Canals	Water holes
Roads and paths	Gullies

These categories will vary from one place to another depending on the type of cover and the range of land uses. For instance, in some cases there may be two kinds of woodland: open grazed woodland and dense forest protected as a conservation area. In the same area there might be several kinds of perennial crop-cover in croplands, including banana plantations, citrus orchards, multi-storey home gardens, and timber trees over coffee and tea. List and label the land cover and land use categories that best describe the range of conditions in the area, in the words of local residents.

Step 2: Who are the land user groups? Identify the land user groups in your particular context. They may be as simple as men or women, or a combination of male/female and child/adult/elder. They may also encompass livelihood, tenure and social groupings as noted in Table 5. List and label the user groups for this specific exercise.

Step 3: On a separate sheet, sketch the distribution of the land cover/land use types in the local landscape. (Sketches by facilitator or participants).

Step 4: In Table 6 note who uses and who controls these land cover/land use types.

Table 5 Subdivision of land user groups[35]

Land users by activity

Producers
    Gatherers
    Hunters
    Herders
    Farmers
        large/small
        paid/unpaid
    Farmworkers
Processors
Market vendors
Consumers

Land users by rights of access and ownership
(Applies to trees and/or land)

Owner (state, group, individual, *de jure* or *de facto*)
Tenant (rent paid)
User by permission or exchange agreement
    Continuous
    Regular
    Occasional
Squatters, 'poachers' (illegal users, occupants)

Land users by management unit/unit of analysis

Individuals or household sub-groups
    Women, men, children; age group members
Households
    Managed by men, women; small/large; young/old; rich/poor
Communities and community groups
    Families, clans, self-help groups
Companies and co-operatives
Administrative units
    States, districts, villages, neighbourhoods etc.

Table 6 Matrix for gendered resource analysis

Place?	Who controls?	Who uses?	Whose labour input?	Who is responsible for managing and/or providing the resource?
Land use/ Land cover				
_____	_____	_____	_____	_____
_____	_____	_____	_____	_____
_____	_____	_____	_____	_____
Water sources				
_____	_____	_____	_____	_____
_____	_____	_____	_____	_____
_____	_____	_____	_____	_____
Plants				
_____	_____	_____	_____	_____
_____	_____	_____	_____	_____
_____	_____	_____	_____	_____
Livestock				
_____	_____	_____	_____	_____
_____	_____	_____	_____	_____
_____	_____	_____	_____	_____
Products				
_____	_____	_____	_____	_____
_____	_____	_____	_____	_____
_____	_____	_____	_____	_____
Buildings				
_____	_____	_____	_____	_____
_____	_____	_____	_____	_____
_____	_____	_____	_____	_____
Other infrastructure				
_____	_____	_____	_____	_____
_____	_____	_____	_____	_____
_____	_____	_____	_____	_____
Tools				
_____	_____	_____	_____	_____
_____	_____	_____	_____	_____
_____	_____	_____	_____	_____

Step 5: Make detailed sketches and inventories. Sketch in symbols of plants, water sources, livestock, buildings, etc. Note on the matrix which places, plants and products are controlled, used and managed by different groups (women, men, children, farmers vs. herders, land owners vs. gatherers). Who is responsible for maintaining the resource or for providing it for the family? Using women and men symbols next to the landscape feature on the list, denote men's or women's labour input (L), control (C) and responsibility to provide (R).

Step 6: Use the sketches and tables to guide planning discussions with individuals and community groups or with technical personnel in order to incorporate the distinct needs, interests and concerns of women and men in resource management.

Step 7: Review the sketches and Table 7 with participants and discuss the possible arrangements for sharing multiple use and multiple user resources.

Table 7 Technology options for multiple users[36]

Parallel technologies (in separate spaces)

    If uses mutually exclusive

        (example: if harvesting fuelwood precludes fruit production)

    If users not compatible (on equitable basis)

        (example: if owner denies access to timber trees for

        fuelwood pruning by gatherers)

Interlocking technologies

    If uses or users conditionally compatible

        (examples: same space or plants, different timing of access;

        same space, different plants; same plants, different

        products)

Fully shared, joint technologies

    Compatible and mutual effect neutral

        (example: two users harvest same product from boundary

        fence; plenty of surplus, fence secure, no competition/

        conflict)

    Compatible and mutually beneficial

        (example: complementary types of labour, share harvest of

        same product)

Examples

Gendered Resource Mapping in Pananao, La Sierra, Dominican Republic

Dianne Rocheleau

Examples abound of the need for sustainable development initiatives to deal with women and men as multiple users and to be accountable to them separately and as a group. The case of Pananao in the Central Mountains of the Dominican Republic illustrates this point in the multiple (and sometimes conflicting) uses of land, trees, and their products by men and women. A particularly graphic example is the use of products from the same palm tree for fibre (women), cheap construction wood (men) and hog feed (men and women) as illustrated on the map.[38]

The gendered division of land use in Pananao entails the distinct division of control, responsibility as providers, and labour, and applies to spaces and activities as well as to specific plants and products. Women's food and fibre processing activities require products from men's fields, herds and woodlands. While women control the cassava, bread, cheese, confectionery and tobacco container processing enterprises, they do not manage source areas of raw materials. Some women's cassava bread enterprises in the same community have been severely curtailed when fuelwood shortages resulted from rapid conversion of woodlands to cropland and pasture [39]. Many women's handicraft operations in the vicinity (straw tobacco containers from palm leaf fibre) also suffered from raw material shortages when swine fever reduced the demand for palm fruit for hog feed and men felled the palms for cheap building material or cash.[40]

Land use planning and technology innovation in such situations clearly require consultations with separate client groups to design practices that cater for

115

Gendered household and community resources in Pananao, Dominican Republic

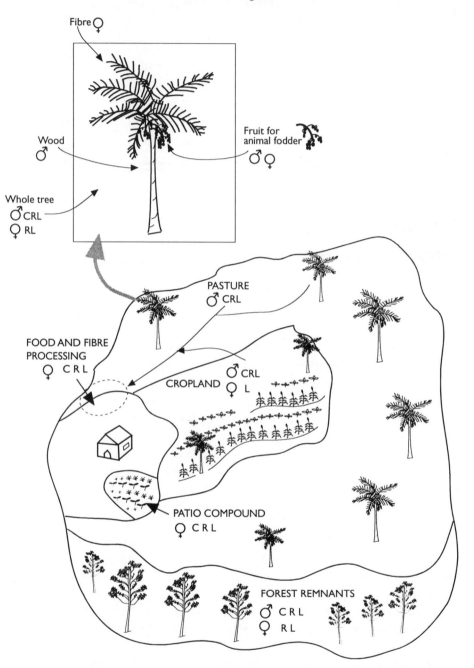

Fibre ♀

Wood ♂

Fruit for animal fodder ♂♀

Whole tree
♂ CRL
♀ RL

PASTURE
♂ CRL

FOOD AND FIBRE
PROCESSING
♀ C R L

CROPLAND
♂ CRL
♀ L

PATIO COMPOUND
♀ C R L

FOREST REMNANTS
♂ C R L
♀ R L

Multi-purpose use of land and trees in Pananao (La Sierra, Dominican Republic). Both men and women are present in this household. R = responsibility to provide a product thereof to the household, L = labour input for the establishment, maintenance or harvest, and C = control of resource or process.

each group, whether separately or jointly. Depending on the compatibility of both the uses and the users, land use systems can accommodate separate, fully shared, or interlocking (partially shared) use by multiple users. The choice between these options and the elaboration of specific practices for multiple users requires a combination of technical and social skills as well as a certain amount of social imagination at micro-scale.

In the case of Pananao, interlocking technology and land use plans for any given household should address processors (usually women) as clients as well as the men who own the land, cultivate the crops, manage the herds and fell the trees. By the same token, this demonstrates that any development programmes to promote income generation for rural women at Pananao should include men and their role as owners, managers, producers and/or competitive users of raw materials (fuel, fibre, milk, crops) for women's home industries. Similar circumstances have been described for other regions where men and women from farm households divide their attention between crops and livestock, respectively [41] or between particular species of both crops and livestock,[42] with a mix of complementary and conflicting interests in land, plants, animals and their products.

Gendered Resource Mapping in Katoma Village, Tanzania

William Rugumamu

Gendered resource mapping was one part of an African Participatory Research Network project in Katoma village, 14 km northwest of Bukoba town on the western shores of Lake Victoria. With the help of the village chairman, we categorized eight households on the basis of socio-economic difference. The categories were rich, middle income, poor and female-headed. We conducted a detailed observation of intra-household interactions at the level of their farms and village land. Using a structured questionnaire, we generated information on gender–resource relationships. Each family member using farm and public resources participated in drawing a map in which they defined control over and responsibility for resources as well as whose labour went into their use.

The village chair facilitated the selection of three teams with eight to twelve members drawn from the four socio-economic clusters. Each team selected a transect line with the intent of capturing the highest degree of resource diversity and land use intensity. The questions guiding the mapping started with what, where, when, why, how, and who? Each team recorded important features with respect to land use, product, how the products were used and distribution of labour, responsibility and control. After the survey, the three teams converged to deliberate on their field findings and to produce a village resource map. All the members of

Gendered household and community resources in Pananao, Dominican Republic

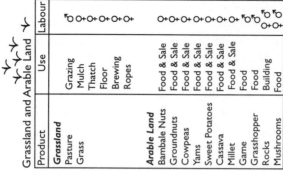

Grassland and Arable Land

Product	Use	Labour
Grassland		
Pasture	Grazing	♂ ♀+♀+♀+♀+♀+
Grass	Mulch	
	Thatch	
	Floor	
	Brewing	
	Ropes	
Arable Land		
Bambale Nuts	Food & Sale	♀+♀+♀+♀+♀+♀+
Groundnuts	Food & Sale	
Cowpeas	Food & Sale	
Yams	Food & Sale	
Sweet Potatoes	Food & Sale	
Cassava	Food & Sale	♂♂
Millet	Food & Sale	♂♂♂
Game	Food	♀+♀+
Grasshopper	Food	
Rocks	Building	
Mushrooms	Food	

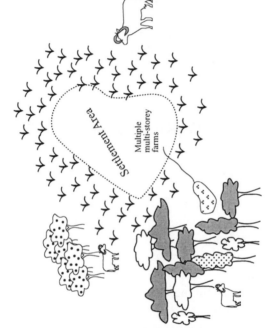

Settlement Area

Multiple multi-storey farms

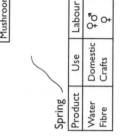

Spring

Product	Use	Labour
Water	Domestic	♀♂
Fibre	Crafts	♀

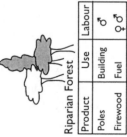

Swampland

Product	Use	Labour
Salt	Domestic	♂
Clay	Trade/Pottery	♂
Medicinal Plants	Medicines	♂
Reeds	Building	♂♂
Fish	Domestic	♀+
Sweet Potatoes	Food	♂
Water	Livestock	♂
Pasture	Livestock	♂

Planted Forest/Woodlots

Product	Use	Labour
Timber	Building	♂
Medicinal Plants	Medicine	♀♂
Fruits	Food	♀+♀+♀+♀+
Fibres	Crafts	
Game	Food	

Riparian Forest

Product	Use	Labour
Poles	Building	♂
Firewood	Fuel	♀+♂

the three teams, occasionally undertaking intense bargaining among themselves, strove to influence the content of the map as it was being created on the dusty playground. Working in collaboration with the village chair, his secretary, two young farmers (a man and woman – both in their late teens), and ten cell leaders, we synthesized the information collected at household and village levels. Decisions were made by consensus.

The final household and village maps showed land use, products and labour, responsibility and control of resources. According to the information we obtained, families with children in secondary school (15+ years) did not consider them as contributors to household labour but instead as an economic burden. At the household level, it was difficult to specify precisely who was responsible for providing certain common resource products, like fuelwood, given their short supply. Some village members learned about the existence of resources such as minor forest products through this exercise. The study also aroused villager suspicions that any private tract of land not planted with trees would be taken away from them.

In future gendered resource mapping exercises, it would be useful to request the village chair to call a village meeting so as to involve the whole community in the follow-up and final resource mapping at different stages of the study. After the transect mapping, I would also present the maps to the village meeting for verification and much more importantly, for community discussion and awareness-building regarding the status of their resource base.

Group Definition

Susan Quass

> **Time**
> Three hours.

Purpose

This exercise allows the proponents of change or project group members to assess themselves in comparison with other groups; to explore the resources and limits of their own group definition; and to consider the impact on outsiders of the group's actions. Society is an interconnected whole of relationships, identities and institutions. When one group makes a change, it affects others. Conversely, the ability of one group to effect a desired change is impacted by other individuals, groups and institutions. Development projects may fail or have only limited success when they do not account for all the members of the community, location or larger societal groups and forces. This exercise offers a self-analysis for members of a group, using a facilitator.

Materials

Paper and markers.

Process

Step 1: Ask the following questions:

1. Who is in this group as it is presently formed? Who is included in terms of gender, class, ethnicity, etc.? What different roles and institutions are represented? What interests do they represent?

2. Who is not included in this group as it is presently formed? Who is excluded in terms of gender, class, ethnicity, etc.? What different roles and institutions are NOT represented? What interests do they represent?

3. Would any of those people and institutions not included in our group be affected by a change in our community? Are there stakeholders we have not included? (This is a question to ask again in the planning stage.)

4. Would any of those currently excluded from the group have resources to offer

in the areas of information, tools or materials?

5. What ways does this group have of interacting with those outside? Should it interact with those outside? Will we recruit others to join our group? Limit participation? Seek representation from other institutions? Report to those outside? Hide information from those outside? Seek regular or occasional input from those outside? Seek support from outside groups or institutions? Form networks?

6. Group size: can we function well as a whole? Can all the voices be heard? If the group is large, how can we use small groups to do some of the work?

7. Where will the authority lie and who can make what kinds of decisions? Will the group as a whole make all decisions? What decisions, if any, can be made by sub-groups? (See Who Decides? p. 223).

Step 2: Record the results: Who are we? How we will make decisions? Who are our potential allies? What are partners resources outside our group?

See also
Who Decides?
Institutional Diagramming and Analysis
Conflict Resolution III
Network Formation

Example
The Rural Federation of Zambrana-Chacuey and the Wood Producers' Association

Laurie Ross and Dianne Rocheleau

The Rural Federation of Zambrana-Chacuey in the Dominican Republic provides an example of a group of small farmers that is actually composed of many sub-groups. Women and men from diverse economic situations, and from three types of movements within the region – based in liberation theology, traditional church groups, and marketing co-operatives – have negotiated their distinct beliefs and backgrounds into a cohesive organization. Social, political, and economic justice for small farmers has been the primary goal of the Federation.

There have been conflicts and hesitant compromises over the years about the best way to promote the interests of the small farmers, and this process has become even more complex as a result of the Federation's partnership with an outside environment and development NGO, ENDA-Caribe. A Forestry Enterprise Project has evolved out of this partnership. The project has focused on the planting, harvesting, processing, and marketing of an exotic tree species, *Acacia mangium*. An ECOGEN research team was asked by ENDA to compile information on the social responses to the Acacia and the forestry project. In this context, the ECOGEN team sought to understand the subgroups which form the Federation; define whose interests are being met, overlooked, or exploited by the forestry project; and the ways that these groups can be better served by trees and tree products.

Our understanding of many of these issues came from focus groups that we convened. We held one meeting with the Wood Producers Association (WPA), a new Federation affiliate organization that was spawned by the Forestry Enterprise Project (the meeting was all men; the WPA is 96 per cent male). A second meeting included the leaders of both the Federation (the leaders were men and women; the organization is about 60 per cent male, 40 per cent female), and the Wood Producers Association (the leaders are all men). We questioned members about the predominantly male composition of the Wood Producers Association as compared with the diverse composition of the Federation. In response, they described the way that this new organization was formed.

A group of farmers from the Federation who were most active in the forestry project decided that a new organization was needed to specialize in timber production. They met over six months to discuss the details of this new organization. They considered whether it should be a part of the Federation and, if not, what the relationship should be. They discussed the criteria for membership. They planned the siting and construction of a local sawmill, and how they would market and process wood. Finally, they wrote the rules and regulations of the group which detailed all these issues. Yet, the excitement surrounding the tree project clouded over the fact that certain sub-groups within the Federation were unable to plant the tree in sufficient numbers to participate in the WPA.

The vast majority of Federation households had planted at least one project tree (roughly 90 per cent) and about half (55.5 per cent) were members of the Wood Producers Association.[43] Yet, through the meetings we convened, we learned that there were discrepancies between women and men, as well as between groups defined by landholding size, occupation and location in terms of their ability to participate in the WPA. In part these discrepancies were due to the fact that the WPA defined who is a tree grower in a way that more closely matched outsiders' technical and commercial visions of forestry than local conceptions. Such discrepancies have created tensions between the Wood Producers Association and the Federation; between men and women; and between people from the different traditions within the Federation.

The ECOGEN team convened meetings with groups that did not often meet together to discuss their organization's mandates, membership, and participation in the forestry project. These meetings taught the team, as well as the Federation/WPA about the experiences of those who were having difficulty – but would like to be – participating in the WPA. The ECOGEN team's outsider perspective on the situation reflected the worries and concerns of many people within both organizations, but they had lacked a framework in which to analyse the structure and composition of both organizations. With a clearer understanding of the different stakeholders in the forestry project, the local organizations as well as ENDA could better plan for the future. An important offshoot of group definition activities is that they lay the foundations for the group to consider – or reconsider – group definition and to continue its own 'self-analysis', without outside facilitators.

Household Interviews

Adapted by the editors from *Tools of Gender Analysis*[44]

> **Time**
> One hour for each interview.

Purpose

Household interviews are a way for an interviewer to gain detailed information about the functioning of a household. They also allow the interviewer to see the house and the surroundings, which provides important insights and information. Interviews in or at the home may involve one or more members of the household, depending on the purpose of the research, planning or organizational effort.

Materials

Note-taking materials or cassette recorder if the participant agrees.

Process

Step 1: Identify yourself and the reason you want to interview a member or members of the household. Ask for a suitable time to conduct the interview and answer questions that household members might have.

Step 2: If you have decided to interview the men and women of a household together and the man is dominating the conversation, explain that you need a woman's perspective on some topic and schedule a follow-up meeting with the woman – ideally outside the home or at a time when she will be alone and free to talk at home. Alternatively, schedule a series of interviews with individual household members, sub-groups and the entire household.

> **Remember**
> Power is a factor in the relationship of interviewer and interviewee.
> In random samples, it is often easier to get interviews with more men than women or more women than men depending on the context – make sure you interview both equally, which may suggest a stratified sample that specifically requires half men and half women.
> Make sure that participants have an hour to spare.

See also

This tool can supplement, complement and confirm information gathered through: Activities, Resources and Benefits Analysis; Conflict Resolution; Gender Analysis Activity Profile; Gender Myths; Gendered Resource Mapping; Land Use Feltboard; Landscape/Lifescape Mapping; Social Network Mapping; Time Line Variations and Wealth Ranking.

Example

The Eastern European Immigrant Oral Life History Project

David Glyn Nixon

The upper Connecticut River Valley in Massachusetts attracted many Eastern European immigrants from about 1880 to 1928. Individuals and families from Slavic groups settled in the Valley and contributed to agriculture, economics, and politics, shaping and influencing the modern social and physical landscape. Unfortunately, their history and experiences have not been rigorously recorded. Beginning in 1991, members of the Pocumtuck Valley Memorial Association (PVMA) and I engaged in a project to record and analyse the lives and backgrounds of Eastern Europeans and their descendants in the Valley. Our task was complicated by hostility and suspicion between a dominant Yankee population and Slavic immigrants as well as inter-ethnic tensions among different Eastern European groups. Such concerns as religion, history and country of origin served to divide rather than unite the different Slavic groups and their descendants.

We conducted a participatory investigation, involving Eastern Europeans in the research design, data collection, and analysis. Our first effort was to assemble a board of advisers drawn from community leaders and prominent citizens representing the three major divisions among the Eastern European communities: Roman Catholic Polish, National Catholic Polish, and Eastern Catholic Ukrainians. With their advice, we hosted the Kulig, a celebration of Eastern European customs of the season around Christmas and Lent. We used the Kulig as a metaphor for sharing customs and information across ethnic and generational lines. We were able to use the Kulig to recruit data-collecting volunteers and informants for the oral life history phase of the project. After training the volunteers in interviewing techniques, we connected them with contacts made at the Kulig. The volunteers meet regularly to share experiences, develop interviewing skills, and receive instructions for the next round of interviewing. Our volunteers have been very successful in entering previously closed communities and have collected valuable data.

Our methodology is distinctive in two ways. First, by including the communities in every stage of the project, our research approach has overcome suspicion and hostility which had defeated a previous project. Second, we have sampled households and conducted interviews in such a way as to elicit different perspectives and tried to relate those differences in the way people see their worlds to significant social processes. We avoided trying to capture 'an immigrant experience' and focused instead on learning the different frames of reference and perspectives of various members of different communities. We tried to find out how different people view their social and physical environments and then discover what resources and strategies would be most effective from any particular point of view. This in turn has given us a better understanding of the links between local-level and larger-order social, political, economic and ethical processes. We expect that as this project continues, we will have the opportunity to make advances in field methodology and social analysis.

Sample questions for grandchildren of Eastern European immigrants

- Were your parents involved with the outside community? How?
- Where did you live as a child? How many times did you move? Describe your neighbourhood.
- Who were your neighbours? Did they welcome you and your family?
- What language did you speak at home? Did all the members of your family learn English? How did they learn?
- Who were your friends?
- What was it like growing up with a Polish (Ukrainian, Russian, Lithuanian) background?
- What were your relationships to your mother, father, brothers and sisters?

Institutional Diagramming and Analysis

Adapted by the editors from *Tools of Gender Analysis*[45]

Time
Two hours.

Purpose

This tool helps a facilitator to understand the roles of local organizations and the perceptions that people have about them. It clarifies which institutions are the most important, which have the respect and confidence of women and men, and who participates in and is represented by which ones. It also helps to identify what outside groups work with which community groups and which groups can effectively engage in sustainable development activities.

Materials

Before beginning, cut 8-15 squares or circles of three to four different sizes. It is useful to use two colours, one for organizations within the community and another for external institutions. Also collect one large sheet of paper, scissors, markers, and pen and paper for note-taking. Alternatively, participants can use coloured markers and large newsprint or coloured chalk and chalkboard.

Process

Step 1: Become acquainted in advance (through key informants) with the names of the community's organizations prior to using the tool, to have an idea of what exists and to know when a focus group has omitted a particular organization from its discussion.

Step 2: Divide the group by gender, age, ethnicity or by whatever other grouping is appropriate. Another useful division is by members of an organization, members of the leadership of an organization, and people who do not belong to any community association. The tool can also be used without dividing people, as for example at a local neighbourhood meeting with representatives from resident households.

Step 3: Ask each group to determine criteria for the importance of an organization and to rank them according to these criteria. Let the participants write the name or put a symbol on the appropriate circle or square. Do not ask them to list all the organizations in the community. Rather, let them note the associations that they think of because those will be the organizations that are the most relevant to them. The size of the circle or square should correspond to the importance of the organization. Allowing the participants to decide on criteria will reveal why organizations are important to them. However, the tool can also be used to understand how people rate internal and external organizations according to pre-determined criteria (e.g. an organization's contribution to community welfare; bringing material wealth; empowering women, the poor in general or a specific ethnic group; or providing opportunities).

Step 4: Ask participants to arrange the shapes on the paper so that they overlap according to whether the organizations are linked in some way to each other. Depending on the group, the diagram can be used to represent not just linkages but the degree to which each organization is linked to another by how much the shapes overlap. Note the types of linkages. Ask how the organizations work together. Some organizations may not work together or have any type of connection. A gender disaggregated institutional diagram can clearly portray gender bias by outside institutions if, for example, a group of women show no connection whatsoever between their organizations and outsiders. Diagrams can also show a presence or an absence of linkages between men's and women's organizations.

A more simple method is to place the internal organizations within a circle representing the community and the external organizations outside this circle. Ask participants to overlap the internal organizations and to draw lines of different widths to indicate interaction between internal and external organizations.

Similarly, arrows of different widths or colours can be used to represent the degree of influence that each exerts on the other. This is also a way to situate oneself (as an outsider) within the diagram. If an outsider is interested in strengthening the capacity of community organizations, the diagram is useful to help the outsider to choose potential partner organizations.

Step 5: Invite discussion about the role of institutions in the community's development. Ask a representative of each local group to describe the activities of her or his association. Questions to ask each representative include:

- What is the history of the organization? How and why was it founded?
- What has its relationship been with other organizations within the community?
- What relationship does it have with external organizations?
- How does the group perceive the various external organizations?
- What actions have external and internal organizations taken together?
- How do the participants perceive the services brought by external groups?

- How long have the internal organizations had relations with external groups?
- Who is involved in each organization? Who is excluded? Why?
- Who does what? Who takes responsibility for what?
- Who leads the group and makes decisions?
- How are decisions made?
- According to the members, how well does the organization function?
- Does the group have a revenue source? How is revenue used?
- Are the organization's decision-making processes and resource management methods transparent?
- How are leaders chosen?
- Have the leaders or members had any (management) training? Was it useful? How?
- What does it contribute to the community?
- How is information transferred? Is it done well?
- How has the institution evolved over time?
- How do the members hope it will be in the future?
- What are the strengths and weaknesses of the organization?
- What are its successes and failures?
- What specific problems has the organization had? Why? How were they overcome or how do the members plan to overcome them?
- What is the degree and range of participation of women and men in community organizations?

Step 6: Bring the groups together and discuss the similarities and differences between the diagrams of the various groups. Ask participants to point out:

- How do the diagrams from the groups differ?
- Why are they different?
- What organizations are more important to men and women (the young, the elderly, the poor, the wealthy)?

Remember
Ask participants to choose criteria for organizational importance but do not try to influence choice unless this is the intention of the exercise.

See also
Group Definition
Who Decides?
Network Formation

Gendered Institutional Diagrams from Choluteca, Honduras[46]

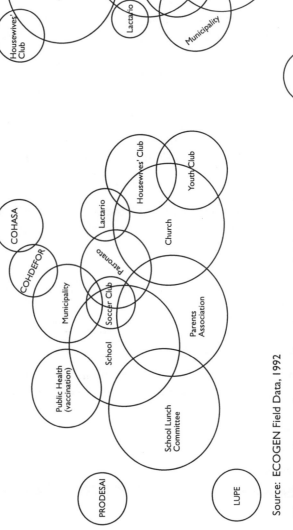

Women's Perceptions

Men's Perceptions

Source: ECOGEN Field Data, 1992

Focus groups of men and women, through a process of dialogue and consensus-building, ranked each organization's importance (represented by the size of the circle). Using paper circles each group constructed diagrams indicating the relationships between and among different community institutions. Men and women ranked the significance of community groups for local welfare very differently. This exercise provided extensive information about men's and women's relationships with and attitudes about local and regional organizations.

Example

Gendered institutional diagrams from Choluteca Honduras[47]

In 1992, a team from Clark University, Virginia Polytechnic Institute and State University, all in the USA, joined with the Land Use and Productivity Enhancement (LUPE) project of the Honduran Ministry of Natural Resources to explore the 'shifting boundaries' of a rural livelihood system in the foothills of Choluteca in Southern Honduras. The project investigated both migration and the management of local resources in the context of existing patterns of gender and socio-economic inequities. In particular the team was interested in the ways in which community organizations involving both men's and women's groups have gradually developed over the past 20 years in an attempt to find group solutions to community-wide problems and to gain greater collective access to natural and financial resources.

Through focus group discussions with both men and women the research team constructed detailed diagrams of each community's network of institutions. The resulting diagram shows the interconnected nature of both local and regional institutions, and also identifies the core institutions with which all other institutions have a significant relationship.

The illustration shows the importance of gathering information about existing community organizations from both women and men. Perceptions of an organization's importance tend to correspond with gender-specific priorities and involvement. For example, men ranked nutrition programmes and church clubs lower than the women did because of their lack of direct involvement in these activities. In addition, the women identified COHASA (Honduran-German Cooperation for Food Security) and COHDEFOR's (Honduran Cooperation for Forest Development) involvement in the community because these organizations were only working with women's groups in El Zapote. In El Zapote, most women had knowledge of all community groups, whereas most men had little knowledge of women's groups and their activities. Both the women and the men perceived LUPE and PRODESAI (Choluteca Integrated Agriculture Development Program) as minimally influential and separate from El Zapote's institutional network, without links to the core institutions. In other communities, where these organizations were connected with the church or school, they were ranked higher by both men and women, and had larger group membership.

Land Use Feltboard

Laurie Ross and Dianne Rocheleau

Time
Two to three hours.

Purpose

The feltboard is a lively way to encourage discussion about land use choices and household resources – what they are, where they are, why these and not others, and who has access to, responsibility for and control over these resources. It provides information different from drawing a map because participants can pick up felt figures of plants and animals and put them where they actually are found on the farm.

This exercise can focus on specific sectors such as livestock, crop production, water management or forestry. It can also explore land use and species changes related to economic or social policies and programmes. The feltboard can be recreated to show changes in number or type of resources depending on changes in the household itself, the environment, resource use regulation, land tenure patterns, and in the local and national economy. This exercise is especially good for 'what if?' discussions of the future or of hypothetical situations in order to understand land use decisions. The feltboard exercise should be used as part of a process, not as an initial data-gathering instrument. Earlier mapping, landscape walks and interviews, as well as discussions with key informants, can help in designing the pieces. This tool can be used to guide technology change, land use and land tenure programmes.

Materials

One or two large pieces of light-coloured felt (about 1 metre by 1.5 metres), scissors, smaller pieces of coloured felt from which to cut animals, trees, plants, houses, water, and any other feature of the landscape, sticks and ribbons to represent linear features and straight pins to attach the cut-out figures to the felt. Camera, video, or cassette recorder are ideal so that the richness and complexity of the information heard and seen is not lost.

Culturally, the feltboard tool worked well in the Dominican Republic with both men and women, but this may not be the case in all areas. Other materials that are locally accepted can be used to obtain the same type of information.

Process

Step 1: Cut out the shapes for all plants, animals, structures and other relevant landscape features on household (or community) lands before meeting with the household or group or do it with them in a separate session.

Step 2: Use the feltboard in one of the following ways.

Option 1: Suggest that one person in the group use the pieces to depict his or her own farm, or ask the group to picture a cluster of farms or a watershed. In the latter case you will need patches that show 'croplands' of different types, or 'forests'. In the single farm case, participants can use icons for individual plants and show more detail. Once the farm (or larger area) is constructed, ask how this would alter if a particular change were introduced: a rise in price of crop X; a change in the forest law; migration of household members to work in cities; a new cash crop; land tenure reform; or other relevant possibilities. Ask one person to make changes in the farm in response to these possibilities, with discussion by the whole group, or ask each in turn to modify the feltboard in response to the change.

   Facilitators can then ask questions concerning why specific resources are in certain areas, who uses or controls which resources, and what impact specific decisions from within the household or outside (local authorities, national policy) would have on the resources represented on the feltboard. 'What if?' questions have proved to be especially useful and the feltboard's easily movable figures can help a researcher to understand household resource choices under different circumstances. The members of the household can also use it to plan according to a choice one might make or a decision made at another scale that will have an impact on their household resources.

Option 2: Pose a hypothetical situation to the group and ask all participants (grouped around a table with feltboard and pieces) to define a realistic case study. For example, suggest that the group set up a farm for a young couple or a widow or a family of a given class. Ask them to be realistic and to choose a location (community), a specific site, the landholding size, and to define the boundaries and physical features on the board or at the edges. Now ask the group to define the land cover and land use already present (for example, a young couple purchases forest land to start a farm or a widow sells half of the land which is currently in garden cropland, coffee and forest). Ask one or two people to 'picture' the original condition and then the changes to be made by the people in the story (animals bought and bred and sold; crops planted and harvested; trees planted and harvested; land cleared; fences built; buildings constructed; water stored or diverted). One or two people can 'play' on the board while the others comment. Then others can use the felt pieces to show, in a separate turn, how they would make different changes in the farm, starting with the same story. This allows for

discussion about why people make different decisions starting with the same resources. It also lets people play out their concerns, aspirations, and knowledge through the experience of a fictional character, which takes away the stigma, for some, of exposing their own poverty. The usual benefits of role-play exercises also apply – people have a safe venue to discuss their distinct perspectives and to experience opportunities and limitations different from their own.

Step 3: Ask group members to note the main findings of the exercise and then share the insights that you gained and exchange comments. Note conclusions.

Step 4: Some groups might wish to make a decorative banner for their meeting place from the felt pieces glued or sewn to a cloth surface.

Remember

The researcher needs to have prior knowledge of the region to create appropriate figures, unless local artists make the figures.

It is important that everyone in the group knows the landscape that will be represented on the feltboard.

Some groups are more quiet than others and sometimes one or two residents dominate the conversation. Back-up plans such as asking people directly to create one section on the farm or asking other members what they would do when faced with a specific decision may help to involve more people in the conversation.

Recording this exercise is tricky. It should be carried out by at least two people so that notes are taken on all that transpires.

See also

Gendered Resource Mapping
Landscape/Lifescape Mapping

Example

Using the feltboard in Zambrana-Chacuey, Dominican Republic[48]

Laurie Ross and Dianne Rocheleau

Drawing maps with individual community members and small groups allowed us to gain an understanding of the multiple uses, biodiversity, and economic diversity of features in the landscape – at both farm and community level. The maps

134

concretely demonstrated how the very space in which men and women work and live is gendered. After looking at this rich information, we wondered how the farmscapes changed over time, how these decisions were made, and why certain people adopted new technologies and others did not. We wanted to enquire 'What would happen if a new tree species was introduced, a cow or a piece of land was purchased or fuelwood became scarce?' Yet, we were confined to the edges of the paper and to pens with their permanent marks. In our search for a more flexible medium that would allow both the participants and the researchers to engage in an interactive conversation around decision-making over time and space, we developed a feltboard exercise.

Both women and men work with fabric in the communities of Zambrana-Chacuey. Women make clothes by hand and machine, and men repair sacks for their products, so the participants felt comfortable using this medium. Based on what we had learned through the group and family interviews and other mapping exercises, we were able to cut out shapes that represented homes and farms in the zone, including structures such as houses, wells, corrals and fences; crops for food, cash, and medicine; trees; animals; water sources; and products such as fuelwood. We brought the feltboard and pieces to individuals, families and groups that we already knew, with an appointment in advance. We set the cutouts in front of the respondent(s), identified them and explained the exercise, then demonstrated with a brief, simple farm example. Then we emptied the board and stacked the pieces for the players.

Unlike ink on paper, the felt figures can be moved, so people were not afraid to make a mistake and they could take time to 'get it right.' People took turns explaining different options. We found that people were more willing to get up and take a piece of pre-cut felt and place it on the board than they were to pick up a pen and draw the same object. Everyone had a lot of fun participating; the discussions often became loud, and best of all, the participants were creating their own or hypothetical farms in felt. We took a fairly passive role, interjecting questions, watching as the image emerged, and taking lots of notes, while letting the participants tell their own or a made-up history and illustrate the processes of farm development.

The feltboard has many applications depending on what information one is seeking as well as the cultural and social context. The following are three ways we used it in the Dominican Republic.

(1) We asked single and married women and men to use the felt pieces to recreate their history on the farm. We enquired why and how decisions were made on resource management; purchase of animals vs. land; investment in land vs. home improvement; and whether or not to adopt a new technology. Felt pieces were added and taken away as needed during the unfolding of the farm history.

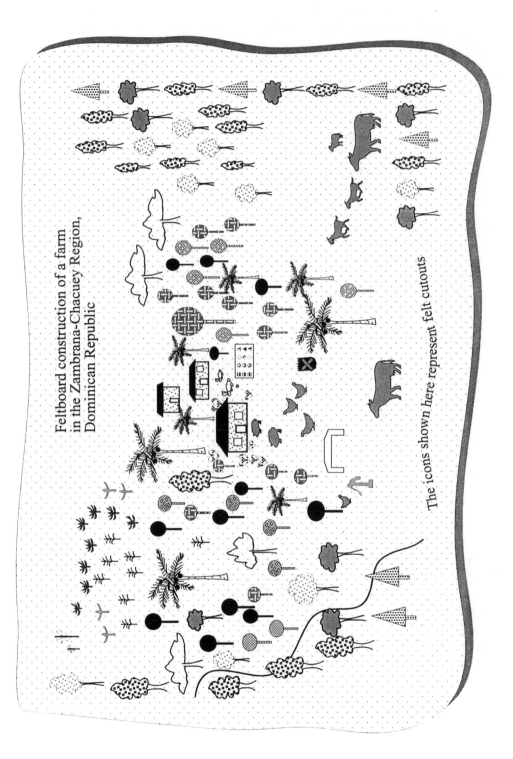

Feltboard construction of a farm in the Zambrana-Chacuey Region, Dominican Republic

The icons shown here represent felt cutouts

(2) With couples we gathered similar kinds of information yet we also witnessed the decision-making process as the couple explained why they built their first home in a particular spot; why they purchased a cow rather than improve their coffee stand; or why they chose to plant timber trees rather than multi-purpose trees. We also asked who made each decision to see which spaces remained the woman's 'property' or the man's 'property' and how and why this changed over time.

(3) With women's and men's groups (separately and combined) we explored 'what if?' questions. With them we created hypothetical families based on social, economic, and ecological characteristics such as stage in the life cycle, quantity and quality of land, family composition, and sources of income. We asked them to create a realistic farmscape given those characteristics. The feltboard is conducive to greater group participation because it can be changed or returned to a blank slate to reflect each person's decision-making strategies, starting with the same stories.

The feltboard helped us to understand ecological and social complexity over time and space by visually constructing what people know and do every day. Unlike listing crops that people plant or telling us where they get fuelwood in a verbal interview, the feltboard provides a concrete space to make the invisible visible. It allows the researcher to understand land use history and decision-making more clearly because the subject of the conversation is in plain view. The image that participants create then leads to further questions, discussion and confirmation by other participants.

The feltboard facilitates a discussion of criteria used when balancing options. Planners can learn from the feltboard what men and women know, do, and have; what they need and want; and what they would or would not accept and why. This information could be used to learn how a new technology might affect the ecological and social domains of men and women. Learning how decisions are made from the participants and having a concrete image as proof leads to better planning by outsiders, and also a better understanding by residents of other people's decision-making processes. Many ideas were shared during these sessions, promoting greater understanding of the complexity of people's situations.

In this case we and the staff and participants in a regional forestry project learned about men's and women's preferences with respect to new timber trees as cash crops. We discussed their priorities among tree species, food and cash crops, their pursuit of cash crop cultivation versus livestock breeding and their choices between gardens and timber lots. We also learned much about the relation between land tenure, land use and land cover.

Landscape/Lifescape Mapping

Dianne Rocheleau and Laurie Ross

> **Time**
> Two hours.

Purpose

This tool is a complement to the Transects. It provides the type of information one could get from an aerial map, unlike transect diagrams which depict landscapes stratified by topography, along a line that cuts across landscape. The transect is a good, quick way to sample the elements of landscape. The landscape/lifescape map serves to discover and illustrate the pattern of these elements centred on one person's or one household's experience and their domains of use and management. Landscape embodies rural people's ideas and actions over time, in space, in relation to each other and to the natural environment. It is a kind of signature in spatial terms that integrates the influence of the past, and provides the geometric point of departure for planning of future land use systems including agroforestry. Landscape is the drawing board for integrated technology and land use design beyond the single farm or the individual plot. Four aspects of landscape are especially relevant: land units of variable scale, a fairly long time frame for development and change, a diversity of species in various configurations and complex systems of land and resource tenure.

Materials

Paper and coloured felt pens or markers.

Process

Step 1: Walk through the farm or landholding before drawing the map. Many people will probably want to show an outsider their farm as a first step.

Step 2: Draw in boundary markers like rivers and roads and ask household members to situate their farm on the map and to describe the different types of plots or areas on the farm.

Step 3: Note all areas of the farm (cooking area, vegetable garden, crop lands, corrals, pastures, forests). Ask all participants to name all plant species (or all trees or crops) and who plants, cares for, processes, uses, harvests, or sells each. Put female and male symbols next to trees, other plants, or particular spaces to indicate who uses the plant or place (optional). Explain to people that detail is important and ask them to help show every type of plant and to point out anything missed in the drawing of the map. An alternative is to do a series of drawings: what was here before? What have you done? What is here now?

Remember

Be sensitive to the need for confidentiality of informants in discussing land tenure and use.

It is helpful to work in pairs where one questions and the other draws, while the participants talk, gesture and direct the drawing.

Participants can also do the drawing, subject to time constraints and the purpose of the activity.

See also

Transects

Gendered Resource Mapping

Land Use Feltboard

Example

Landscape/Lifescape in Zambrana-Chacuey, Dominican Republic

Laurie Ross and Dianne Rocheleau

Map drawing exercises proved to be an invaluable component of almost every stage of our fieldwork in the Dominican Republic. We found that drawing maps during household interviews took pressure off the verbal dialogue and allowed the answers to many of our questions to flow visually on to the sketch map image in a more integrated and detailed way. Through the images on the maps we obtained a local landscape dictionary with visual references. This allowed us to frame resource questions in later interviews and enabled us to notice certain landscape patterns during subsequent transect walks.

During household interviews, we asked people first to help us locate their house on paper. To do this we drew in boundary landmarks such as rivers, roads, and fences. After drawing the house, we worked our way out to include all land use areas such as the patio (compound), gardens, *conucos* (mixed croplands), annual cash crop plots, plots of coffee, cocoa, fruit and timber trees, and remnant riverine forests. We noted all the species of trees, crops and medicinal plants that grew in each place and who planted and cared for them, as well as who harvested, processed, used and/or sold them. We followed the same procedure for livestock. We prompted the respondents to fill in any blanks and to confirm that the image was correct. We found that it was very important to the respondents that we understood how the farm appeared – right down to specific trees.

The final product is a map depicting the plants, animals, land uses and land users at the household level and can be useful for structuring discussions about who does what in a more complex context. For example, the landscape/ lifescape map could serve as the template for future discussions of source areas for particular resources such as water, fuelwood and fodder. It can be expanded to show the movement of goods, services, money, and labour both in and out of the farm; and it can inform the feltboard exercise by providing the groundwork on which to base the preparation of icons and the proposals for hypothetical situations to simulate with groups (see Land Use Feltboard p. 132).

One particularly valuable way we used landscape/lifescape mapping was during our final random sample questionnaire. When we initially piloted the survey we had not included the maps. After having lively household interviews and mapping exercises with community members, these pilot surveys were dry for us and uninteresting for the respondents. We quickly decided to add the map to these interviews. After completing basic demographic information, we spent about an hour drawing the map. (After doing so many maps in earlier phases of research we had a system which allowed us to draw an inclusive map very quickly.) Many of our survey questions could be answered by referring back to the map.

The map facilitated a process in which information was elicited, coded, quantified and then analysed. Analysis can be done in the field as well as back in universities or development agency headquarters because the maps are a concrete representation of the actual farmscape. Both our qualitative and quantitative analysis of species diversity, location, uses, and users drew upon the complex information embedded in the maps.

Both in household interviews and in the survey we worked in pairs so that one person could pose questions and take notes while the other drew the sketch maps. Some familiarity with the flora and fauna as well as spatial and landscape terms enabled the team to quickly record and draw in the midst of the running story and description of the farm. Such familiarity can be obtained by first conducting walking interviews and transects of the communities with several key informants or through participant observation. These maps later served as a basis for feltboard exercises and gendered resource mapping.

While understanding biodiversity in the landscape and social diversity in its users can be valuable for researchers and community groups, such explicit documentation of resources, quantity of land, and outside resource locations can be very sensitive and difficult information for residents of rural areas to disclose. We need to take care when introducing ourselves and the research as well as assuring respondents that their identities will remain confidential.

Landscape/Lifescape sketches of Rolando and Marta's home and lands

Homestead and main plot

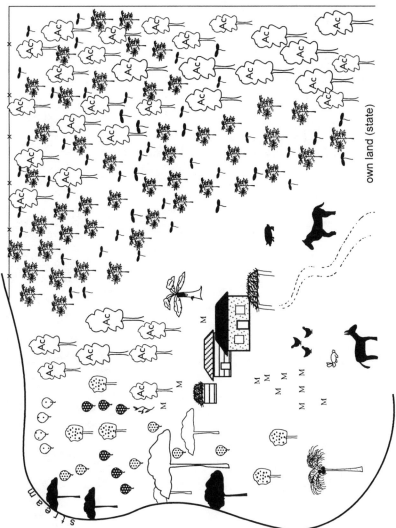

own land (state)

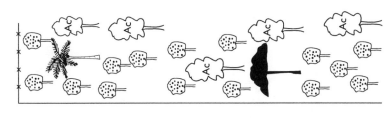

Landscape/Lifescape sketches of Rolando and Marta's home and lands

Other holdings removed from main plot

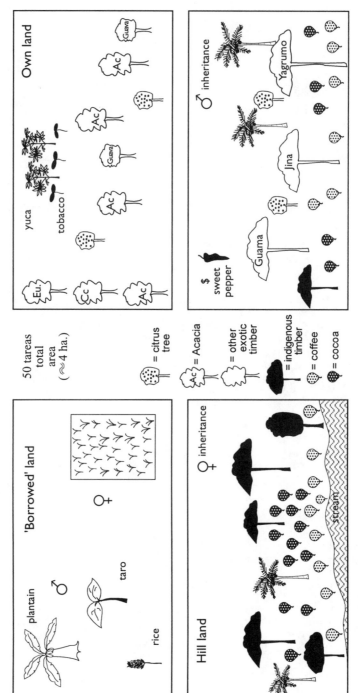

50 tareas
total
area
($\approx$4 ha.)

Own land

'Borrowed' land

Hill land

= citrus tree

Ac = Acacia

= other exotic timber

= indigenous timber

= coffee

= cocoa

Outlying plots include: taro, plantain, and rice; cassava, tobacco, fruit and timber trees; and coffee and cocoa with indigenous trees and a pepper garden.

142

Legal Rights I: Education

Adapted by Rachel Slocum from *Navamaga: Training Activities for Group Building, Health, and Income Generation*[49]

> **Time**
> Several hours, preferably over the course of a few days or weeks.

Purpose

Legal rights education facilitates critical awareness about rights and obligations under the law, the ability to assert those rights, and the capacity to mobilize for change.[50]

Materials

The facilitator must have a good knowledge of law, particularly those laws that concern the group, but she/he need not be a lawyer. Large sheets of paper and markers may be useful to present information.

Process

Raising awareness about legal rights is a long-term process. Using this tool once, alone, will not be adequate to do more than raise some ideas.

Step 1: Find out if there is an area of the law in which the group is particularly interested. Ask the group members whether they have specific questions or cases they would like to have explained. Some examples include women's legal rights, marriage law, taxation, laws on forest product use, land tenure laws, or employee rights. Find out whether the participants know the difference between state and customary law.

Step 2: Then do one of the following.
- Research and present the laws or rights.
- Help one or more of the group members to research and present the information.
- Bring in an outside resource person for the purpose. Legal literacy facilitators

have found that an interactive approach is preferable to simply giving participants information about the law.

Step 3: Discuss what rights these laws accord participants and what they do not. Discussion of rights and responsibilities could lead to a broader discussion of human rights, possible positive and negative implications for those who stand up for their rights, limits of the law, struggles inside and outside the court, and others.

Step 4: Ask whether anyone can think of examples in which her own rights, or those of someone she knows, were violated or abused by someone who acted contrary to the law. Will the law be useful for addressing these violations?

A facilitator could devise scenarios or participants could do role plays and ask, 'what would someone do if...?' For example:

- The forestry department officer tells you that you must pay a fine or pay for a permit to cut a dead branch off a tree on your land, but the law says you do not have to pay.
- By law a woman cannot own property so when her husband dies, she is left with nothing. Is this just?
- If a husband beats his wife, which is illegal in some countries, what recourse does she have? Where can she go? What can she do?

It is important to discuss recourse as well as resources within or near the community that people can turn to if they feel their rights have been violated.

Remember

Know the country or area context very well.

It is essential to follow up a legal literacy workshop in the districts or villages of the participants.

Think about possible repercussions for participants or yourself.

See also

Legal Rights II: The Woman's Walk
Communicating with Officials and Outsiders

Some questions to consider before beginning:[51]

- What problems do women and men in the community face?
- What are their root causes?
- What role has law played in the existence or continuation of the problems?
- What is the nature of gender relations in the community?

- What impact do gender relations have on the nature and the magnitude of the problems?
- Can legal rights awareness play a role in reducing or eliminating the problems?
- What resistance is a legal literacy facilitator likely to face in trying to address, through education, the problems raised?
- What does the community suggest to deal with the obstacles or resistance?
- Who should be involved in further legal education?

Example
Legal literacy workshop in Karnataka, India

Adapted by Ratna Kapur from *Legal Literacy: A Tool for Women's Empowerment*[52]

A government-sponsored education programme for women's empowerment held a three-day knowledge fair for over 1300 village women. I was asked to help facilitate a law workshop involving three to four hundred women in sessions of four hours per day. The workshop format had both strengths and limitations. Ideally it should have been conducted with small groups of women in spaces specifically for women over a long period of time.

As facilitators, we had to work out methods that did not reduce the workshop to merely giving information to women about the law. We focused on our objective of enabling women to challenge the understanding of law as a solution to the problems and violations that they experience in their lives.

Different communities of rural women attended the workshop, including *devadasi*, *adivasi* and scheduled caste women.[53] They experienced a range of problems including the dedication of women to temples, the expulsion of tribal women from their forest dwellings, sexual assault, domestic violence, cruelty, bigamy and desertion. Accordingly, we decided to address the specific concerns of a different community of women each day. For the purposes of this discussion, I will elaborate on the discussion we had on the second day with *devadasi* women who practise prostitution on the basis of traditional and historical factors.

We decided to use only one hour to convey some information on the issue of particular concern or relevance to the group being addressed. In the second hour, we divided into smaller groups to explore the issue in detail and to allow women to listen to one another's experiences. We formulated stories for the women to consider and to explore the extent to which law could assist or limit their efforts to address the violations. In the final half hour, the groups then reported back to the group as a whole.

In the discussion on *devadasi* practice, prostitution and child marriages, some *devadasi* women shared their experience with the group. They were rural *harijan* women who had little economic security and frequently had to resort to

145

prostitution. They were unable to find employment or participate in society because of social stigma and rejection from other women.[54] We looked at the different legal provisions governing prostitution and governing the dedication of women as *devadasi* and the extent to which such laws help protect or further hurt these women. We attempted to illustrate how the law continues to reinforce the stigma attached to *devadasi* and prostitutes, as it penalizes them for the kind of work they do. The law is concerned with protecting public rights; it does not protect the rights of these women or attempt to address the economic conditions, constraints or class interests responsible for their situations.

We presented small groups of participants with different situations and asked them to respond in light of the knowledge that they had acquired about the law.

- Situation 1: In your village there is a woman with two children who is a *devadasi*. How do you treat her?
- Situation 2: You see a 12-year-old girl in the village being dedicated as a *devadasi*. A pimp will take her to Bombay. What will you do?

The group of *devadasi* women were asked: How do you view yourselves as a group? Do you see yourselves as workers? Are you different from prostitutes? Should the law treat prostitutes as immoral?

The purpose of this discussion was to encourage women to question the assumptions on which the law is based and whether the distinction between prostitute/*devadasi* women and all other women is a legitimate distinction. Should women be denied their rights because of the nature of their work? Furthermore, it challenged the distinctions that women themselves practised and revealed the need to break down these distinctions between women if there were to be any possibility of solidarity among women.

For future work in legal literacy, we need to explore more deeply the role of rights as a tool of empowerment, our role as facilitators, power and women's relationship to it, and the idea of interlocking or interrelated oppression. A deeper understanding of each of these conceptual areas needs to be communicated in the course of giving practical information about the law. How do rural women define their rights? What is our understanding, as trainers and educators, of a right? Is it a language we feel comfortable with? To what extent is it empowering or liberating? To what extent does it merely introduce the power of the state into our lives? Is the idea of individual rights a radical notion for those who have not had the privilege or power to be recognized as individual agents? These questions will assist our understanding of rights and in moving beyond a formal notion of rights.

Both participants and facilitators need to understand the role of law in reinforcing existing power relationships. Further, we need to talk more about the use of rights both inside and outside the courts. It is important to come together to relate struggles of women in court, both successful and unsuccessful, and to try to understand the reasons for success or failure. We also need to share the struggles that have taken place outside the courts. Our purpose is to explore the full potential of rights and use them in ways that can be more effective and practical for rural women in particular. Legal information must be placed in context if we are to understand its full potential and its limits. To tell a woman that bonded labour is illegal is to provide her with information that will make no difference to her life. To work toward formulating strategies for social and economic empowerment with the knowledge that bonded labour is illegal must be the goal of an effective legal literacy strategy. Lastly, in a legal literacy process, we must be acutely aware of how gender is mediated through other forms of oppression, such as class, caste, or religious community.

Legal Rights II: The Woman's Walk 🔲🔲🔲

Florence Butegwa of WiLDAF (Women in Law and Development in Africa)[55]

> **Time**
> Three hours.

Purpose

This tool may be used after the participants in a legal education process have discussed a legal rights issue and the applicable law. The aim of the activity is to enable participants to bring the rights they have learned about into their real life situations. It helps them to appreciate the fact that knowing the rights is only the first step. Through this activity they appreciate possible stressful situations that c 'd arise as they exercise their rights. It enables them to pool their various expe   ∙es, resourcefulness and ingenuity to find ways of coping. The activity can be used to discuss other types of obstacles. For instance, instead of relationships, the participants may focus on structural obstacles like the police or courts. While WiLDAF designed this tool for women, it can be used with men as well.

Materials

About ten sheets of paper, markers and, if necessary, props to represent obstacles to enjoyment of rights.

Process

Step 1: Ask the participants to identify significant relationships in which they are involved which might have a negative impact on their effort to realize and enjoy the legal right(s) they have covered in the earlier legal education session. Compile a list of these relationships (marriage partners, children, neighbours, family...).

Step 2: Facilitate a discussion in which participants talk about the different ways in which each of the relationships might create obstacles in the realization of a particular right.

Step 3: After this general discussion, ask each group to select one relationship and one legal right and discuss it in some detail. For example, if a woman knew that she had a right not to be subjected to any form of violence, in what way would members of her immediate family present obstacles to her enjoyment of that right? Discuss ways of overcoming the obstacle.

Ask the group to choose one person to note on paper or by memory the relationship and issue being discussed. As the discussion continues, the group will see two categories, one of obstacles and another of possible actions that the participants think might be useful in overcoming the obstacle or in reducing its impact on their rights.

The facilitator should help each group and also try to ensure that each group works on a different issue and/or relationship.

Step 4: Reassemble the participants and ask each group to report on its work. Encourage a general discussion and seek a consensus on a list of obstacles for each relationship.

Step 5: To sum up the session and also to help participants remember the lesson, try a game. Ask the participants to stand in line with each person in the line representing one obstacle. Obstacles can be represented on paper or symbolically. One participant volunteers to do the 'woman's walk' trying to overcome each obstacle in order to enjoy her legal right.

Step 6: As the volunteer walks up to each obstacle, she declares what she will do to ensure that the obstacle does not interfere with her rights. If time allows, the woman's walk can be repeated with different volunteers, relationships and issues so that the nature of the obstacles and their solutions change.

Remember

Facilitators must know the details of the laws and rights participants will be discussing.

This tool assumes that participants have previously been engaged in a process of education on legal rights.

Follow-up is important, to know whether the participants have found this activity useful in their daily lives.

See also

Legal Rights I: Education
Problem Solving: Trees, Ranking, Assessment

Example
Using the Woman's Walk

Florence Butegwa

Eleven professional women, including lawyers, from different African countries convened in a hotel in Uganda. What they had in common were two things: many years of experience in implementing community education programmes seeking to promote the exercise of rights by women in their respective countries and a general frustration that very few women acted on the information they gained. They had come together to explore ways of making the programmes more effective.

I, as facilitator of their effort, had to provide a framework for analysing the low level of actual exercise of rights by women. This was done by asking the participants to identify obstacles which have prevented women whom they know to exercise or enforce their rights. A formidable list of obstacles was the result. The group attempted to classify them into obstacles linked to relationships, economic status, procedures, culture, attitudes, and so on. Taking on one category at a time, participants stood in line, each representing an obstacle. As 'the woman' walked by, each participant blocked her way with a threat or actual restraint (acting out how the relationship creates the obstacle). At a later stage we attempted to show the interrelatedness of the different categories of obstacles and to highlight how difficult it is for a woman to surmount them in order to act upon the information on rights.

The ultimate aim was for the participants to appreciate the idea of going beyond simply giving information in their education programmes. They should work with the communities or groups to identify potential or actual obstacles and work out ways of minimizing their impact on capacities to exercise legal rights.

Mapping the Body

Gouri Choudhury

> **Time**
> One day or half day.

Purpose

The concepts of pleasure and pain are universal. However, the expression of our feelings differs within and between cultures, class and gender. Since women's and men's gendered roles in many cultures are intimately linked to biological processes and experience, ideas about the body are an important component of self concept. Discussing body concepts relating to work, sex and reproduction illuminate how people see themselves as both sexual and gendered social beings. The body workshop creates a space to explore people's perceptions of their limitations and their powers. In enacting their own lives and sharing their personal experiences, they begin to question the norms and values and the roles set out for them in patriarchal society. They move from acceptance – 'this is how it has always been' – to 'there must be a way to change these inequalities.' However, the game is not an end in itself. It merely provides a tool for discussion. It creates an environment for reflection and introspection and requires a skilled facilitator to carry forward the discussion towards conceptual analysis. This process requires time so that the day is allowed to move spontaneously without a rigid schedule. If, at the end of the day, the participants have raised and reflected on new questions, it is a good beginning.

Materials

Large piece of paper, coloured markers or crayons.

Process

This exercise must be done in gender disaggregated groups with women facilitators for women's groups and men facilitators for men's groups. Groups of 8 to10 people are best.

Step 1: Make a full-size outline of the back and front of a woman or man as appropriate. Ask everyone to sit around the drawing of the body and to think about how we use our body.

Step 2: Ask the group, 'What gives us pain? Where is the source of this pain?' Ask one of the participants to colour in red the part of the body where the source of her or his pain lies.

Step 3: 'How is the body affected by fatigue or stress from the work you do?' Colour in red those parts of the body affected by work.

Step 4: 'What gives us pleasure? Where do you feel pleasure? What part of your body do you like? What part of your body helps you to feel pleasure?' Colour in these parts with green.

> **Remember**
> Discussing pain and pleasure is a way to approach more difficult topics of power, equality and reproductive rights.
>
> **See also**
> Legal Rights I and II

Example

Body mapping as part of a training with the Ghad Kshetra Mazdoor Morcha[56]

Gouri Choudhury

A team of four women from Action India, Delhi, consisting of two middle class activists and two community health workers, took on the Women and Equality Training Programme with the Vikalp social organization in Saharanpur.

We began with an exploratory visit to familiarize ourselves with the area and to enable us to conceptualize the content and methodology of the training programme. The three-day exploratory workshop was held in Nagal Gaon. There were 28 women from 12 villages, the majority of them *chamars* or other disadvantaged castes. Only five of the women were literate.

We found the women to have a strong sense of identity. Their life is intimately linked with the forest; their livelihood depends on the *bhabbar* grass which they process to make rope. The *bhabbar* is their common bond – a question of their survival.

The Ghad Kshetra Mazdoor Morcha organized groups in the villages to fight the Forest Bill which appropriated forest from the people and declared it a national reserve. The movement to regain access to the forest was strengthened by

152

women joining the struggle some years ago. These women have realized their collective strength in their struggle to win back the *rammannas* (customary forest rights granting access to forest resources taken away by the Forest Bill) which were traditionally theirs, and have no fears of the forest officers, contractors or the police. They are in the forefront of the struggle. They are the Ghad Kshetra Mazdoor Morcha women, militant, fearless and ready to die.

What kind of workshop on Education for Equality would meet the needs of these women? We began by playing a game where all the women sat in a circle with one blindfolded woman in the centre. We turned her around and then pointed her toward a woman sitting in the circle. She had to guess who the woman was by touching her. Then we asked the women, 'What did you feel when someone touched you?' Their answers were: 'I liked being touched', 'It reminded me of my childhood,' 'I thought this is how the blind must feel.' 'I liked being touched by a woman. I was comfortable even when she touched my chest.' We asked, 'Can men and women play this game together?' 'Men,' they said, 'can touch us on the arms and legs and not our body,' and 'We can play this with our co-workers here; we trust them. But we couldn't do this in the village.'

Sona said, 'The father gives his daughter to a man, for this purpose and only this purpose. The man will have her whenever he wants. A woman cannot say no. Never. Not even if she is ill or tired. He will beat her.'

'Can a woman say she wants the man if she feels the desire?' we asked. 'If the woman feels desire, she can never say it.' 'Bread can never say eat me.' 'Women can indicate with their eyes and bodies – that is, they can be inviting or seductive,' Sona said. The woman can never refuse the man. He can do whatever he wants, whenever he wants. If the woman says anything, the man will take it badly. 'He will bury his penis in the earth and spit on the woman's tongue' – he would rather deny her than give in to her needs. 'Always the woman has to keep her mouth shut. If she opens her mouth she gets beaten. The woman is just like a shoe of the man.'

At this point we asked, 'Do you think men and women are equal?' 'We work together, we struggle together,' they said. 'Women work harder than men. Men can rest after the day's work, women must go on, take care of children, take care of husband, elders, take care of animals and do all the household chores. And after all that he will ask her "what are you doing at home?" and he will find some excuse to beat her.'

After we took a break, we played a trust game where six women carry a woman as if she were on a stretcher, three on either side. After walking in a circle, they put her gently on the ground. Each woman described being lifted: 'I felt I was flying; I didn't want to come down'; 'I was flying like a bird'; 'I was floating in the air in a giant wheel'; and 'I was flying in an aeroplane without a ticket'. Many barriers were broken. We felt we knew each other more closely because we could feel safe in trusting ourselves to others. One woman said it is like 'picking up something that has fallen and sharing the burden together.' 'It's a matter of women supporting – holding – one another.'

We went on to find areas of pain and pleasure in the body. On a double sheet of brown paper, we made an outline of one of the women present. The women chose two crayons, red for pain and green for pleasure. We asked the women, 'What gives us pain?' Usha said 'The womb is the source of women's pain; the womb is where the greatest sorrow rests for a woman,' Rajbala said, 'It's in the stomach that all the sadness of the woman lies.' They drew in the womb and coloured it red. Sona talked about the process of making rope from the *bhabbar* grass. Each action affects a different part of the body – the neck, arms and shoulders, waist, the small of the back, the knees, feet and legs. She coloured these areas red. 'In a woman's life, work is the greatest sorrow; she can never talk about her tiredness.' 'Nobody ever tells her to rest. She wants to rest but no one ever tells her to rest.'

We asked, 'How about pleasure?' I coloured the lips green because laughter gives me joy. Bharati made the hands green saying that 'touching makes me feel nice'. Chandru coloured the ears green because she likes wearing earrings. Poonam said, 'I like to smell flowers' and coloured the nose green. Tripta said, 'When you embrace someone, you get great happiness' and coloured the chest green. 'And how about this,' one of us asks, pointing to the genital area. Bala says, 'This is where the most pleasure rests.'

But moments of pleasure are few and the discussion quickly turned back to pain and the pain of being beaten. Usha's husband, who is an activist, beat her last week. If she were his equal, she said, she would hit him back. The discussion became intensely personal. For the first time, we felt, the women were able to move from the framework of struggle and organizing to themselves: 'Only a woman can understand what a woman feels when she is beaten'; 'A woman cannot fight back'; 'At the most she can raise her hands to defend herself'. Perhaps the women had not talked about their personal experience of beating before. That evening as the sun went down and we sat huddled around the drawing of the body, the dimensions of our discussion changed and the personal became political. Darkness enveloped us in each other's confidence. Rajkumar, a Mazdoor Morcha activist, lit the gas lamp and placed it in the centre, shattering the intimacy with the bright light.

Network Formation

Susan Quass

Time
Three hours.

Purpose

A network is an alliance between two or more groups. Each group remains autonomous but co-operates with other groups toward the achievement of the mutually specified goals of the network. Networks are formed to further the work of each organization by joining with others to increase strength or expand impact of the organizations in some way. A network may be highly structured and formal or it may be loose and informal. The structure may depend in part on the purpose of the network. There may be a single purpose or a set of goals for the network. Networks have formed to advertise or publicize an issue of concern to all the network members; raise money for all the network members; increase political support for a candidate or a policy; raise awareness or educate specific constituencies or targets; share physical labour; advocate for or against specific policies or programmes that impact all the members of the network; share perspectives and information internally among network members.

Materials

Paper and markers.

Process

Step 1: Identify the issue(s) for which you would like to have support or on which you would like to expand work.

Step 2: Identify the sectors of society which have an impact on that issue. Make a list of the groups or institutions that may share your perspective or may have a complementary view of the issue. Include religions, age-groups, cultural, ethnic or economic groups.

Step 3: Ask all members of your group to think of one other person who may want to join and invite him/her.

Step 4: Scale up or down as appropriate to network with groups larger or smaller or in different locations; national, local or international.

> ### Remember
> Who is involved? Whose interests are at stake?
> Who is in control of the process?
>
> ### See also
> Chapter 3
> Advocacy Planning
> Group Definition
> Institutional Diagramming and Analysis
> Personal and Household Resources
> Communicating with Officials and Outsiders

Functions of a network[57]

* Communicate ideas and information internally or externally.
* Develop a network-wide analysis, vision, and strategy.
* Carry out concerted actions or advocacy.
* Provide a channel for groups to challenge and discuss the merits of other member groups' actions.
* Provide aid (social, political, financial or physical) for local groups in crisis situations.
* Do outreach to new people or groups on a wider level (national, international, or sectoral).
* Make decisions on wider policy objectives which may be approved by the member groups.

Examples

An international network for women's health

Susan Quass

The Women's Health Documentation Centre Network was formed in 1992 to create more formal links among five documentation centres which had co-operated for several years. Each of the five Network member groups in Chile, Mexico, Malaysia, Brazil and United States serves as both a local and regional information and action centre on women and health. Each group decided it was in its interest to join the Network to advance its own work on women and health more effectively. Goals include:

- Exchange of documents to strengthen each group's collection of reproductive health information. While the groups all work on a wide variety of health topics, this one topic area was considered the highest priority for all the groups.
- Exchange of technical information about documentation processes and electronic resources. As each group expands its own computerized database it shares with the other groups major learnings and discoveries.
- Documentation of impact on the media. Each group is documenting its contacts with the media, to demonstrate the wider impact of the information exchange on local, national and international policy issues.
- Mutual referrals. Each group will promote the work of the other groups, especially to the public, the media and funding agencies.
- Co-operative work on specific areas of policy. Currently the Network is working to combat population control policies with a feminist analysis of women, health, and environment.

The Network was designed both to serve the internal information exchange needs of the groups and to target specific issues and constituencies for concerted action and outreach.

Local social service networks in the United States

In a number of communities in the United States there is an informal network of social service groups offering assistance to poor families. The network member groups represent different sectors of the community: synagogues, churches and other religious organizations; some local businesses; and the local government offices and non-profit groups involved in providing free food or meals, low-cost housing, assistance with utilities, education and job training.

Such networks serve some important functions. For the member groups, it is a way to see that services are not duplicated; and it provides a way to keep information about clients that all the groups may serve. It makes a difference not only for the groups but for their clients too: any client seeking help from one group will receive information about services available from other groups in the area.

The network may also provide a place for discussion about pressing social service needs of the community and for research and planning about how to meet new or newly recognized social needs.

The Gardner Area Interagency Team: A local social service network

Octavia Taylor

In the early 1980s the mother of a teenage runaway met with the two social service agencies (the Departments of Social Services and Mental Health) that had been providing services to her daughter. This was the first time that representatives of these organizations had sat at the same table in an attempt to resolve a problem common to both. Out of this initial meeting evolved the Gardner Area Interagency Team (GAIT), a forum for about two dozen local governmental agencies, churches, and health and social service organizations to assess community needs and plan actions to address these identified needs. Located in a rural area of central Massachusetts in the United States, and comprising a small city and five surrounding towns, GAIT at first served as a network for these organizations to:

- support each other in crisis situations;
- educate one another about their services and clients;
- eliminate duplication of services; and
- collaborate on a variety of projects.

GAIT achieved these goals by holding regularly scheduled monthly meetings with an agenda determined by membership and rotating leadership. Meetings typically featured an information-sharing session, reports of subcommittees and special presentations on identified problems, programme plans or innovative solutions. In addition, GAIT periodically sponsored seminars and workshops for service professionals. All of these occasions provided opportunities for members of the network to communicate ideas informally and become aware of dilemmas facing other organizations. As a consequence, co-operation and collaboration became valued.

Although the network was strong and useful among health and social service providers, members perceived that representation from business groups would be critical in giving GAIT a voice beyond local boundaries, especially in a climate of shrinking aid to cities and towns. A business and social services partnership developed in the late 1980s enabling GAIT members to flex their political muscle and make decisions on wider policy and legal issues affecting the provision of health and social services. More than twelve years after its inception, GAIT continues to be a vital and dynamic local network, providing members with an opportunity to serve their clients better and giving life to the old adage that there is strength in numbers.

Oral Life Histories

Adapted by the editors from *Learning to Listen: Interview Techniques and Analyses*[58]

> **Time**
> One to two hour sessions over several days or weeks.

Purpose

Collecting life histories is useful as a learning tool for researchers – a check on the researcher's assumptions and biases. Applied by feminist researchers, oral life histories are a tool to recover women's words and experience. (Clearly, this tool can be applied to men, too, but in deference to the authors of the source material we have quoted their process verbatim.) They have been used in research, action and advocacy, and provide a way to understand the roots and long-term trends of issues that people confront in the present.

Materials

Pen and paper or cassette recorder.

Process

Listening to the narrator

1. If the narrator is to have the chance to tell her own story, the interviewer's first question needs to be very open-ended. It needs to convey the message that in this situation, the narrator's interpretation of her experience guides the interview. For example [from the source study] 'Can you tell me, in your own mind what led up to your experience of depression?'
2. If she doesn't answer the interviewer's question, what and whose questions does the woman answer?
3. What are her feelings about the facts or events she is describing?
4. How does she understand what happened to her? What meaning does she make of events? Does she think about it more than one way? How does she evaluate what she is describing?

5. What is being left out; what are the absences?

Listening to ourselves

1. Try not to cut the narrator off to steer her to what our concerns are.
2. Trust our own hunches, feelings, and responses that arise through listening to others.
3. Notice our own areas of confusion, or of too great a certainty about what the narrator is saying – these are areas to probe further.
4. Notice our personal discomfort; it can become a personal alarm bell alerting us to a discrepancy in what is being said and what the woman is feeling.

> **Remember**
> Honour the integrity and privacy of the narrator and do not intrude into areas that she/he has chosen not to discuss.[59]
>
> **See also**
> Chapter 4
> Time Line Variations

Examples
A life history recorded in Tubod, Siquijor, The Philippines

Dale Shields

Exploring the life history of Engracio Ongcol on Siquijor Island clarified the social and physical processes associated with the pressure of too many people on too little land. It revealed land tenure and inheritance patterns, migration patterns, the nature of parental aspirations for children, the marked decline in the natural resource base on Siquijor, and the struggles of one household over a lifetime.

Sixty-one years old at the time of the interview, Engracio was enthusiastic about the prospect of this discussion and even prepared notes so that important details would not be forgotten. Details of his youth included his parents' support for training in auto mechanics on the nearby island of Cebu so that he would not have to depend for his livelihood on the small farm which they owned. Despite this training, Engracio wished to farm and he spent four years struggling with his wife to make ends meet by farming one of his father's plots of land and also by fishing. This effort failed, and was followed by two years on Mindanao – a favoured destination for migrating Siquijor residents – in various carpentry jobs. He then returned to farming and fishing on Siquijor with his family. When the opportunity arose, he bought a small plot of land on the neighbouring island of Negros Orien-tal. For four years he migrated seasonally to tend his crop, leaving his family be-hind.

In 1968, Engracio's father was elected to the municipal council and asked Engracio to return home to work in the mayor's office, which he did between 1968 and 1983. His responsibilities included various semi-permanent positions such as tax collector, accounting clerk, and municipal mechanic. During this period, the family depended on his salary for income, but they also continued to farm both for household consumption and for additional income.

Since 1983, Engracio and his wife have made their livelihood from farm-ing, livestock keeping, and ploughing other people's farms with their bullock. Their farm is now quite a bit smaller than before because their daughter and her family are farming half of it. Her husband is a mechanic but they also need land to make ends meet. Their son is married and has relocated to Mindanao where he works as a factory mechanic.

The cycle of pressured livelihoods, insecurity, diversified strategies for se-curing a living, divided families, and both short and long-term migration continue in what is, for the present, an unending pattern for residents of Siquijor. This pat-tern is captured in the life story of Engracio Ongcol.

Using life history techniques to reconstruct Kyevaluki's history

Barbara Thomas-Slayter

Kyevaluki is a sublocation in Machakos District in rural Kenya. It was the focus of a participatory rural appraisal exercise conducted by Egerton University and Clark University in 1989. One afternoon two members of the research team sat in the sunshine with three elders, all in their seventies, reconstructing Kyevaluki's local history. These 'Mzees', as respected male elders are called in Kenya, were eager to talk about their community. Born around the time of World War I, they had memories extending back more than 60 years. They gladly recollected events, con-sidered changes which had come to their community, and reminisced both indi-vidually and collectively about their lives and about their community.

The discussion opened with the research team's expression of interest in learning about the local community from seniors who had personally observed the changes over the last half century. Specific topics of interest were identified, but the discussion flowed as a conversation. The team members occasionally directed the group towards a new topic or probed for details. All three Mzees were enthusi-astic participants in what was a lively meeting.

Topics included changing access to land and land use patterns, the impact of colonial policies on land and livestock management, the coming of independence, land privatization, household food security, changing responsibilities of men and women, community and government responses to famines, water availability, the introduction of coffee production into the area, the first primary schools, changing educational opportunities, the impact of roads on the community, employment opportunities within and beyond Kyevaluki, and inter-generational questions and conflicts.

In rural Kenya, the collective memory is an oral memory. Even in Machakos District, there are few local written records, and those are largely constructed by outsiders. The opportunity to collect and reconstruct a community's history through listening to its own elders is valuable, providing insights into the past and observations on its transformation into the present.

Oral life histories in collaborative research with the Rural Federation of Zambrana-Chacuey, and ENDA-Caribe, Dominican Republic

Dianne Rocheleau and Laurie Ross

Oral life histories were part of a multi-method approach to a study of the past, present and potential effects of an innovative forest enterprise project sponsored by the Federation and ENDA – Environment and Development Alternatives, an international NGO headquartered in Senegal. Stories of individual lives helped us[60] to grasp the meaning of our daily observations and, through the patterns in people's lives, to understand better the logic and spirit of the landscapes and livelihoods of individual smallholders, their households and their rural communities. In particular we gained a sense of the diversity of life experiences, choices and situations, not only between men and women but among women and among households normally lumped together as smallholders. We also gained insight into the dynamism of peasant economies, ecologies and culture and the rapid and varied responses of rural households and individuals to the changing economic and political context.

Several women and men recounted their own lives, including where they were born and their parents' situation at the time; the migrations of the family, if any; their training by parents; their childhood, youth and adult participation in domestic, subsistence and commercial pursuits as well as religious and community service and leadership; their affiliation with various organizations; and their own life choices with respect to marriage, education, family division of labour, other occupations (farmer, livestock breeder, charcoaler, artisan, day labourer, farm caretaker, small business owner, wage worker, factory worker, merchant/trader) and vocations (midwife, herbalist, community organizer, community elder). Their experiences, their analysis of their life course and their future aspirations for themselves and their children allowed us to understand better the context for daily and long-term decisions about forestry, agriculture, water management, transportation and other elements of rural land use and resource management. These life stories helped to explain the links between life in rural communities and national policies, and the connections between the daily practices of individuals and the economic and ecological well-being of whole communities.

One of the most dramatic results of this process was a deeper understanding of the gender division of labour, land and authority and its relevance to land use change and farm forestry. Unlike some other parts of the country, in Zambrana-Chacuey the gender division of labour is far more flexible and leaves considerable scope for choice – sometimes by women themselves and sometimes by their spouses – to identify and work as 'farmers', as commercial traders, as artisans or as housewives.

Through the juxtaposition of several women's personal histories we learned that many women who were the eldest children or part of a family with many daughters and few sons became apprentices to their fathers and participated more actively in crop production and land management than girls with older brothers or with many brothers. Both the father's and the mother's needs for assistance affect the occupational training of girl children. Likewise the women who spoke with us were affected by the number and gender of their own children in their occupational options and choices as adults. Many of the women were the main farmers and tree planters in their households while others relegated that work to men. One woman who had worked with her father in his coffee nurseries and plantations was now the main farmer in her household, while her husband worked in a nearby mine. Yet, she could not plant timber trees due to his reservations about regulation of tree harvesting and his lack of faith in the administrative and marketing assistance of the Federation. The women's experience showed us that women's participation in forestry and land management was far more complex than simple gender equity or inequity, or a fixed norm for the gender division of labour. Two other women (both heads of households, one widowed and well-off and one divorced and near landless) planted their own timber lots, and others had either relegated this activity to the men, had planted their own trees as well as their husband's plots, had helped with their husband's plantations, or had chosen not to participate. Beyond the gender division of labour, the life histories – as well as each person's recent experience with the forestry initiative – explained the complex gendered constraints and opportunities in forest enterprises based on gendered property, land management, authority and affiliation with the Federation and ENDA.

Personal and Household Resources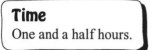

Adapted by Katie Nye from *Navamaga: Training Activities for Group Building, Health, and Income Generation*[61]

> **Time**
> One and a half hours.

Purpose

People do not often recognize the breadth of personal skills, resources, and knowledge in themselves and their own households. Being clear about one's own strengths can lead to self-confidence, self-awareness, and better planning of one's role in group activities.

Materials

Two large pieces of paper, markers, glue.

Process

Step 1: Cut one piece of paper into enough puzzle pieces so that each participant has one. Mark the top side of the pieces. Leave the other piece of paper whole to be used as the base of the puzzle.

Step 2: Explain that the purpose of this exercise is to identify the resources that each person possesses, and make it clear that personal resources can take on many forms: historical knowledge; skill in a trade, traditional art, or farming technique; organization or leadership abilities; personality traits such as patience or tenacity; access to financial resources outside of the community; many friends within the community, and so on.

Step 3: Ask each participant to write down or think of as many personal resources as she can within five to ten minutes. Emphasize quantity not quality.

Step 4: Ask the group members collectively to identify an issue or problem in their homes, groups and/or community that they need to or would like to address, such as voter apathy, poor health and sanitation, or land tenure disputes.

164

Step 5: Once the group has a particular problem in mind, they can focus on solving that problem. Ask each participant to write or draw one personal resource on the marked side of a puzzle piece that they feel will contribute to solving the problem. The group then works together to assemble the puzzle with the resources written on the top of the pieces. When the puzzle has been assembled, the pieces can be glued to the base, and the puzzle hung for the group to view and discuss. Notice who participates in the activity and who does not.

Step 6: Lead the group in a discussion of the exercise, addressing questions that may include:

- Are there some personal resources listed that people did not previously think of as valid or useful? Why?
- Are there any resources that the group feels that it does not have?
- How can the group use individual members' resources to gain access to these 'missing pieces'?
- What group dynamics occurred during the exercise?
- Did the group work together to make decisions and solve the puzzle?
- Did anyone take a leadership role?

Example

Women's unrecognized skills and contributions in Calansi, Camarines Sur, The Philippines

Andrea Lee Esser

While conducting in-depth household interviews in the coastal community of Calansi in the Philippines in 1994, it became evident to me that people underestimated the number of ways in which they earned their livelihoods. Similarly, the skills required to diversify income sources were not recognized as important or useful.

Calansi residents have traditionally relied on both farming and fishing for their livelihoods. Increasing pressures on traditional resources have pushed residents to seek alternative sources of income to supplement earnings from fishing and farming. New income sources include working for wages at tasks such as clearing land or mending nets. Small-scale handicraft work is increasingly common. Residents make brooms, palm roof shingles and sleeping mats, and sell goods – such as cooked foods, fish, and ice – door-to-door.

While men and women have both diversified their livelihood bases, women have been almost twice as likely as men to expand their work beyond fishing and agriculture. Some women were involved in as many as eight different types of money-making ventures. Yet when women were asked about other sources of income, they often did not immediately think of their multiple small-scale tasks. They did not consider these efforts particularly important and did not recognize the skills involved in carrying out the varied schemes.

For example, from time to time some women in Calansi sell cooked goods such as fried bananas or sticky rice cakes door-to-door. This undertaking involves specific skills, resources, and knowledge. Women must know how to cook the food and they must know how to market it. They must secure the money to obtain the raw ingredients and then establish a fair price so that their earnings exceed their inputs. The personal resources which enabled women to carry out such a venture were not readily recognized or valued by the women.

The Personal and Household Resources exercise can help to raise group and individual consciousness of existing strengths, thereby fostering empowerment. While I did not engage in group discussions with women on this topic, I did conduct in-depth interviews with individual women, eliciting information about their livelihoods. Frequently, the women I was interviewing registered both surprise and amazement as they recounted their numerous livelihood strategies and observed my response to their impressive entrepreneurial skills.

Remember

What are the relations of power at play in the local community, both in the larger social context and in the activities planned?

See also

Communicating with Officials and Outsiders
Group Definition
Problem Solving: Trees, Ranking, Assessment
Who Decides?
Who am I?

Photography

Maria Protz

> **Time**
> One day.

Purpose

Photography can be used to enhance participatory methods and the tools that are used to implement them. Participants can use media – photography, video, computers, tape recorders, radio, etc. – in conjunction with each tool found in this book. Photography (or any other medium) cannot easily stand on its own, but should be tied in with other tools and project efforts. Too much emphasis on photography/media, without stressing other benefits or activities, will over-dramatize the relative usefulness and importance of the tool. It should not become an end in itself, or a burden to the participants.

The purpose of this tool is to provide participants with the basic skills necessary to operate a simple camera, including camera functions, film loading and photo composition. Easy-to-use cameras are helpful as a starting point for building confidence and for achieving early success.

Materials

Each group should be provided with a simple, automatic-focus SLR camera with a built-in flash. Disposable and Polaroid cameras are also available in many areas.

The materials needed include a roll of exposed film and enough unexposed film to allow your groups to shoot their pictures; negatives, slides and magazines or newspapers with a variety of photographs which provide examples for the various shot compositions; a large binder with photo-album sheets to keep photographs; files for meeting sheets, equipment sign-out sheets, field notes; large canvas (or other) bags for storage; adhesive tape, scissors, rulers, pens, markers, pencils, large and notebook size paper and other graphic supplies.

Have drawings of the camera you will use ready to display with the parts labelled (if you use disposable or Polaroid cameras, this session is still useful because it demonstrates the basic principles of photography).

Process

Step 1: How the camera works

Explain the functions of the camera to the participants, then ask them to divide into smaller groups. Hand out a camera to each group, then demonstrate how to hold the camera properly and review each part of the camera and how it functions (what the lens does, the shutter, the aperture, etc.). A larger SLR camera with detachable lenses can be used to show internal camera functions.

Step 2: Introduction to film

Provide each group with a roll of exposed film and negatives so that they can see which parts of the film have been completely exposed to light. Explain the chemical nature of film and the function of light in 'exposing' the film. Taking a picture is really a process of keeping the film inside a light-tight box, and quickly exposing the film to light to snap the picture. If there is more light outside, the film needs less exposure time. If it is dark out, the film needs more exposure time or a flash.

Step 3: Shot composition

The next step is to introduce shot composition. It is important for participants to realize that successful photography is more than simply going out and snapping a picture. Care and planning should be involved both to get a good shot and to avoid wasting film. You can cut out pictures (or let the participants select the photographs themselves) from magazines and newspapers illustrating different types of shot compositions (long shots, close-ups, etc.) and ask participants which sorts of pictures they like and why.

Next, review line drawings of all the various types of shot compositions and discuss what types of shots are good for different types of visual information that the participants might want to express. The different types of shot compositions are as follows:

- Very long shot (or establishing shot)
- Long shot
- Mid-long shot
- Mid shot
- Mid-close-up
- Close-up
- Extreme close-up

The next step, if possible, is to have a slide or photograph show covering a wide assortment of shot compositions and subject matter: people, plants, landscapes, still lifes, crowd shots, extreme close-ups of parts of faces, and so on. The groups can return to the photos they chose from the newspapers or magazines and determine the photo composition of each. As the slides or photographs are shown, the participants should determine what type of shot it is and whether or not the composition was the best one chosen for what the picture was trying to express. A set of over-exposed, under-exposed, and out-of-focus shots should also be included in the slide show. Participants can practise making different shot compositions without film in their cameras.

Step 4: Snapping photographs
The groups should now load film into their cameras on their own. Make sure everyone knows they will have an opportunity to do this eventually. With each camera loaded, each participant should recompose their 'pretend' shots and take one each of all the different shot compositions. With four people per group and a roll of 36 exposures, everyone has enough film for seven shots, allowing for mistakes. Once everyone has completed their shots, the film should be processed right away.

> ## Remember
> You should budget for wasting film at the beginning of the process.
> Showing early the effects of exposing film to light will save money later.
> Make sure adequate time is given to explaining proper care and maintenance
> of the equipment, especially for humid and dusty environments.
> Preparing simple 'troubleshooting' lists will help participants with some
> technical problems that they may have on their own.
>
> ## See also
> Video I and II

Example
Integrating photography into a workshop in Jamaica

Maria Protz

The overall goal of the workshop was to document existing agricultural practices with respect to fertility and soil conservation, both to give those indigenous practices which are positive more status in the design of soil fertility technologies and to ensure that rural women food producers' information needs are addressed throughout the project.

Photography was used in conjunction with an audiotape recording of oral histories and with community publishing as a basis for participatory training. We provided communication training to a select group of people from each community, who were then involved in photographing various aspects of indigenous agriculture and cultural practices, as well as interviewing and audiotaping community members who are the real experts in these areas. These stories were then transcribed and published in a project newsletter and other booklets. Some cases involved videotaping these techniques to produce short video programmes that will be part of community-based resource centres.

We were working with three different communities. A few months into the project we found that although we were mainly working with rural women food producers, the rural youth (both young men and women) needed to be involved in the project. As parents of these young people, the women were very concerned about their lack of interest in and respect for agriculture, even though this was the main way that their families provided for them. Parents also wanted a better future for their children and thought that communication training would make it easier for the young people to find an office job – something that all rural people seemed to aspire to here. We also hoped that, through the training, the younger people would better understand the older people in the community, and vice versa. As a result, four people from each community were selected to receive training: two women farmers; and one young woman and man who were not farmers.

We organized the training over a two-week period with practical exercises for each community to perform between sessions. The sessions were held in classrooms at the local JAMAL (Jamaica Movement for the Advancement of Literacy) office.

Participants identified community resources first because far too often people complain about problems while failing to credit the resources they have. After each group completed their list, the groups shared their findings and were surprised to learn that they differed quite a bit in terms of the resources they had. The groups were also surprised to discover that while they did have many things in common, they also had different problems and priorities. Reflecting on available resources proved to be an eye-opener for some of the community members who said they had never actually stopped to think about all the people who had skills and knowledge that could benefit the community as a whole.

The next exercise was to identify community problems in general, with particular emphasis on agriculture. We asked participants to match their existing community resources with the problems they had identified. Were there local human or physical resources that could be put to use to alleviate some of these problems? In some cases this question revealed deeper community issues. In cases where human resources were available, a lack of co-operation and community cohesion were seen as the underlying problems. Leadership training and community development skills were identified as the real training requirement.

Four discussion groups were then created, based on age and gender. Each group was asked to list all the problems they could identify from their perspective with regard to agriculture. The sharing of these lists was also interesting because they revealed gender and age differences which are important for understanding problems. For example, young women and men consider agriculture to be dirty work, while older women do not attach a stigma to farming.

At this point we introduced the photography skills session as described in the Process section.

Each person produced a storyboard illustrating one of the lists showing community problems and resources. For example, one person chose community physical resources, one chose human resources, one agricultural problems, and another community problems. Then they were asked to decide which type of photograph would best illustrate their points, and to produce a simple drawing.

Once the storyboards were completed and reviewed, the groups returned to their respective communities and used them as a plan for taking photographs. They had reviewed the previous day's photos so they could learn from their mistakes.

Along with photography training there was training in the cassette recording of oral histories so that participants could both photograph and interview people back in their communities.

Some individuals have embraced the training and are using their new skills, while others have dropped out. The selection of participants is very important. In our case we underestimated this aspect, especially with regard to the younger participants. We had left the selection of the young people to the women farmers, in a spirit of 'participatory decision-making'. Unfortunately, some of the young people were chosen not for their skill or commitment but because they were related to the women farmers in some way. In addition, the younger women have different interests and are more enthusiastic about subjects that they like. One of the main benefits was for rural people from different communities to have such an exchange and to learn more about each other.

In conclusion, there need to be immediate outlets for photographic activities – for example, newsletters. Photographic research can be used as a lead in to other participatory research activities to get a wider and deeper community analysis.

Problem Solving: Trees, Ranking, Assessment

Adapted by Rachel Slocum from *Tools of Gender Analysis* and *PRA Handbook*[62]

Time

One day or shorter periods spaced over several days. It may help people if the time is extended over a few days because then they can discuss the ranking among themselves within groups of trusted family, friends, co-workers and without the presence of the facilitator or more powerful individuals.

Purpose

Problem Trees, Pair-wise Ranking and Options Assessment are tools for identifying issues of concern and their causes, prioritizing these problems and choosing solutions. Facilitators can use these tools to ensure that the problems of less powerful groups are at least discussed and perhaps also acted upon. There may not be a concern common to the entire community, rather there may be priorities and solutions that differ according to gender, class, ethnicity, age and race and within different ecological, political, economic and historical contexts.

Materials

Several large sheets of paper and markers. Paper of different colours and tape as well as cassette recorder.

Process

Divide participants by gender and/or any other relevant category.

I. Identifying problems, causes and consequences

Step 1: From focus group, household and key informant interviews, a facilitator can learn of various topics of concern. Discuss these issues or ask the group to suggest several problems common to all. Avoid yes/no questions and leading questions like 'Do you need X?' or 'Is X a problem?'

Step 2: One method to encourage reflection on the causes and consequences of a problem is to use a Problem Tree. The trunk represents the problem, the roots are the causes, and the branches are the consequences. Also useful is the Freirean method to arrive at the root causes of problems by asking 'But why?' after each explanation. Ask participants to draw a tree, and using symbols or words, fill in the issues of concern, their causes and the consequences as the group agrees on each during the discussion. If it helps, write on coloured pieces of paper and attach them to the tree in the appropriate places. Repeat the tree exercise until the group has a list of five to ten primary issues of concern.

Step 3: Practise going through the results of the discussion and then ask the group to choose one or two people who will present the results to the larger group.

Step 4: Return to smaller groups to prioritize problems.

Example
Problem Tree

Adapted by the editors from *SEGA Manual* and *Manual for Participatory Planning*[63]

The obstacles to equitable and sustainable development are numerous, but so are the opportunities for change. For example, violations of human rights occur in many ways, often through gender bias or adherance to inequitable roles ascribed through cultural norms and reinforced through economic constraints. Such conditions can be addressed through consciousness-raising and training, grassroots organizing, access to information and media, clarifying power structures, and seeking legal changes. Solving problems of environmental degradation requires respecting local knowledge, addressing inequitable power relations, recognizing livelihood interconnectedness, and acknowledging the need for concerted action which respects all people's needs and rights.

We can demonstrate these obstacles visually in the form of a problem tree which identifies the main problem as a broad range of socio-economic and gender inequities existing throughout the world today. The underlying cause of these inequities is the disenfranchisement of the vast majority of people who have little control over the decisions and resources which affect them. The impacts of this situation are numerous, ranging from the devaluation of their knowledge systems to the concentration of these resources in the hands of a privileged few.

We can then use this analysis to formulate an objective tree which suggests ways of redressing the conditions specified above. The underlying objective of any development effort should foster socio-economic and gender equity through the empowerment and participation of the disadvantaged groups. This involvement

Problem Tree: inequitable and unsustainable development

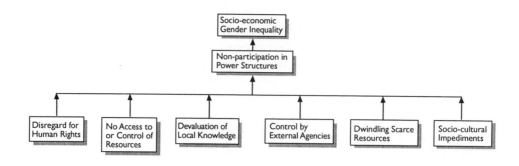

Objective Tree: equitable and sustainable development

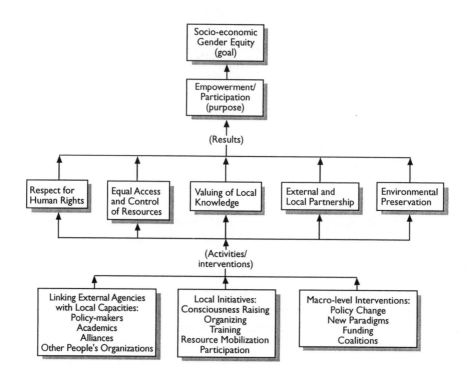

can result in a variety of beneficial outcomes as shown in the example. The enabling interventions include local participation, macro-level policy, paradigm, and organizational changes, as well as fruitful links between local and external capabilities. Given this analysis it is essential to turn next to a discussion of empowerment as the key to achieving equitable and sustainable development.

II. Pair-wise Ranking

Step 1: Set up a matrix listing the most important five to ten issues of concern along the horizontal and vertical axes. Give each topic a letter or symbol chosen by the participants.

Step 2: Ask each small group to compare the urgency of issue 1 on the horizontal axis with issues 2, 3, 4, 5, 6 and 7 on the vertical. Write a letter or symbol in each box that corresponds to the most important issue of the two which are being compared.

Step 3: Add the number of times each letter or symbol appears in the matrix. The more times it appears, the higher its rank.

Step 4: Ask the group to choose someone to present the list of ranked priorities to the larger group. Discuss similarities and differences in the problems and priorities of each group.

Example
Gendered priority ranking

Adapted by the editors from *People, Property, Poverty and Parks: A Story of Men, Women, Water and Trees in Pwani*[64]

Table 8 Women's Priorities: Pwani, Kenya

	Family Planning A	School B	Water Supply C	Soil Erosion Control D	Fuelwood E	Seed Bank F
Family Planning A						
School B	A					
Water Supply C	C	C				
Soil Erosion Control D	A	B	C			
Fuelwood E	E	E	C	E		
Seed Bank F	A	B	C	F	E	
Issues of Concern	Family Planning A	School B	Water Supply C	Soil Erosion Control D	Fuelwood E	Seed Bank F

Number of times occurring	Ranked priorities
A = 3	Water
B = 2	Fuelwood
C = 5	Family Planning Services
D = 0	Secondary School
E = 4	Indigenous Seed Bank
F = 1	Soil Improvement

176

Table 9 Men's Priorities, Pwani, Kenya

Livestock A					
Water Supply B	B				
Hospital C	A	B			
Roads D	A	B	D		
Sustainable Agriculture E	E	B	E	E	
School F	F	B	F	F	F
Issues of Concern	Livestock A	Water Supply B	Hospital C	Roads D	Sustainable Agriculture E	School F

Number of times occurring	Ranked priorities
A = 2	Water
B = 5	School
C = 0	Sustainable Agriculture
D = 1	Livestock Disease
E = 3	Roads
F = 4	Hospital

III. Options Assessment: opportunities and solutions

Step 1: If the participants have previously addressed the issues of concern they listed, discuss how they did so. What worked, what did not work and why? What opportunities and resources are available for dealing with each problem, need or issue?

Step 2: Make a list of possible solutions. Questions to ask for finding opportunities and solutions include:

- What needs to change to overcome this problem?
- What can you do to bring about this change?
- What are the necessary steps?
- What resources do you have that could bring about this change?

Step 3: Ask the participants to discuss the criteria they have used to choose solutions. Ask whether there are other criteria they could use. For example, if the participants have not considered how equitable a solution is for both men and women, encourage them to reflect on this issue. It is important for outsiders offering solutions to reflect on equitability as well. Some questions to consider include:

How would the solution affect the following:
- gender, class, ethnic and race relations
- income levels
- economic opportunities
- workload
- status
- access to and control of resources
- decision-making power (household and community)
- gender roles
- gender division of labour
- the ecosystem
- nearby communities
- the local economy
- relations with other communities
- relations with local authorities or the government

How much will it cost compared to the benefit it will bring?
Who will pay? How much?
What will the group contribute?
What support is necessary from outside?
How long will the solution last?
Does it need to last a long time? Is a short-term solution more practical? Why?

Step 4: From the answers to the above questions, draw several key criteria (such as equitability and sustainability). Ask the participants to rank each solution according to these key criteria using a scale such as:

> Highly favourable
> Favourable
> Not enough information
> Unfavourable
> Highly unfavourable

Discuss why and for whom a solution is favourable or not. If not enough information is available, ask the participants if and how they plan to obtain more information.

Step 5: Ask the group to choose one or two people who will present the ranked solutions to the larger group. Ensure that differences in the solutions of each group are discussed.

Table 10 Ranking solutions against participants' key criteria

Rank	Solution				
	A	B	C	D	
Highly favourable					
Favourable					
Unfavourable					
Highly unfavourable					
Not enough information					

Above table refers to one criterion; repeat for multiple criteria

Remember

Search for ways to ensure that the priorities and solutions of one group (gender, age, class, ethnicity etc.) are not always dominant. Consider doing this exercise in smaller groups if necessary, then negotiate to choose the final list of action priorities.

See also

Advocacy Planning
Personal and Household Resources
Conflict Resolution I, II and III
Who Decides?

Example

Mbusyani Options Assessment, Machakos District, Kenya

Adapted by Barbara Thomas-Slayter from the *PRA Handbook*[65]

In 1988, the Mbusyani Sublocation Development Council invited the National Environment Secretariat to conduct a Participatory Rural Appraisal, similar to the activity which had been carried out in the neighbouring sublocation of Katheka. The groundwork was laid with numerous visits by NES staff to the community early in 1988 for discussions with Assistant Chief Kaku and his colleagues on the Council. The team, along with participants from Clark University, conducted the PRA in mid-1988. In the course of data-gathering and analysis, it became apparent that the community regarded water as its number one problem.

The NES team established a sub-group of specialists to work with the Divisional Water Officer to carry out a technical survey of various water sites, including three springs, three wells, four dams, one borehole, and two dams located at coffee factories. The specialists presented their findings at the public meeting in which problems and priorities were being ranked by the community. To the list of options pertaining to water was added the roof catchment option. These choices were discussed and debated by the community members attending the meeting. Participants then ranked the options for water resource development. The two dam-related options (rehabilitate dams and new surface dams) were ranked first with roof catchments second. Although the Options Assessment Chart does not reveal 'follow-up,' in fact village members started shortly after the meetings to gather the materials for use in building roof catchment water tanks for the local schools.

Mbusyani option assessment chart

BEST BET OR INNOVATION	PRODUCTIVITY	STABILITY	SUSTAINABILITY	EQUITIBILITY	TIME TO BENEFIT	COST	TECHNICAL AND SOCIAL FEASIBILITY	PRIORITY
BOREHOLES	?	0	-	0	3	3	3	6
ROOF CATCHMENT	+	+	++	+	1	1	2	3
NATURAL SPRINGS	+	+	+	++	1	2	2	
REHABILITATE DAMS	++	+	++	++	1	2	2	
SHALLOW WELLS	+	+	++	0	2	1	2	
NEW SURFACE DAMS	++	+	++	++	1	2	2	

KEY				
? Unknown		Time	Cost	Feasibility
- Negative Impact	3	Long	High	Low
0 No impact	2	Medium	Medium	Medium
+ Positive impact	1	Short	Low	High
++ Very positive impact				

Seasonal Activities Calendar

Adapted by the editors from *Working Together*[66]

Time
Two hours.

Purpose

A seasonal calendar helps to identify livelihood tasks and to categorize responsibilities by season, gender, age and intensity of activity. It highlights heavy work periods as well as times of rest, seasonal peaks of illness, drought or flood seasons, and hungry months. The information is useful for project planning as well as a means to begin a discussion of gendered responsibilities, the gender-specific difficulties associated with work in each season, the uses of revenue from collective work, and gendered time allocation and workload.

Materials

Large sheets of paper and markers. Sketches can be made on the ground but it helps to have someone who can copy while the other facilitator continues the discussion, otherwise the conversation does not flow and the participants are made to wait. Sketching on the ground or drawing with coloured sands may also be a better medium for people who are not used to working with markers and paper. Different colours of paper for the different seasons is optional.

Process

Separate participants into groups by gender and age, if necessary.

Step 1: Ask the participants to describe the primary activities in each season. Using words or symbols, mark off the months of the year or a (crop) cycle on the horizontal access or in a circle. Participants may not use a 12-month calendar nor will they necessarily begin with January.

Step 2: Add the activities using words or symbols directly on the paper or on coloured paper of different lengths using a different colour for each season. There are many ways of graphically representing the information. One way is to arrange the months on a horizontal axis and the activities on the vertical axis. The months and activities could be arranged in a circle if the participants prefer.

Step 3: Ask when the workload is heaviest and lightest. If the participants have noted activities that are part of a crop cycle but which they do not take part in, ask who does each task. Using symbols or words, note alongside the activity whether women, men, boys or girls are responsible for the task. Heavy workloads can be represented by the height of each activity block, or with a heavier line as in the Siquijor example.

Step 4: Ask for volunteers to present the information. Possible discussion topics to follow the presentation are listed below.

Elements to include on the calendar

Depending on the objective, some elements that it may be useful to include on the calendar are the seasonal cycles of:

*   human, crop and animal diseases (or pest attack)
*   food shortages/surplus
*   forage shortages/surplus
*   cash and subsistence cropping activities
*   livestock breeding and management tasks
*   water/rainfall availability
*   religious/cultural events
*   influx/exodus of people
*   heavy/light expenses

Questions and topics for discussion

For a discussion of gender roles, some questions include:

*   How have your seasonal activities changed over time? Why?
*   Do women/men have more work now than before?
*   Have women's/men's household consumption crops changed over time?
*   Have technologies been introduced that lighten or increase your workload? By whom? Why?
*   If you have more work now or if you contribute more labour time to cultivation for the household, do you have more decision-making power over the use/sale of the produce?
*   What difficulties do men/women have during the seasons because of their work?
*   How have you tried to alleviate these difficulties?
*   How do you perceive the division of labour? Do you have too much work compared to other family members?
*   Compared to young women/men nowadays, did you have more or less work

when you were younger?
- What do you gain for your work on the household plot?
- What do you gain for your work on your own crops?
- Do you manage credit taken to pay for inputs? Do you manage the use of revenue from the sale of the crop?
- What are the consequences of one gender having to devote most of her/his time to X activity?
- What would you prefer to do with your time?
- Would you be able to cultivate X if your husband/wife did not help you?

The Seasonal Activities Calendar can help to begin a discussion on:

- gender roles
- unequal workload, causes and consequences
- use of, access to and control of land, trees, water and other resources
- pasture rights
- profitability of activities
- reasons for times of sickness
- gain versus workload
- pesticide use
- household financial management

Remember

Activities calendars may differ within a community according to gender, age, ethnicity, class, race, religion, ecological zone, caste, education or occupation.

After completing the exercise, cross-check the information using key informant interviews.

Depending on the objective, an involved discussion using the tool as a starting point may be more useful at times than filling the calendar with details.

See also

Activities, Resources and Benefits Analysis
Gender Analysis Activities Profile
Time Line Variations
Division of Labour
Gendered Resource Mapping

Seasonal Activities Calendar from Tubod, The Philippines[67]

	Jan	Feb	Mar	Apr	May	Jun	Jul	Aug	Sep	Oct	Nov	Dec
Season	Wet	Dry Season				Wet Season						

Activities

STRESS PERIODS
- Heavy Workload
- Hunger/Illness — fevers, dysentery
- Many Expenses — food, school fees, fiesta, farm inputs

HOUSEHOLD PRODUCTION
- Cooking
- Childcare
- Small Livestock — regular maintenance

FISHERIES — best season · process · market · typhoon season

MAJOR CROPS
- Dried Coconut — process/market · process/market
- Rice (2-3 crops) — harvest 1 · plough · trample · harrow/level · transplant seedling · weed · plough · harvest 2 · fertilize · spray · harvest · seed plot prep · process/market · plant seed plot · harvest 3 · process/market
- Corn (1 crop field) — plough · weed · row · plant · plough · weed · harvest · plough/row · plant · plough · weed · harvest

Legend

○ Adult female
● Female youth/child
□ Adult male
■ Male youth/child

↑ continuous activity
↑ sporadic activity
▬ heaviest activity

Source: Shields and Thomas-Slayter, 1993.

184

Example
Seasonal Activities Calendar from Tubod, The Philippines

Dale Shields and Barbara Thomas-Slayter

There is considerable crossover and sharing of domestic responsibilities between women and men and between the old and young. Lines are not sharply drawn between heavy and light work. Arrangements between the sexes often seem somewhat ad hoc, dependent upon the schedules and responsibilities of household members rather than their gender and age. Although the final responsibility for household chores is a woman's, all members of the household usually help accomplish them. Some activities are clearly gender specific. Women, for example, do not gather coconut sap or fish; men do not bake and sell foodstuffs. Generally, heavy tasks are undertaken by men, including ploughing and managing large livestock; women care for the small livestock and manage the household. The figure opposite is a condensed version of a gender-disaggregated seasonal calendar created by focus groups in Tubod. It illustrates the division of labour by gender and age for several major household activities.

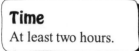

Social Network Mapping

Christel Weller-Molongua and Johannes Knapp

Time
At least two hours.

Purpose

Donating, loaning and exchanging materials, labour and other resources occur in many communities as a result of complex economic, social and cultural ties. Mapping these relationships can help facilitators and researchers to understand them and the needs of community members. More importantly, it allows facilitators to see which, if any, families are excluded from these networks. The tool reveals the most important items of exchange. The map can also be used to understand ties between sub-groups (ethnic, religious, class, extended families) and between adjacent communities.

It is important to use this tool from the beginning. Many project teams make contact with the chief of the village assuming that the village is one united community. It is also useful to see if there are different communication systems for women and men. Often women exchange information only among the women in the extended family. Unlike men, women in some areas, without outsiders encouragment of their participation, do not take part in village meetings.

Materials

Large sheet of paper, pieces of cardboard, markers, paste or tape, or coloured chalk and a chalkboard.

Process

As the social networks of women and men often differ, it may be appropriate to make two separate maps. Networks may also differ according to religion, ethnicity, socio-economic status or other factors.

Step 1: Ask a representative group (three women, three men) from the community to define household or family within the specific country or regional context. Ask the same group to list the most important resources exchanged between households. Select no more than eight households for the mapping. Write the name of the household or one of its members on a card for the exercise.

Step 2: Draw the community boundaries, compass headings, and neighbouring communities. Paste the cards on the paper according to the households' actual locations in the community, but leave enough space between cards. Practitioners have found it is often easier to understand the exchange networks if the houses are placed in a circle rather than at their precise location. In some cases a diagram might be useful; in others, a map will be more appropriate.

Step 3: Ask each household representative which kind of relationship links her or his family with others. List the types of resources that women or men exchange. Using coloured pens or different types of lines, indicate what each member of each household exchanges with the others. Draw arrows at both ends or one end of these lines to show reciprocity or a one-way exchange.

Remember

Use this tool with representatives of no more than 8 households. The purpose of this tool is not necessarily to reveal every last detail about the exchange network, but to see whether there are households excluded from this network.

See also

Activities, Resources and Benefits Analysis
Wealth Ranking
Household Interviews

Example
Social Network Mapping in villages of southern Mali

Christel Weller-Molongua and Johannes Knapp

Communication and exchange are the typical signs of good relations in the villages of southern Mali. One way to improve the organizational capacity of a village is to use participatory research to discover the patterns of interdependence among the different families living in the village. The results of this research can help to show whether:

- The social system in the village is intact and what means of communication and exchange exist between all families.

- There are outsider families not included in village matters who do not receive information through village meetings.
- There are poor and wealthy families.
- There are ethnic, religious or cultural groups which have their own systems of communication and exchange.
- There was a change in the exchange networks as a result of project intervention. In this case the tool is useful for evaluations.

Typically, the first steps, 'definition of household' and 'list of resources exchanged' are done in the project (Promotion of Local Initiatives – PRODILO – a GTZ[68] project) with a mixed group of villagers. If the group of facilitators (also composed of women and men) notices any differences between the answers of men and women or young and old people, they arrange separate meetings. We have found individual interviews useful when we ask about money loaned or received. Participation of young women is very difficult in many villages in southern Mali because they are seen as people from outside the village (due to patrilocal marriage) who might be divorced or leave the marriage at any time and return to their own village. They are considered as such until they have had a certain number of children and have reached a certain age.

The maps drawn by both the men and the women revealed a divided village. The village consisted of 5 extended families and 17 households. Members of one household work on one collectively owned field together, have a common granary and eat together according to both men and women. We saw that there was almost no exchange or communication between the two neighbourhoods but that women and men in the same neighbourhood had established exchange networks among themselves. We learned that the families in neighbourhood 2, Diallo, a Fulani family, and Diarra, a Bambara, were perceived as foreigners. Even though they had settled in the village over one hundred years ago, because they were not among the founding families of this village, they will be considered outsiders forever. The other issue is that both these outsider families are rich. Jealousy is a significant factor explaining village divisions. The men in neighbourhood 1 said that they do not share the same problems so why exchange with the families in neighbourhood 2. The women discussed the aspect of wealth less but said, simply, this is the way it is. They said, further, that all the other projects that have come to the village have accepted that the village is divided such that when one project brought shea butter presses, they gave one to each neighbourhood. The women asked, 'Why do you want to change us now?'

We understood that the families of Samake 1 and Dumbia support the family of Samake 2 which is considerably poorer. Small families are typically the result of a larger family splitting up often over the lack of transparency in management of household resources. These small families have difficulties because they do not have enough people to do all the work. The exchange of labour for shea

Social Network Mapping

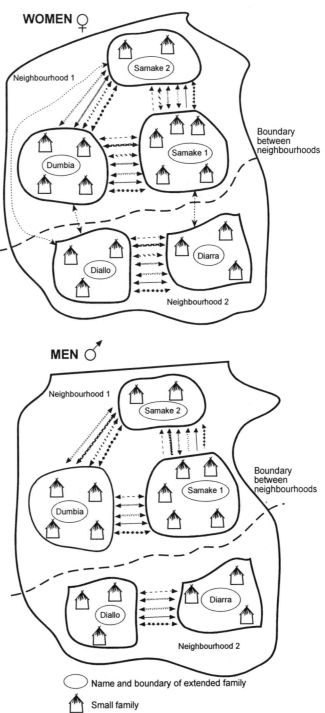

WOMEN ♀

Neighbourhood 1

Samake 2

Dumbia

Samake 1

Boundary between neighbourhoods

Diallo

Diarra

Neighbourhood 2

KEY

Men

Exchange of work tools ————
Exchange of labour - - - - - - -
  for field work
Land loans ︿︿︿︿︿
Seed exchange ●●●●●
Credit ∿∿∿∿
Millet exchange ✕✕✕✕✕✕
Information exchange 〉〉〉〉〉〉

Women

Exchange of work tools ————
Exchange of labour - - - - - - - -
  (housework in case of sickness)
Collective work in rice field ﹀﹀﹀﹀
Rice seed exchange ●●●●●
Credit (for clothes, ∿∿∿∿
  medicine, small enterprise)
Collective work to ✕✕✕✕✕✕
  prepare shea butter
Information exchange 〉〉〉〉〉〉

MEN ♂

Neighbourhood 1

Samake 2

Dumbia

Samake 1

Boundary between neighbourhoods

Diallo

Diarra

Neighbourhood 2

⬭ Name and boundary of extended family

⌂ Small family

189

butter production between Samake 1 and Dumbia on the women's map was another indication that these families were better off because the shea butter production is extremely labour intensive. The women of Samake 2 do not have enough time to produce it.

The women's map revealed the only exchange between the two neighbourhoods – collective work on the rice fields. This work does not require exchange so much as collective time organization. There is one larger rice field divided into small parcels for each woman. These parcels were marked out long ago and they were not segregated by neighbourhood so the women have to work side by side. The spatial arrangement requires women to organize collectively when to plant so that they will all be transplanting, weeding and harvesting at the same time. If everyone were on different schedules, it would be difficult because it is rain-fed rice and they would risk damaging the plants of others. Another issue concerning land use that we learned from the men's map is the fact that two families in neighbourhood 1 use land on loan from a neighbouring village which means that there is a lack of land. Eventually, both neighbourhoods agreed to discuss their differences in a meeting facilitated by PRODILO staff.

After two years of project intervention, training the community in communication, organization and management, all households worked together and the separation of the neighbourhoods no longer existed. The villagers decided that at least one representative of each extended family has to participate in each management committee for both women's and men's activities.

Study Trips

Johannes Knapp and Christel Weller-Molongua

Time

For women, one day (or more if overnight is possible). For men, one to several days depending on the distance and the theme.

Purpose

Study trips provide a way to encourage learning by seeing and to promote the exchange of ideas between one group that has particular knowledge or experience and another that seeks to learn. Study travel is a way for project facilitators to see another village or project's work and its relative success. The tool is a means to enhance discussion of new ideas and methods because participants first observe and then discuss. For women, an excursion can be the starting point for greater self confidence and empowerment. Often the culture prevents women from having much contact with other communities and ideas. Travel may be especially difficult for women due to a variety of restrictions on their movement (such as lack of time or transport). Also, the preparation for study trips encourages analysis and can be used in other problem-solving discussions.

Materials

Pen and paper for preparation and discussion.

Process

Step 1: Let the group determine who will participate in the excursion. If women will participate, make sure they have permission to go. Choose excursion participants who are respected in the community and to whom the community will listen upon their return. This may include representatives of the poor or of groups normally excluded from such activities. Ask the participants to choose someone who will take notes, another who will serve as the group leader during the visit and at least one who will present the information to the community when they return home.

191

Step 2: Facilitate a discussion to define the objectives of the excursion. Questions that should frame this discussion include:

- What don't we know?
- What are we unsure about?
- What do we want to know?

Prepare a list of questions that the participants could ask but encourage them to come up with these questions on their own. Use role play to train the group in asking questions. Prepare the participants over the course of several days if necessary. Preparation of the group is especially important to ensure that they learn something from the trip.

Step 3: Travel to the site. Be sure that the visitors verify answers to their questions through direct observation.

Step 4: Facilitate an evaluation and interpretation of the findings and assist the group in preparing a final presentation for the community.

Step 5: Facilitate a presentation of the results of the excursion and new perspectives to the community.

Remember
Be sure that the community has chosen someone to present the results of the trip prior to leaving. Devote significant time to the presentation and community discussion following the excursion.

See also
Focus Groups
Communicating with Officials and Outsiders

Example
The Sotiguila Bougouni women's group visits Falan, Mali

Christel Weller-Molongua and Johannes Knapp

As part of the GTZ[69] project, Promotion of Local Initiatives (PRODILO), we facilitated a study excursion for a group of women from Sotiguila Bougouni, Mali – a small, isolated village about 45 km from the closest major town. The women of this village work collectively on the fields of well-off farmers during the rainy season. This women's association consists of 53 women who work for a total of 10,000 - 12,500 fCFA ($20-$25) per day. Their annual collective income amounts to about 100,000 fCFA ($200). Traditionally, these women turned over most of this money to the village elders to purchase a bull for the annual festival marking the founding of the village. When PRODILO implemented a revolving fund for small loans, women began not only to use this credit, but also to think about how they could better use their collective income. They asked the PRODILO facilitator what they could do with their money. In the ensuing discussion, the women outlined two objectives: that the women's group would make more money each year and that individual women would also increase their income. They proposed investing the collective money in a mill, a shea butter press, rice cultivation and soapmaking.

Rather than choose among these proposals, the facilitator suggested a study trip to Falan (the site of another project) about 30 km away where women were already investing money from their collective income. Six women were available to participate. The facilitator planned an evening of role play to acquaint the women with the process of asking questions and to gain some self confidence before embarking. The women practised for four evenings because the trip and the idea of posing questions to strangers were so new to them.

In Falan, the group asked the prepared questions about the mill and other activities. But seeing that the women of Falan had a revolving credit fund for which they maintained written records, the visiting group began asking new questions about record-keeping that they had not thought of during the practice sessions. They realized that they first needed to become literate and numerate in order to effectively manage a similar revolving fund.

Back in the village, the women presented what they had learned to the community. They then approached the village elders and told them that they would no longer donate the majority of their earnings to the festival. The women asked PRODILO to help them organize a literacy centre and they decided to use 70,000 of their 100,000 fCFA to open a credit fund for women. With the remaining 30,000 fCFA, they decided to start a soapmaking business like the one they had seen in Falan. Within half a year, these women more than doubled the original 30,000 fCFA with the soap they produced.

Several aspects of village life changed after the excursion. The men were at first reluctant to accept the idea that the women would no longer purchase a steer for the feast but later changed their minds when they saw how successful the women were in investing the money. Furthermore, prior to the group visit and subsequent economic activities, only two women attended village meetings. Now women sometimes outnumber the men at these meetings and they participate as well. Finally, the women's activities helped to reactivate the village market, dormant for some 50 years. With the new opportunities, fewer youth are leaving the village and some have even come back.

Time Line Variations

Rachel Slocum and Dieuwke Klaver

Time
One to two hours.

Purpose

Time lines are a way to note the important historical markers of a community or household. It is important to consult both women and men of different age, race, ethnic, and socio-economic groups because women and men often mark time by different events. Time lines are also useful as an introduction to a discussion of changes in gender roles and relations. One way to approach change over time is to ask questions about the past, present and future. Futures possible or 'what if?' questions can also reveal the degree of openness to change as well as the potential impact of an intervention.

Materials

Pen and paper for notes, markers and large sheets of paper for time line, and three or four suitable containers for a confidential poll of responses to 'what if?' questions.

Process

Step 1: Time lines
Ask participants to use symbols or words to denote important historical events. Some time lines begin with the founding of a community or with an event that the oldest people remember, but they can start at any point. Time lines may also be represented in a circular rather than linear fashion depending on the participant's perspective. Years can be estimated and exact numbers are not necessarily important.

Step 2: Change over time
Use the time line to discuss the situation of women and men before and after a certain year or event. Ask groups of men and women to list activities they did 'traditionally' and to describe what they actually do now. If there have been changes, encourage them to determine the reason for the changes and the consequences for

personal and community life.[70] It may be easier to start with a discussion of activities and from there move to a discussion of changes in gender relations. Also, take care to ask people of different age groups about changes they have noted over particular time periods. Some questions include:

- What changes have occurred in your life in the following categories?
    - Access to resources (land, water, information, credit, education, etc.)
    - Control of resources
    - Decision-making at the individual, household, community or organizational level
    - Personal self-esteem and confidence
    - Control of your own revenue
    - Control of your time
    - General workload
    - Standards of behaviour for 'good' women and 'good' men
- Have these changes been positive or negative and why? What changes in these categories do you hope for?

Step 3: Possible futures
Discuss changes that participants hope for or think possible. Some questions include:

- What would you do if you had more time (because you did not have to do a particular task)?
- How do you hope your children's lives will be different from yours?
- Are there specific resources you hope to have access to or to own in the future? Why and how will you gain access?
- What responsibilities would you like to have? Which ones would you prefer not to have?
- What would you do if there was 'X' intervention by the government or an aid organization?
- What would you do if there was 'X' political, economic, social or environmental change?
- What would happen if 'X' plant, animal, technology or other resource was introduced?
- What activities do you think women or men will have in the future?

Step 4: Confidential polls
If necessary, use a secret poll to determine the answers to sensitive 'what if?' questions. Pose a question and suggest two to four possible responses. Interview each person separately. When she or he has decided on a response, ask her or him to put a pebble in the appropriate container. You can come up with alternative ways of responding as well.

Step 5: Ask segregated or mixed gender groups to guess at the final tally. Reveal the results and discuss them and any differences between what the group guessed and the actual response.

> **Remember**
> It may be easier for participants to respond about the past, so more effort may be necessary to encourage discussion about the future.
>
> **See also**
> Land Use Feltboard
> Gender Myths
> Division of Labour
> Gender Analysis Activity Profile
> Oral Life Histories
> Seasonal Activities Calendar
> Chapter 3

Example
A confidential poll on alternative uses of time in Sanambele, Mali

Dieuwke Klaver

While working in a UNIFEM-financed grinding mill project in Mali, I used the confidential poll to ask women about preferred time use. My question was, 'If you had extra time, what would you do?' I gave them three choices:

- Help my husband on his millet field.
- Work for myself (small enterprise, working on her own field, making shea butter, gardening).
- Rest.

At a meeting in Sanambele, Mali, involving groups from six villages (four women and three men per group), Malian facilitators posed my question to each woman and asked her to put a pebble in the bag corresponding to her time use preference. The facilitators then asked a mixed group to guess at the majority response. Men and women said uniformly that the majority of women would choose to help the men on their fields.

However, when the stones were counted, first place went to 'work for myself' (41 women). 'Rest' received 13 votes and only four women wanted to help their husbands on his millet field. Everyone was surprised. The men declared that even if the women wanted to work for their own gain, the men would use the money the women earned. Unfortunately, despite my encouragement, none of the six facilitators (two women and four men) wanted to lead a discussion with the villagers about the results of the poll and the difference between what was said publicly and what was voted privately. They were sure a conflict would ensue if they pursued the issue further. The difference between the group response and the poll result demonstrates that sometimes, in discussing gender relations, a confidential means of expressing opinions is useful.

Transects

Adapted by Lori Wichhart from *The PRA Handbook*[71]

Time
A few hours to a few days depending on the size of the area, its diversity, and the time available.

Purpose

Transects portray the interactions between the physical environment and human activities over space and time. They are useful for identifying a community's natural characteristics, both current and historical.

Materials

Paper and pen. Some form of transportation may be appropriate depending on the area the transect will cover. (Video camera optional.)

Process

Step 1: Gather information by walking/driving in a line through a cross-section of the landscape. The line may extend in any direction (north to south, high to low, east to west, forest to desert) as long as all major ecological and production zones are covered. This ensures representation of maximum topographical, resource, and socio-economic variation in the community. It may be necessary to do more than one transect, depending on the pattern and complexity of the landscape or the size of the community. Ways to select a transect line include remote sensing imagery, random sampling, or reviewing a map to estimate the line of greatest diversity, as well as viewing the landscape from a lookout point.

Step 2: Select a group of about six to ten people representing a cross-section of the community. Discuss the exercise with the group. Look out on the landscape from an overlook point with local residents to choose a representative path. Depending on the selected route, this point could be a high spot in the landscape or a community boundary.

Step 3: If members of the group will conduct informal interviews with community members along the transect path, the questions need to be clear and some practice may be necessary.

Step 4: Ask the group to divide into three observer teams for: soils, cropping patterns, and farm size; water points, slope and drainage; and socio-economic indicators. Encourage the groups to make general observations even if the topics overlap. Local residents can do the transect but inviting government extension officers is also a possibility. If the area is large and a vehicle is not available, subdivide the transect and assign the parts to two or three smaller groups.

Step 5: During the walk, take time for brief and informal interviews of residents in each of the ecological zones. During these open-ended interviews, focus on such resource issues as soil management, land tenure, access to and availability of water, fuelwood problems or others that residents identify as issues of concern. Interviewers should ask questions but let residents steer the discussion and ask questions of group members.

Step 6: At the end of the exercise, compile field notes and construct a landscape/land use profile. The information from the interviews can also be used later to help determine problems and opportunities.

Remember
Consider what are the appropriate spatial and organizational scales for analysis, action, advocacy, policy change and follow-up.

See also
Gendered Resource Mapping
Landscape/Lifescape Mapping

Examples
Creating a transect in Ghusel Village, Nepal

Nina Bhatt

The transect was critical in providing the research team with a quick understanding of our research site's physical nature (terrain, soil types, topography, water systems, forest areas, agricultural land) and social characteristics (ethnic and caste settlement patterns, government vs. private ownership of land, who owns what and why). The tool's participatory nature gave us an opportunity to meet and interact with community members in a very informal manner.

Two researchers, along with a local Tamang research assistant, proceeded to walk from Ward 7 (our home base) to Ward 2 which was the furthest point of our research site.[72] The morning of the transect, our Tamang research assistant, who was native to the area, began 'walking us through' the several wards. This 'walk through' consisted of careful observations and discussions of the surrounding environment (landslides, soil erosion), the best forest and fodder collection sites, and types of water sources. Walking and observing gave us a clear idea of the terrain, the length of time required to cover the distance, the areas which community members accessed for resources on a regular basis, and how far these sites were from their homes.

At a point about an hour's walk from our base village, we arrived at a high ridge which gave us an excellent cross-sectional view of our entire research site. We stopped there. A few other community members had joined us as we walked to the ridge we were on (we encouraged them to come with us since we knew we would pause to sketch). Others joined in as the drawing process began. Not only did we know that this ridge gave us the best possible view of Ghusel, it was also an area through which community members passed with considerable regularity. We wanted as large a group as possible. In the end, there were about eight people participating, which is a fair-sized group in the Nepalese hill context.

Our local research assistant initiated the sketching process. My counterpart was busy discussing with the group at large, while I observed the drawing, listened to the conversations about Ghusel, its territory and people, interjecting questions and asking for clarification as the discussion and drawing progressed. This was very much a group effort. We used big, colourful sheets of paper, and coloured markers, which generated much interest and curiosity, especially when community members were encouraged to use them.

The final transect was a visual map which gave us a cross-section of our research site. This map showed resource availability and constraints as depicted by community members. These included landslides, severely eroded sites, important water sources, as well as tracts of land which are still abundant with fodder and fuelwood. The transect was also excellent for illustrating some social and cultural dimensions of Ghusel such as caste and ethnic determinants of settlement – who lives where, and how that facilitates or hinders their access to natural resources.

Transect of Ghusel, Lalitpur District, Nepal[73]

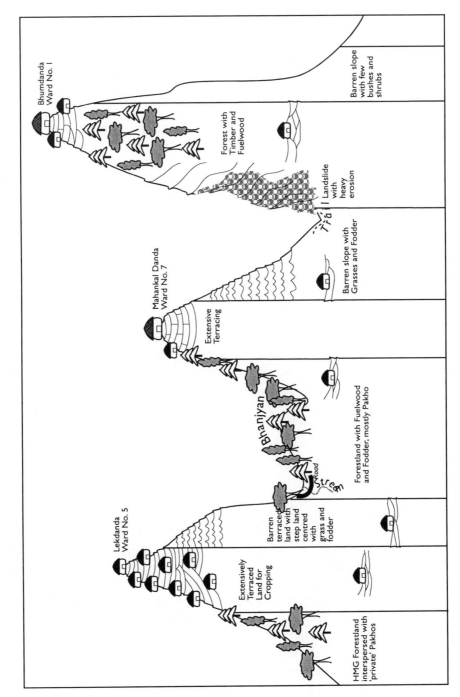

Historical transect in Diak Lay, East Kalimantan, Indonesia

Mark Poffenberger

Historical transects provide an approximate visual description of changing land use profiles. A time series of transect lines may be used to illustrate changes in the natural vegetative cover, including structure and composition, or human land use patterns in the study area. The area (distance) covered by the transect depends on the types of changes the figure is meant to reflect. Changes in the species composition of a home garden or a rainforest may be best represented in a transect covering from ten to several hundred metres, while migratory human settlement shifts within a watershed may require ten kilometres or more. The points in time covered in the transect series depend on key events or changes which the researchers and community deem important and desire to illustrate, as well as on information available for preparing the transect.

Historical transects can also be used in conjunction with time lines and trend line graphs. This enables the researchers to relate changes in land use profiles to demographic, rainfall, resource flow and other types of data often depicted in trend lines, or to political and natural events shown in time lines.

Opposite is an example of a historical transect showing changes in the landscape surrounding Diak Lay village in East Kalimantan. The purpose of the transect was to illustrate the long-term system of rotational swidden (slash and burn) farming, and the period when settlements and commercial gardening were introduced in the area. Consequently, the spatial frame selected for the transect bounded it on one side with the village and, at the far side, with the primary forest just beyond the furthest swidden fields, approximately six kilometres away. The transect was prepared during discussion with the Wehea tribal community who had migrated into the area in the late 19th century. The historical data was generated through in-depth discussions with members of the council of elders and other older women and men.

The transect covers 1870 up to the present, since prior to 1870 the area was said to have been under old growth forest. The elders reported that they lived approximately 5 kilometres up-river from the Diak Lay site, using it only for swidden farming from the 1880s until the 1940s. Towards the end of the Second World War, due to expanding population pressure in the old settlement, a number of villagers established a new settlement in Diak Lay. The transect shows how the primary forest was cleared for dry rice fields at increasing distances from the Telen River. These swidden fields were fallowed as new swidden paddy fields were opened. Regenerating secondary forests emerge in fallowed areas in the early 20th century. After the settlement was created in 1945, and in response to growing market opportunities, Diak Lay villagers began manipulating fallowed swidden plots through

Historical transect [74]

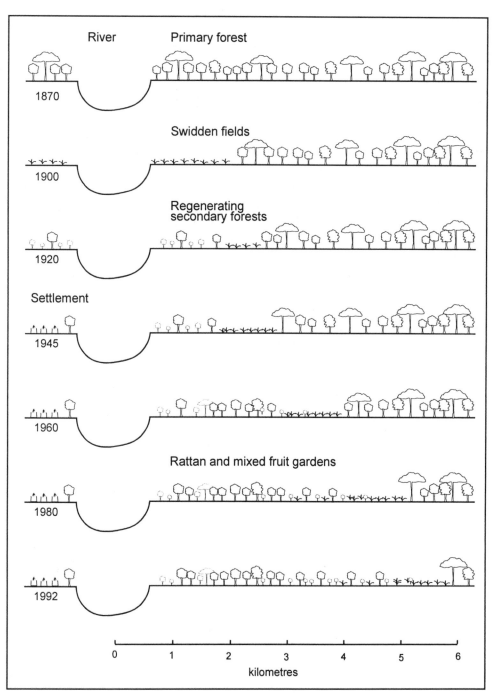

enrichment planting with fruit trees and rattan. This is illustrated by the depiction of rattan and mixed fruit gardens in the transects from 1960 to 1992. By 1992, many of the swidden fields were located up to six kilometres from the settlement.

The transect presented is a generalized representation of the basic changes in land use in Diak Lay over a 120-year period. Covering an area of 6 kilometres, this transect provides only a very gross picture of changes in land use. It would be desirable, with additional time, to attempt to reconstruct more accurately, and in greater detail, changes along a shorter, specific plot line. To do so would require walking the transect line with a group of older women and men who have knowledge of how that land area was used in the past. In addition to community recall, current vegetation, especially the age of fruit trees or secondary growth, would give some verifying data regarding the number of years each forest patch had been fallowed and the types of human manipulation it had experienced during regeneration. Locally significant events, determined by the villagers, could be used to mark the time points more accurately, for which each transect line would be drawn. Sometimes these important points in time differ by gender, race, ethnicity and class, so it is important to consult with a broad cross-section of the community. Time points might include year of settlement, before and after a large fire, before and after the loggers came, and the present. In summary, historical transects provide a useful technique for depicting land use changes. These promising methods need to be further developed and tested in a variety of applications.

Video I: Developing a Community Project

Elizabeth Fabel

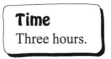

Time
Three hours.

Purpose

Video is a medium with great potential power that holds both promise and limitations for participatory development. Its appropriateness to the purpose, setting and audience, as well as potential costs or negative impacts, must be considered along with the benefits. Training fieldworkers in video, for example, should include dialogue about the impacts of communication technologies as applied to development. Often, the very experience of using the camera and mastering the technology is what helps participants to think about the role of communications in development and the nature of mass media versus community media. Through this kind of awareness, participants can arrive at ways of using video in their own setting that are inclusive, participatory and engage audiences in an interactive way. This is a planning tool designed to help groups think about their communication needs and the appropriateness of video to meeting those needs. The objectives of the tool are:

- To identify existing communications and needs.
- To develop a plan for using video that fits with the organization's objectives and communication needs.
- To generate an action plan for a video project.
- To identify needs and resources for carrying out the plan.

Materials

Flip-chart paper and markers.

Process

There are four sets of questions corresponding to the objectives. The questions are designed to help participants move through the process of developing a rationale

205

and generating concrete ideas for a video project and the resources they need. This tool can be facilitated by someone from the group, but will be most fruitful as a group activity. The group should engage representatives of staff and project participants who might be involved in the project as well as those who make decisions about the allocation of resources. Assign roles in the group for facilitator, notetaker, and timekeeper.

Expect to encounter some scepticism about video like 'It's too complicated,' 'It's too expensive,' or 'We don't know how to use it' and so on. Try to start the process with a positive statement about those barriers. Before starting on the questions, ask people to brainstorm the positive aspects as well as the obstacles to using video. Take notes on these and return to these ideas or concerns at appropriate points in the exercise.

Summarize your answers at the end of each step.

Step 1: Identify existing communications resources and needs. What groups/constituencies does the organization communicate with (participants, funders, officials, other)? Underneath each category, identify the kinds of materials, media or approaches you use to communicate with these groups. For example:

- Print (newsletters, posters, training materials)
- Oral (meetings, theatre, folk media such as songs, storytelling)
- Audio/Visual (photographs or slides, video, film, audio cassettes, radio)

Discuss how effective you think each material or approach is. Address these questions in your discussion:

- Who creates these materials or does the communicating? Who communicates with whom?
- Are programme participants involved in these communications? How?
- What do you think the communication needs of the organization are? (Consider internal and external needs. Consider the media environment in your area. What media are available locally and to whom? How is the media environment changing?)

Step 2: Develop a rationale for developing video. Ask yourself the following questions:

- Do you currently or have you ever used video as part of your work? What is or was your experience with it?
- Are there particular goals/objectives that could be met?
- Are there particular audiences that could be reached?
- Why do you think video would be appropriate?
- What ideas do you have for making it participatory?

- Do you anticipate any obstacles or problems with using video? Any negative impacts?

Discuss your answers to these questions. Work as a group to develop a rationale for using video.

Step 3: Develop a plan for a video project. Through discussion and brainstorming, come up with an idea and a set of objectives for a video project. Address the following questions:

- How do you propose to use video?
- Who is your main audience?
- How will the content, messages, and approaches of the videos be developed?
- How will participation in the project be nurtured and sustained? (Consider all aspects from planning and research to scripting, logistics, shooting, editing, screening and evaluating.)
- How will video tapes you produce be used?
- What are the intended outcomes?
- How will you evaluate the project?
- How do the objectives, approach, and outcomes fit with the organization's overall goals and objectives and communication needs already identified?

Consider operational issues such as:

- How will the project be carried out?
- Who will be responsible for implementing the project?
- What is the time frame?
- Who will do the training?
- Who will receive training?

Develop a preliminary time line for the project, from planning to implementation to evaluation.

Step 4: Identify needs and resources. List three resources that you will need for this project. Think in terms of tangibles like equipment, as well as technical assistance in training, writing or drama development and interview skills.

- Which of these do you already have or have access to?
- Which of these do you need to get?
- How will you get them? (donations, loans, grants, rentals?)

Using this list, estimate a preliminary budget. Identify up front and/or one-time costs of the project for one year. Identify ongoing costs of the project over the proposed lifetime of the project.

Step 5: Generate a preliminary proposal. Pull together your summaries from each of the steps. You will find that you have the beginnings of a proposal: a statement of need, a statement of purpose and objectives, a description of activities and intended outcomes, a plan for implementation and a budget.

Discuss your next steps: these include further exploration of the feasibility of the project (can you get what you need?) and sharing the plan with others in the organization.

Benefits and potentials

- The immediacy of video means that footage can be shown on the spot.
- Immediacy allows for simultaneous feedback when used in a learning process.
- Video can act as a mirror of a community or allow the community to portray itself as it chooses.
- Video can capture what is witnessed; it is proof of positive or negative actions.
- Video is a channel of communication across geographic, social, economic and political boundaries.
- Video can bring together groups that might not otherwise meet face to face.
- Video can be used to portray a sensitive issue in a way that externalizes it so the issue can be discussed 'at a safe distance'.

Costs

- Tariffs and import restrictions.
- Videos obtained through foreigners may have strings attached.
- Up front costs of acquiring the equipment are high.
- Support may be needed for initial and ongoing training.
- Producing and using videos requires access to a reliable power source, even when using batteries in the field.

See also
Chapter 5
Video II: Demystifying the Technology
Communicating with Officials and Outsiders
Community Drama

Example
Video SEWA, Ahmedabad, India

Adapted by Lori Wichhart from *Video SEWA: A People's Alternative*[75]

In 1984 several SEWA members took part in a three-week video training workshop. One-third of the participants were illiterate and another third had less than a high school education. The group included women of all ages, Hindus and Muslims, craftswomen, vendors and carpenters as well as several senior SEWA leaders. Many of the women were members of the Manekchowk Market.

'I did not know what video was,' one women explained. 'Still, I learned to make programmes, to operate equipment and to do replays. I am illiterate and do not have electricity in my house but I learned to make video programmes and become a producer.'

Several months after the initial video workshop the Municipality of Ahmedabad began, under court orders, to negotiate with the vendors of Manekchowk Market. The negotiations centred on the rights of small-scale street vendors to claim space in the market place where they had been earning their livelihoods for generations. In the eyes of the municipal authorities, these vendors obstructed the traffic and were to be cleared off the streets.

A meeting to inform representatives of the vendors was called and Video SEWA decided to tape it. The vendors were comfortable with the women who were taping and thus the taping did not inhibit or interfere with the meeting. The women's reactions to the municipality's offers were manifold: some were sceptical; some expressed concern about political pressures; some felt no price was too heavy to pay to escape police harassment; some were very emotional and enthused. Eventually they formulated a list of conditions and concerns. All of this was captured on video – the words of women making decisions about their lives.

Ela Bhatt, General Secretary of SEWA, wondered if the municipal authorities would be so indifferent to the problem of these women if they had been present at the meeting? She invited the Municipal Commissioner to view the tape informally. As he watched the agitated faces of the women, he was moved by their fear of the police, their sense of solidarity and their distrust of the municipal authorities. Listening to them on video meant that he could be open without betraying his emotions; he could be himself and not the Municipal Commissioner. The women would never have spoken to him directly as they did on the tape and he would not have been able to hear them in the same way. The tape proved invaluable to the negotiations between the vendors and the Municipality. It also shaped the way the market women and the members of Video SEWA understood the potential of video.

Video II: Demystifying the Technology

Elizabeth Fabel

Time
At least three two- or
three-hour sessions.

Purpose

Participatory video involves people as both subjects and producers in a process of community reflection and action. Alongside movements to regenerate popular theatre for social development, participatory video and participatory radio programmes began during the 1970s as part of a movement to use modern electronic media in a way that incorporated indigenous communication such as folk song, dance, story-telling and people's theatre. Such efforts have been particularly effective with populations where oral traditions prevail, where illiteracy is widespread and among groups who do not traditionally have a 'public' voice, such as women, squatter communities, or marginalized ethnic and tribal groups. Video is an accessible technology; it is relatively low-cost, portable and provides the immediacy of an audiovisual image. This tool attempts to demystify video technology. Uses of video in the context of social change and development include:

- As a reflection tool for raising awareness and building confidence among women and men.
- Training, education and information.
- Horizontal communications between NGOs, villages, and projects.
- 'Communicating up' with policymakers at national, regional or international level.
- Monitoring, documenting and advocacy.

Materials

Camcorder, video cassette recorder, film, props.

Process
Step 1: Think about the What, Why, Who, When, Where and How questions.

Make a plan for use, dissemination and evaluation. How will you use the video? Does it need an introduction or discussion afterwards? Are there other materials (print, pictures) that will go along with the video? How will you measure its effectiveness? Is it feasible? Is it a good idea? (See Video I: Developing a Community Project.)

Step 2: Develop a script
Message: What is the main message you want to communicate and your objective in communicating that message?
Content: What information will be included in the video? What is the logical way to present that information?
Audience: Whom do you want to reach with the video? What effect do you want the video to have?
Format: What is the best way to convey the message and the information to your primary audience (interview, drama)? What is the point of view?
Get feedback from the target audience.

Step 3: Pre-production planning
Choose and visit the places where you will be shooting; make a shooting schedule and arrange all equipment and props.

Step 4: Production
Rehearse with participants and crew on location. Consider lighting and try to avoid back-lighting. Be aware of sounds you do and do not want. Know where the action will be. Consider the best places to put the camera. Practise timing of the scene. Practise cues and communications. Be prepared for action in the scene. Shoot the video.

Step 5: Post-production
Play the video. Make a time log of the footage and note which are good and bad scenes. Write a script for editing that will tell you where to find those scenes you want to include. Record any additional sound and complete the edit.

Step 6: Screen the video to an audience
Test the video on an audience to make sure that message and content are clear and that it has the effect you want. Share the tape with participants for their comments.

See also
Video I: Developing a Community Project
Chapter 5
Advocacy Planning

Example
Village video workshops, Trichy District, Tamil Nadu, India

Elizabeth Fabel

The Association for Rural Education and Development Services (AREDS), an NGO working in Tamil Nadu in non-formal education, health care, and institution building, has long used street theatre, song and dance to stimulate discussion on a number of issues. With the invasion of television and video into villages in the past five years, AREDS felt the need to recapture rural people's attention with video dramas that reflect their reality and the value of local culture. I designed three one-week workshops in Development Communications and Participatory Video to train AREDS literacy workers, village facilitators and health workers in basic video production.

The technology we used was a single home video recorder and cassette recorder. No additional lighting, sound or editing equipment were used to produce the videos. I introduced 'In-camera editing' along with scripting techniques as a way to tell a story by collapsing events or processes that happen over time and space. In-camera editing involves shooting a video in sequence by stopping and starting the camera. This precludes the need for editing. The key to in-camera editing is careful scripting and planning with attention to the logical sequence of images and sound, the pacing and variety of shots. In this way, a finished piece can be made in a short time. Editing decisions are either predetermined or made on the spot and can be controlled by the people involved in making the video.

In choosing techniques, we assumed that a simple, low-cost and fast production process, requiring intensive rather than extensive training, would be most appropriate given the time constraints and multiple responsibilities of fieldworkers and members of the community. Also, we considered realism and the ability of the viewer to identify with the story as key to engaging the viewer beyond the level of entertainment.

Participants in the workshops produced a series of village video dramas using local actors and focusing on literacy, landlessness, non-formal education, collective action and political participation. As a series, the eight village video dramas represent a range of issues with which participants grapple daily. They encapsulate and depict processes of struggle, learning and empowerment in a way that affirms experience but also calls for continued action and education. Rather than emulating cinema, television, or ethnographic videos, participants created videos in the spirit of street theatre while taking advantage of the authority of the video medium.

To gauge the effectiveness of these videos for stimulating discussion and reflection of village reality, the video dramas were screened in four villages. The fact that the content of the videos was based on local events and issues and that local people represented themselves in the videos was critical to the credibility of the videos to local audiences. As one woman said, 'This is our village and our people we are seeing here. It is not a movie; it is like a real story to us... We can understand this video, because it is our own people speaking in our own language.' The production and screening of village video dramas revealed the expressive capacities of rural women and men as they acted out their collective struggles and told their own stories.

The empowerment of local teachers and learners as media-makers, actors and change agents along with the actual production of village video dramas were the outcomes of this workshop. Based on a participatory evaluation of AREDS' four-month experience with video, we generated a few ideas about how to apply video to AREDS' work:

- Confidence building among women's groups through video letters to strengthen links among these groups and between them and outside groups.
- Strengthening communication skills in the context of non-formal education.
- General education about health issues.

Although video cannot replace the value of indigenous forms of communication or of human interaction, it can be an effective tool for engaging people around the discussion of local issues and for revealing a dynamic local culture. Because of its accessibility and immediacy, video has been shown to be an effective tool for grassroots and bottom-up communication, particularly when put in the hands of the people themselves.

The use of video as a participatory tool was pioneered by Martha and Sara Stuart who introduced video to the Self-Employed Women's Association (SEWA) in Ahmedabad, India. They demonstrated that non-literate women can not only master the technology, but can be effective and articulate communicators in this medium. Perhaps more important, the process of becoming video-literate proved to be a very empowering experience for the women in itself. Video has been taken up by a limited number of NGOs around the world as a tool for training, health and literacy education, and formal skills transfer and by Northern NGOs as a tool for global education and cross-cultural communication.

Wealth Ranking

Adapted by Dale Shields and Rachel Slocum from *Wealth Ranking in Smallholder Communities*[76]

> **Time**
> Approximately one day for every 100 households.

Purpose

Once a facilitator has established wealth criteria and is able to see who is in what socio-economic layer, she/he can better understand the local power structure, decision-making processes, access to and control over resources. Wealth ranking[77] is also useful to determine how a particular action might affect or has affected people of different economic groups.

Materials

Pieces of paper or small cards upon which household names will be written.

Process

Step 1: Choose four or five key informants from the community to do the exercise. The informants should be people who have lived in the community for a long time and who know most if not all of the residents. They should represent a cross-section of the community along social and environmental lines which might include age, gender, ethnicity, agro-ecological zone, kin affiliation and religion.

Step 2: Since the concept of 'household' varies between cultures and communities, meet separately or individually with your informants to discuss how they define this concept. There may be confusion because of a variety of subdivisions like neighbourhoods, residential compounds, and independent households within the compounds or extended families. The difficulty of how to deal with married children living with their parents may be raised. In previous research, they have been listed as dependents and numbered as, for example, household 20 for the parents and 20A for a dependent. The cards were then kept together and it was up to the informant to group them together or separately. Try to develop a consensus on the definition of the household, but if a consensus cannot be reached, take note of the differences in your research design.

Step 3: Obtain a list of all the households in the community from one of your informants or another local source such as a village leader (most often a local source is more accurate than census data because they are aware of new arrivals).

Step 4: Write the names of all the households on pieces of paper. If the community is too large to include all the households in the exercise, then choose a random sample.

Step 5: Meet individually with each informant. Read off the cards one by one and have the informant form piles representing different relative levels of well-being between the households.

Step 6: When all the cards have been put in a pile, read off the households in each pile giving the informant the chance to review where each has been placed. Informants may want to move some cards from one pile to another or divide a group in two. As a rule, no pile should contain more than 40 per cent of the households.

Step 7: Discuss the characteristics associated with each pile the informant has made and the reasons for assigning a household to a particular cluster. In general, it may be easier for informants to discuss first the characteristics of the groups to which they do not belong. Indicators of wealth may include the availability of labour, the amount of land, the number and types of animals, higher educational levels, money for inputs or savings, and more well-developed social relationships. Before leaving the interview, record what households were in what piles.

Step 8: After leaving the interview, calculate an average score for each household for that interview. If there are five piles and the piles are numbered 1 to 5 from richest to poorest households, a household in the fifth or richest pile would have a score of 1/5. Multiply this by the number of households in the sample (100 in this case) and round off if necessary, for score of 20. A household in the fourth pile receives a score of 4/5 x 100 = 80.

Step 9: After all the interviews have been done, calculate an average score for each household. Add up the scores given to each household by all the informants and divide by the total number of rankings given to that household. If there were five informants and three gave a household the score of 80 and two gave it a 70 (as calculated above) then its average score would be 80 + 80 + 80 + 70 + 70 = 380/5 = 76.

Step 10: With these average scores for each household, group them loosely into wealth strata. Formulate the strata utilizing your knowledge of the wealth ranking criteria used by your informants combined with the average scores you have generated. To use absolute scores would represent a false degree of accuracy. Three lev-

215

els (rich, average, poor) are typically sufficient, but not always. The number of households in each stratum should be roughly equal or, if this is not possible, the middle group should include the most households. This should give you a stratified sample of your community. If possible confirm your results with your informants.

> ## Remember
> Some of this information may be very sensitive.
> ## See also
> Activities, Resources and Benefits Analysis
> Social Network Mapping

Example
Wealth Ranking on Siquijor Island, The Philippines

Dale Shields

For Wealth Ranking in two barangays, Napo and Tubod, on Siquijor Island, the ECOGEN research team from Clark University and the Visayas State College of Agriculture used the following steps.

Through discussions with local informants, we first determined how people in the two communities defined the household since the ranking needs to apply to the household as a unit.

We met with the leadership in each barangay and obtained from each of them a list of households, in each case approximately 160. We then chose a random sample from this list. Between 50 and 70 names seemed to be a good sample size. The names took our informants about 30 minutes to sort. With more cards people grew weary and did not have energy for discussion. The best exercises did not run to more than about one hour. Another hint: some of our informants did not recognize the formal names of many of their neighbours on the cards they sorted during the exercise. It would be helpful to ask an informant ahead of time (or your first informant) to help write some nicknames on the cards.

When selecting informants, we were quite concerned about two issues: the risk of the community responding negatively to an exercise that asked them to talk about their neighbours and the possible consequences for the rest of the research; and that in trying to minimize this risk we would bias our choice of Wealth Ranking informants towards people known to the team or towards the educated. We were also aware that we had to choose informants from a cross-section of the community for an exercise which was supposed to tell us just what such a cross-section looks like.

We decided that a field test using two people we knew and trusted in the community was appropriate. After they had completed the exercise and we had their feedback on the process, we then asked them to suggest others who would represent the categories they had sorted; include both men and women; and include the full range of agro-ecological zones. This approach seemed to work well and gave us a pool of informants to approach. We ended up needing this pool because not all suggested informants wanted to participate. We found this particularly true of the poorer members of the community and of women, especially those living alone. Although some of the hesitation was linked to being extremely busy, we also hypothesized that these sectors had more at stake if their neighbours found out they were talking with us about them. No matter how many times we assured them we were not interested in the stories of individuals, they were not satisfied, and although they participated, they shared only the bare minimum of the information.

Male informants, on the other hand, seemed quite willing to speak up, although we did note a similar class effect. The richest and the poorest men were hesitant to make public judgements about the personal end of the spectrum, while those in the middle range were the most talkative. A rich man hesitated to say why the rich were rich; and the poor man was quick to point out the richest but then lumped all the rest of the households into one 'poor' category. The most comprehensive description of the stratification came from a wealthy female councilwoman.

On Siquijor, the tendency was for people to describe everyone as poor. We told the informants that yes, this was true, when the community was compared to the rich in other countries, but that in order to understand all the problems in the community, we needed to know about the different problems of rich and poor households and those in between as they compared to each other. We asked them only to group people, and not to provide sensitive information such as amount of land or income. If an informant seemed reluctant or ill at ease, it was best to ask another.

Actual informant ranking

Following Barbara Grandin's directions, we met in separate sessions with each informant, asking him or her to put the cards in a series of piles representing households of similar circumstances. The informants decided how many piles they wanted to make. If the informant was not sure of a name or a household, that card was put aside. If the informant hesitated, we encouraged him/her not to rank that card: no information is better than guesswork.

Once the cards were sorted, it was easiest to begin with the richest group, asking not about specific households, but rather what the members of this group have in common. What makes them rich? This was repeated for each pile. If the informant wanted to give information about individual household circumstances, we had to rephrase the question to 'What do the households in this pile have in common?'

Who Am I?

Adapted by Rachel Slocum from *Women Working Together for Personal, Economic, and Communtiy Development* and *Tool Book: Gender Analysis and Training*[78]

Time
One hour.

Purpose

Raising awareness about one's identity enables women and men to reflect on their lives, critically analyse and evaluate their experiences, and appreciate the possibility of transforming their lives.

Materials

Large sheets of paper, markers, cards of four different colours.

Process

This exercise is best done in all women's or all men's groups. Afterwards, the participants may want to discuss what they have learned in a mixed group.

Step 1: Ask participants to make a list (or lists) of their roles at home, at work and in their communities. One variation is to ask men, for example, what roles women have and then pose the same questions listed below.

Step 2: On the cards, divide the roles participants have listed according to:

- Which of these roles or responsibilities did you choose yourself? (green)
- Which do you have to fulfil because of your gender – given to you without choice? (blue)
- Which roles or responsibilities do you like? (red)
- Which do you dislike? (yellow)

Discuss as well:

- Who decided you have to fill this role? Why?
- What would it take to change roles or responsibilities you dislike?
- Are there roles you would like to have or things you would like to do that you

cannot do now?

- Who has more roles or responsibilities that are chosen and more that are given? Why?
- What responsibilities do you have now that you did not have before?
- What roles and responsibilities did your parents have that you do not have?

Step 3: Attach the cards from each group to a wall or to a display board, ask for a volunteer to present the results to a mixed group and discuss.

Remember

For best results, try to combine this activity with another that is more concrete such as the preliminary work for a group problem-solving process.

See also

Gender Myths
Group Definition
Personal and Household Resources
Time Line Variations
Division of Labour

A poem by Honduran women in an Oxfam training manual written by and for women:[79]

If I don't know who I am,
If I don't know what my virtues are.
Or my strengths and abilities,
Then nor do I know
My weaknesses and shortcomings
I can't value myself for what I am,
I have no self respect, I don't even like myself.
I need to get to know myself
So that I can grow and develop as a person.
If I know myself better,
I can help other people.
And I'll be able
To help myself.

220

Examples

Getting to Know Myself: A women's educational programme in Honduras

Adapted by Luisa Maria Rivera Izabal from *Half the World, Half a Chance*[80]

Many women in Honduras live demanding and difficult lives. Unable to migrate to look for work on the banana and sugar plantations, many work tiny plots of marginal land in the mountainous regions of the western provinces. There they cultivate a subsistence crop of maize, beans, and the occasional coffee shrub. Woman-maintained households are common, yet land reform laws rarely favour women. From birth onwards girls imbibe the values of machismo culture and grow up believing that they were born to serve others – their children, their husbands and other menfolk. The socialization of rural women makes it extremely difficult for them to put their own needs first, or to even recognize that they have legitimate needs.

In 1985, an organization called the Women's Educational Programme (PAEM) began its work under the auspices of the Catholic Church. Its co-ordinator, Maria Esther Ruiz, came to believe that one of the main constraints on women grew out of the culture in which they were socialized, a constraint that lay first and foremost within their own minds: 'From when we're tiny they told us so often that we're stupid, that we ended up believing it ... Fear stops us thinking properly, so we make mistakes. It's fear that makes us get things wrong. It's not because we're stupid.' The consistent failure of 'projects for women' – whether welfare projects, income-generation or food-for-work projects – reinforces the same message: 'women are too stupid to want to improve themselves.'

The idea of producing a manual grew slowly over several years. We developed a methodology for working with small groups of semi-literate women. The group co-ordinator reads passages aloud and passes round photographs to encourage free discussion. The women begin to consider power relations which work against them but which they have always considered to be natural. A range of techniques, such as role play and group work, encourage the women and children to become fully involved.

Getting to Know Myself is essentially about enabling women to find a language with which to talk about shared experiences encoded in their gender role, their sexuality and the oppression they suffer because of it. It is a step in giving women back their right to themselves.

Knowing our roots: Eastern European immigrants to the north-east United States

David Glyn Nixon

Preliminary analysis of household interviews among descendants of Eastern European immigrants to the upper Connecticut River Valley in Massachusetts revealed several important dimensions of difference in people's experiences. One is that Eastern European men and women and their descendants experience and define ethnicity differently. Men experience ethnicity most strongly as an identity formed in clashes with governments and other peoples in Europe, so when a man was interviewed about himself as, say, a Ukrainian, he was often referring to his place in a historical struggle taking place in the old country. His relations with other people in the Valley, while not always harmonious, did not contribute to the formation of an ethnic consciousness to the same degree.

When one interviewed a woman, however, a different picture emerged. Women experienced ethnicity most strongly as an active struggle with people in the Valley. Slavic peoples imported a gender division of labour by which young women were sent out of the home to work as domestics in affluent Yankee households. There they had to care for Yankee children, while often lacking skills in English, and uncertain about cuisine and other New England customary preferences. Many of these women recounted their relations with dominant groups as being exploitative, disagreeable, and even frightening. Furthermore, marriage among Yankees and Eastern Europeans was exogamous, so young wives left their homes to live either with the husband alone or with his parents. These conflicts and tensions in women's lives created new forms of opposition and self-identity which were much more community-based than men's European-derived ethnic consciousness.

Who Decides?

Rachel Slocum

Time
Three hours.

Purpose

Who makes decisions at the household, organizational, or community level often depends on gender, status, age or other markers of identity. The elements of this tool are useful both to understand decision-making processes and to promote reflection on the degree of transparency and fairness in this process.

Materials

Pen and paper, two colours of powder paint for pie charts, markers, large sheet of paper (cassette recorder optional).

Process

Step 1: One option is to focus the discussion by choosing a specific problem or issue about which the group is concerned. Ask people to divide into groups by gender or other relevant categories.

Step 2: The following are possible questions that must be adapted to the context. Formulate more subtle questions depending on your objective.

Household decision-making

- What decisions do you make which are based on your particular responsibilities?
- What decisions do you make as a result of your gender (or other identities)?
- What decisions are you not allowed to make?
- Are there aspects of household life that you are responsible for but on which you do not make decisions?
- How are decisions you make similar to or different from those made by other family members?

- Who makes decisions on the use of which resources? Why?
- What information useful to the entire household is shared fully or partially?
- How are decisions made that will affect the entire family?

Community/organizational decision-making

- How is information shared?
- Which groups receive information sometimes, most of the time, always?
- How does access to information affect decision-making power?
- If you make a decision that will affect others, with whom do you discuss the options?
- Is the decision-making body representative of one, a few, or many interests in the group or community?
- Are there aspects of the decision-making process that you would like to change?
- How are decisions made?
- Who is involved? How?
- Who is not officially part of the process but is consulted?
- Does the decision-making body represent you?
- How is your group/organization connected to decision-makers in the community?
- How do you choose decision-makers?
- What positions in the organization do women and men hold?

Step 3: Bring the groups together and encourage a discussion on the points raised. Ask the men and women to draw a pie chart either jointly or separately. The circle can be left whole or divided into several sections to represent aspects of decision-making responsibilities. Give powders or paint to the women and men. Ask them to divide each section to indicate the overall level of involvement of men versus women in different aspects of decisions.

> **Remember**
> For discussion of organizational decision-making processes and transparency, separate groups into members and non-members of leadership bodies.
> Consider the effect of elites in the group discussion.
> Recognize hierarchies in the local decision-making process.

See also
Activities, Resources and Benefits Analysis
Group Definition
Problem Solving: Trees, Ranking, Assessment
Conflict Resolution I, II and III
Institutional Diagramming
Gender Analysis Activity Profile

Examples

Decision-making regarding responsibilities for Panchamganipatti water tank, Madurai, India

Nina Bhatt

Panchamganipatti is a scheduled caste village located near Madurai in South India. The village was part of a research project undertaken in 1992 by Ford Foundation and its South Indian grantees to investigate gender roles in participatory management of tank systems.

The Panchamganipatti water tank is a small rainfed system with two sluices and five distribution channels serving a command area of ten acres. Overall, formal participation by women in tank water management is absent although many of them are involved in a very active women's credit and savings group. This is partly because the Water Users' Association is restricted to farmers with title to land in the command area. In most cases title holders are men.

In an exercise to analyse decision-making in regard to tank management, men and women jointly drew a pie chart. The chart, in this instance, was divided into four quarters each representing one aspect of decision-making regarding water tank responsibilities:

- Tank water use.
- Physical work on the tank.
- Decision-making within the home about tank issues.
- Decision-making within the Water Users' Association about tank issues.

Men were given blue powder and women yellow. They were to divide each quarter to indicate the overall level of involvement of men *vis-à-vis* women in respect to the four categories.

The exercise revealed that decision-making power within and outside the home regarding tank issues was more or less equal. Women attend the WUA meetings although they are not formal members. Joint decision-making for tanks takes place within the household since issues such as cash payment for the tank, physical labour, and irrigation usage affect both men and women equally.

Differences did exist in the water use quarter where men were given more leverage. This was because the primary use of tank water is for agricultural purposes. In physical tank work, women were given more prominence as the ratio of women to men in physical work on this tank was 3 to 1.

Men and women had strong but differing views regarding tank work, representation and formal participation. Some women felt that WUA should be exclusively a men's group and stated that they would join if a separate women's group was formed. Others felt there was no need for the women of Panchamganipatti to form a group as they were already part of a credit group. Others mentioned they would join if the need arose and would carry out all the responsibilities that men currently undertake.

Men's responses about women's participation in tank decision-making differed greatly. At this particular tank men were mostly amenable to the idea of women formally participating or playing a greater, more active decision-making role. (This was not the case at other tanks.)

Issues concerning the relatively high ratio of women to men involved in the labour connected with tanks merited further investigation. We identified four issues arising at this and other tanks:

- Are women more involved in the physical labour on tanks because they constitute a cheaper form of labour and men's opportunity costs for tank work are greater?

- What are the implications of the high ratio of women to men labourers in tank work for women's decision-making roles, especially where physical labour is used for in-kind payment?

- Are women greatly displaced from their normal activities/sources of income by tank work or does it provide a source of income?

- What other issues surround the use of free and paid labour on the tanks, wage rates, and so on?

This exercise can bring out gender differences in resource use and perception of problems as well as gender differences in involvement in decision-making and in labour requirements. It can assist in addressing issues of gender inequities through sensitizing the community in this regard. It can enable the NGO to be more effective in building gender equity into its projects as it replicates them. These exercises can be useful for formative evaluation processes as well.

Decision-making in Pwani, Kenya[81]

Dianne Rocheleau

During a Participatory Rural Appraisal (PRA) exercise in Pwani, Kenya, residents identified water, fuelwood supply, lack of family planning services, low crop yields, livestock disease, transgression of the park boundary, poor road conditions, lack of healthcare facilities, lack of employment opportunities, and lack of a secondary school as the primary problems in their community. Water scarcity was regarded as the most pressing problem crossing class, gender and age lines. However, people experienced and ranked other problems differently. These differences, the power structures, the presence of outsiders, and the local decision-making process all affected what finally became the PRA Community Action Plan.

Discussion about problem definition and priority ranking involved more men than women and a disproportionate number of wealthier members of the community. Among these households, construction of a dam was the priority solution for the widely shared water problem. The PRA's village resource management plan also gave top priority to dam rehabilitation which implied a diversion of self-help group resources away from home water tanks and toward the dam as community infrastructure. The choice to give first priority to the dam was forged from the convergence of men in general as cattle owners, wealthy or influential women who already had water tanks and very poor women with little or no chance of building a home water tank through group efforts. The group which would have placed home tanks as the first priority were those women who did not yet have household tanks, but hoped to build them with group assistance in the near future.

Throughout the PRA problem-identifying process, women raised the issue of fuelwood scarcity but men tended to accord it low priority. In a PRA discussion, the relationship of fuelwood and gender issues was clearly demonstrated. The discussion took place in a church with officials, outsiders, the combined presence of women and men and a high proportion of wealthy and influential community members. This mixing of groups produced a struggle over the meaning of women's work, women's resources, and women's voices in public affairs relating to resource management.

Women generally favoured setting fuelwood as the second priority after water. The men, however, talked about roads and markets. By the end of the meeting, decision-makers had disregarded fuelwood needs and had listed a secondary school, roads, a hospital, and improved agriculture as the priorities. The hospital was derived from women's complaints about the lack of family planning services. 'Family planning' was renamed 'hospital' by the men.

The next day, community leaders and residents asked the PRA team and officials to let them meet alone to resolve the confusion of the previous day. After the meeting, community leaders announced that roads and a hospital were beyond the community's resources. They further noted that there is more to trees than fuel, such as timber, fodder, food, medicine, soil fertility, and soil conservation value. Thus was born the 'tree planting and tree protection' priority rather than the fuelwood problem and fuelwood solution. They included this priority within sustainable agriculture.

The distinct interests reflected in various water development options, in spite of a consensus on the problem, demonstrated the importance of proportional representation of different groups, by gender and class, in the overall community meetings. Alternatively, it may be more effective to determine priorities of distinct interest groups in separate sessions and to use a community-wide forum to negotiate the terms of joint or complementary efforts from these separate viewpoints. In either case, it is critical to determine the nature of the interest groups; the relative number of people in each group; and the nature of the interests at stake.

In the case of the fuelwood controversy, the dynamic set in motion by the presence of outsiders and the unusual nature of this forum had firmly separated participants in the room by gender. It became clear that the matter being discussed was not merely fuelwood, but rather women's place – in the household, in the landscape, and in community meetings. This experience also supports the need for separate meetings with distinct interest groups followed by careful negotiation of just solutions acceptable to all parties.

ENDNOTES

Preface

[1] Thomas-Slayter and Rocheleau, April 1994.

[2] We recognize the significant limitations of the terms North and South but prefer them to the Third World and First World which implies a hierarchy – first before third. We would like also to note that within all countries there exists a 'South' and 'North' where those in the figurative South are disenfranchised, subject to punitive measures, and cut off from a fair share of the resources available.

[3] We draw here on the distinction made by Kate Young between practical needs and strategic interests. See Young, 1993, p. 154. Young's analysis derives from Molyneux, 1985.

[4] Korten, 1989; Korten and Klass, 1984; Ghai, 1989; Escobar and Alvarez, 1992; Parajuli, Pramod, February 1991; Shiva, 1989 and 1994; Agarwal, 1988 and 1992; Mohanty, 1991.

Chapter 1

[1] For a discussion about participation in development processes, see Lisk, 1985; Chambers, 1983; Uphoff, 1986; Ghai and Vivian, 1992.

[2] Rocheleau, 1994, p. 1.

[3] Dei 1993, pp. 97-98.

[4] Esteva 1992, p. 10.

[5] Fowler, forthcoming, 1995.

[6] Rocheleau, 1994, p. 21.

[7] Martin, from Woodhill *et al.*,1991.

[8] Sharp, 1992.

[9] Thomas-Slayter and Rocheleau, 1994.

Chapter 2

[1] For a thorough discussion of the various types of local institutions and organizations, see Uphoff, 1986.

[2] Bergdall, 1993, p.7.

[3] Chambers, 1983; Korten, 1980; Korten and Klass, 1984; Cohen and Uphoff, 1977

[4] Cohen and Uphoff, 1977, p.6.

[5] Coady International Institute, 1989, p.17.

[6] Freire, 1970.

[7] Schumacher, 1973; Sachs, 1976.

[8] Uphoff, 1986; Uphoff, Cohen and Goldsmith, 1979; Uphoff and Esman, 1974.

[9] Korten, 1980, p.480.

[10] Korten and Klass, 1984; Chambers, 1974; Chambers *et al.*, 1989.

[11] Bergdall, 1993, p.13.

[12] Fals-Borda, 1991, p.4.

[13] Rahman, 1991, p.13.

[14] Polestico, 1988.

[15] Bergdall, 1993

[16] Chambers *et al.,* 1989; Conway, 1986.

[17] Chambers, 1994; Thomas-Slayter *et al.,* 1993.

[18] Hope and Timmel, 1984.

[19] Hope and Timmel, 1984. Book I, p.6.

[20] Philippine Partnership for the Development of Human Resources in Rural Areas (PhilDHRRA), 1993, p.3.

[21] MYRADA, August 7 and 8, 1990.

[22] MYRADA, no date, p.8.

[23] Moser, 1993; Braidotti *et al.,* 1994; Leach, 1994.

[24] See Kabeer, 1991; and Coady International Institute, 1989, p.9.

Chapter 3

[1] Escobar, 1992; Esteva, 1992; Shiva, 1988.

[2] Batterbury, 1994.

[3] Rocheleau and Malaret, 1987; Poats *et al.,* 1989; Chambers *et al.,* 1989; Fortmann, 1993.

[4] Rocheleau, 1994

[5] Stamp, 1989; Escobar, 1992; Sachs, 1992; Shiva, 1988; Esteva, 1992.

[6] For additional methods for determining local categories of wealth and well-being and who belongs to each group, see case studies of PRA by Ian Scoones and others at International Institute for Environment and Development and writings on wealth ranking by Barbara Grandin (1988, 1994).

[7] See Scoones and Thompson, 1994.

[8] Pradervand, 1989, p.190.

[9] Lecomte, 1986.

[10] Rocheleau, 1987; Rocheleau, 1988; Thomas-Slayter and Rocheleau, 1994.

[11] The CIP Manual and other articles by Rachel Polestico address the methods used in the land tenure reform project and gender consciousness-raising exercises with both men and women.

[12] Rocheleau, 1991.

[13] See Rocheleau, 1991 and 1994; and Davison, 1989 for discussions of oral histories and life histories in group and individual contexts.

Chapter 4

[1] Ostrom, 1990.

[2] Standard scholarly practice requires that I refer to her as Puerta, but this is a feminist reflection of feminist methods and the development of human connections and networks. In that spirit, I refer to her as Ivette.

[3] The Centre for Applied Social Sciences at the University of Zimbabwe has replicated this method and found it effective in communicating research findings.

[4] Whose extraordinary patience with my inexpertly preserved specimens I gratefully acknowledge.

[5] This is not to suggest that village researchers should not also be paid living wages. Obviously they should.

Chapter 5

[1] None of the terms used to designate the world's economically poorer societies is very satisfactory. None accounts for the enormous economic, political, and cultural differences among societies. For this discussion, 'the South' will be used as a general term for the world's economically poorer societies, with an acknowledgment that the term comes from a 'Northern' sense of what is 'developed'.

[2] Dowry is an illegal though widely practised custom in South Asia where the woman or her family gives money and/or presents to the prospective husband and his family at the time of marriage. The burden can be so great that families with daughters are bankrupted trying to get them married. Husbands seeking money often use violence or threats of divorce to extort more dowry from the wife or her family.

Chapter 6

[1] Auvine *et al.*, 1978, pp. 4-5.

[2] Shields, 1994, p. 95.

[3] Bergdall, 1993.

[4] Adapted from Francis, 1992.

[5] Francis, 1992, pp. 87-88.

[6] Thomas-Slayter *et al.*, 1993; Overholt *et al.* 1985.

[7] Buenavista and Flora, 1994, p. 27.

[8] From Bhatt *et al.*, 1994, p. 24.

[9] Adapted from Svendsen and Wijetilleke, 1983.

[10] Mda, 1993.

[10] Mda, 1993.

[12] Auvine *et al.*, 1978.

[13] Fisher, 1994.

[14] Adapted from Shields, 1994, p. 59.

[15] Fisher, 1994.

[16] Ford *et al.*, 1994.

[17] Ford *et al.*, 1994.

[18] Kreidler, 1993.

[19] Fisher and Ury, 1991.

[20] Carpenter and Kennedy, 1988, p. 91.

[21] Coover *et al.*, 1985.

[22] Thomas, 1994.

[23] See section on PRA/RRA, p.13.

[24] Ford *et al.*, 1992, p. 18.

[25] Flora, 1994, pp.63-64.

[26] Bilgi, 1992.

[27] GTZ/WID, forthcoming.

[28] Thomas-Slayter *et al.*, 1993, p. 12-13; Morgan, 1988.

[29] Morgan, 1988.

[30] Thomas-Slayter *et al.*, 1993; GTZ/WID, forthcoming.

[31] GTZ/WID, forthcoming.

[32] Moser, 1989.

[33] Kindon, 1993.

[34] The Bali Sustainable Development Project (BSDP) is a collaborative research endeavour between the Faculty of Environmental Studies, University of Waterloo in Canada and Gadjah Mada University in Yogyakarta with the assistance from Udayana University in Bali. The BSDP is part of the University Consortium on the Environment (UCE) project, an initiative funded by the Canadian International Development Agency (CIDA) through the Environmental Management Development in Indonesia (EDMI) Project.

[35] Rocheleau, 1987.

[36] Rocheleau, 1987.

[37] Rocheleau, 1987, p. 60.

[38] Georges, 1981; Rocheleau 1984; 1988.

[39] Rocheleau, 1988.

[40] Georges, Eugenia, 1981 (personal communication); Rocheleau, 1988.

[41] Fernandez, 1989.

[42] Sumberg and Okali, 1989.

[43] Rocheleau and Ross, 1995.

[44] Thomas-Slayter *et al.*, 1993.

[45] Thomas-Slayter *et al.*, 1993.

[46] Urban and Rojas, 1993, p. 35.

[47] Urban and Rojas, 1993, p. 35.

[48] Rocheleau and Ross, 1995.

[49] Svendson and Wijetilleke, 1983.

[50] Agimba *et al.*, 1994; Schuler and Kadirgamar-Rajasingham, 1992.

[51] Agimba *et al.*, 1994, p. 24.

[52] Schuler and Kadirgamar-Rajasingham, 1992.

[53] *Devadasi* refers to women who have practised prostitution as a consequence of certain traditional and historical factors; *adivasi* refers to the indigenous people of South Asia; and scheduled castes are groups which have historically been disadvantaged.

[54] D'Cunha, 1986.

[55] First published in Agimba *et al.*, 1994.

[56] Translation from Hindi by Shalini Nataraj, Programme Associate for India, Unitarian Universalist Service Committee. Ghad Kshetra Mazdur Morcha translates as Ghad Region Workers' Union.

[57] Coover *et al.*, 1985.

[58] Anderson and Jack, 1991, p. 24.

[59] Anderson and Jack, 1991, p. 25.

[60] Two geographers from the United States – both women – and one forester and one historian from the Dominican Republic – both men.

[61] Svendsen and Wijetilleke, 1983.

[62] Thomas-Slayter *et al.*, 1993; National Environment Secretariat *et al.*, 1988.

[63] Thomas-Slayter *et al.*, 1995. Polestico *et al.*, unpublished.

[64] Adapted from Rocheleau *et al.*, 1991.

[65] National Environment Secretariat *et al.*, 1988.

[66] Feldstein and Poats, 1989.

[67] Shields *et al.*, 1993, p.21.

[68] *Deutsche Gesellschaft fur Technische Zusammenarbeit* (German Agency for Technical Co-operation, GTZ)

[69] *Deutsche Gesellschaft fur Technische Zusammenarbeit* (German Agency for Technical Co-operation, GTZ).

[70] Technique used by ACORD Mali and described by Saoudata Maiga.

[71] National Environment Secretariat *et al.*, 1988, pp.18-20.

[72] This research was undertaken collaboratively by the Institute for Integrated Development Studies (IIDS) in Kathmandu and Clark University through the ECOGEN project.

[73] Bhatt *et al.*, 1994, p.8.

[74] Poffenberger, 1993. Figure 12, p. 41.

[75] Stuart, 1990.

[76] Grandin, 1988.

[77] Wealth Ranking is a very effective way to determine socio-economic groupings in a com-

munity by measuring households. However, it is more difficult to determine whether the men and women of a household separately fall into the same economic category as the whole household. First, women and men may have different criteria for measuring wealth. Second, research has shown that household resources are not shared equally among men and women, boys and girls. Also, it is sometimes true that women are not remunerated commensurate to their contribution to household resources. If one uses Wealth Ranking to categorize the inhabitants of a community as part of an evaluation to see what project resources reach whom and the data reveals that the rich benefit the most, this does not answer the question of whether the project equally benefits rich men and rich women. Wealth Ranking by gender disaggregated groups might reveal additional information concerning these issues, although it may be more difficult to obtain.

[78] Kindervatter, 1987; GTZ/WID forthcoming.

[79] Mosse, 1993, pp. 179-180.

[80] Mosse, pp. 180-181.

[81] Rocheleau *et al.*, 1991.

Bibliography

Agarwal, Bina. 1992. 'Gender Relations and Food Security: Coping with Seasonality, Drought, and Famine in South Asia,' in Lourdes Beneria and Shelley Feldman (eds)*Unequal Burden, Economic Crises, Persistent Poverty, and Women's Work*. Boulder, Colorado: Westview Press.

Agarwal, Bina. 1988. 'Neither Sustenance Nor Sustainability: Agricultural Strategies, Ecological Degradation and Indian Women in Poverty,' in Kali for Women (eds). *Structures of Patriarchy. The State, The Community, and The Household*. New Dehli: Kali for Women. pp. 83-120.

Agarwal, Bina. 1986. *Cold Hearths and Barren Slopes: The Woodfuel Crisis in the Third World*. New Delhi: Allied Publishers, Ltd.

Agimba, Christine, Florence Butegwa, Grace Osakue and Sydia Nduna. 1994. *Legal Rights Awareness Among Women in Africa*. Harare: Zimbabwe: Women in Law and Development in Africa (WILDAF).

Anderson, Kathryn and Dana C. Jack. 1991. 'Learning to Listen: Interview Techniques and Analyses,' in Sherna Berger Gluck and Daphne Patai (eds). *Women's Words: The Feminist Practice of Oral History*. New York: Routledge.

Anglin, Mary K. 1993. 'Engendering the Struggle: women's labor and traditions of resistance in rural southern Appalachia,' in Stephen Fisher (ed.) *Fighting Back in Appalachia: Traditions of Resistance and Change*. Philadelphia: Temple University Press.

Auvine, Brian, Betsy Densmore, Mary Extrom, Scott Poole, and Michel Shanklin. 1978. *A Manual for Group Facilitators*. Madison, WI: The Center for Conflict Resolution.

Barndt, Deborah, Ferne Cristall and Dian Marino. 1982. *Getting There: Producing Photostories with Immigrant Women*. Toronto: Between the Lines Press.

Barndt, Deborah. July 1977. 'Just Getting There'. Working paper 7. Participatory Research Group. Toronto: International Council for Adult Education.

Barndt, Deborah. July 1977. 'Visual Interventions in a Participatory Research Process: How a Camera Can Enrich Interaction and Inquiry'. North American Regional Participatory Research Team.

Batterbury, Simon. April 1994. 'Changing Ecological and Social Dynamics of Mossi Livelihood Systems: Assessing the impacts of soil and water conservation and "village land use management" schemes.' Paper presented to the Annual Meeting of the Association of American Geographers. San Francisco.

Bergdall, Terry D. 1993. *Methods for Active Participation, Experiences in Rural Development from East and Central Africa.* Nairobi: Oxford University Press.

Bhatt, Nina. August 1992. Evaluation projects in South India funded by the Ford Foundation. New Delhi: Ford Foundation, unpublished report.

Bhatt, Nina, Indira Koirala, Barbara Thomas-Slayter, and Laju Shrestha. 1994. *Managing Resources in a Nepalese Village: Changing Dynamics of Gender and Ethnicity.* ECOGEN/ SARSA case study. Worcester: Clark University.

Bilgi, Meena. 1992. 'A PRA in Boripitha Netrang'. The Aga Khan Rural Support Programme, Ahmedabad.

Braidotti, Rosi, Ewa Charkiewicz, Sabine Hausler, and Saskia Wieringa. 1994. *Women, the Environment and Sustainable Development Towards a Theoretical Synthesis.* London: Zed Books.

Buenavista, Gladys and Cornelia Flora. 1994. *Surviving Natural Resources Decline: Explaining Intersections of Class, Gender and Social Networks in Agbanga, Leyte, Philippines.* An ECOGEN Case Study. Blacksburg: Virgina Polytech and State University.

Burbidge, John (ed.) 1988. *Approaches that Work in Rural Development.* Munich: K. G. Saur, Inc.

Carpenter, Susan L. and W.J.D. Kennedy. 1988. *Managing Public Disputes.* London: Jossey-Bass Publishers.

Chambers, Robert. 1994. 'Participatory Rural Appraisal (PRA): Challenges, Potentials and Paradigms.' in *World Development.* Vol. 22, No. 10.

Chambers, Robert. 1983. *Rural Development: Putting the Last First.* Harlow: Longman.

Chambers, Robert. 1980. *Rural Appraisal: Rationale and repertoire.* Brighton: Institute of Development Studies.

Chambers, Robert. 1974. *Managing Rural Development: Ideas and Experience from East Africa.* Uppsala: The Scandinavian Institute of African Studies.

240

Chambers, Robert, A. Pacey, and L.A Thrupp. (eds). 1989. *Farmer First: Farmer Innovation and Agricultural Research.* London: Intermediate Technology Publications.

Chidari, Gift, Francisca Chirambaguwa, Patricia Mastsvimbo, Anna Mhiripiri, Hilda Chanakira, James Chanakira, Xavier Mutsvangzwa, Angeline Mvumbe, Louise Fortmann, Robert Drummond, and Nontokozo Nabane. 1992. 'The Use of Indigenous Trees in Mhondoro District.' NRM Occasional Paper 5. 120pp. Centre for Applied Social Sciences, University of Zimbabwe.

Coady International Institute. 1989. *A Handbook for Social/Gender Analysis.* Ottawa: Social and Human Resources Development Division, Canadian International Development Agency.

Cohen, John and Norman Uphoff. 1977. *Rural Development Participation: Concepts and Measures for Project Design, Implementation and Evaluation.* Ithaca: Cornell University.

Conway, Gordon. 1986 *Agroecosystem Analysis for Research and Development.* Bangkok: Winrock International Institute.

Coover, Virginia, Ellen Deacon, Charles Esser, Christopher Moore. 1985. *Resource Manual for a Living Revolution: A Handbook of Skills and Tools for Social Change Activists.* Philadelphia: New Society Publishers.

Cornwall, Andrea, Irene Guijt and Alice Welbourn. 1994. 'Acknowledging Process: Challenges for Agricultural Research and Extension Methodology.' in Ian Scoones and John Thompson (eds). *Beyond Farmer First: Rural People's Knowledge, Agricultural Research and Extension Practice.* London: Intermediate Technology Publications.

Cunningham, James and Milton Kolter. 1983. *Building Neighborhood Organizations. A guidebook sponsored by the National Association of Neighborhoods.* Notre Dame: University of Notre Dame Press.

Davison, Jean. 1989. *Voices from Mutira: Lives of Rural Gikuyu Women.* Boulder, CO: Lynne Rienner Publishers.

Davison, Jean. (ed) 1988. *Agriculture, Women, and Land: The African Experience.* Boulder, Colorado: Westview Press.

D'Cunha, Jean. 1986. ' The Suppression of Immoral Traffic in Women and Girls Act. 1956: A Critical Review.' Bombay: Research Centre for Women's Studies SNDT Women's University Working Paper 13.

Dei, George J.S. 1993. 'Sustainable Development in the African Context: Revisiting Some Theoretical and Methodological Issues.' *African Development*, V. 18, 2, p. 97-110.

Escobar, Arturo, and Sonia Alvarez. (eds). 1992. *The Making of Social Movements in Latin America: Identity, Stratification and Democracy.* Boulder: Westview Press.

Escobar, Arturo. 1992. 'Culture, Economics and Politics in Latin American Social Movements Theory and Research' in Arturo Escobar and Sonia Alvarez (eds). *The Making of Social Movements in Latin America*. Boulder: Westview Press.

Esteva, Gustavo. 1992. 'Development' in Wolfgang Sachs (ed.). *The Development Dictionary.* New York: Zed Books. p. 6-25.

Fals-Borda, Orlando and Muhammad Anisur Rahman. 1991. *Action and Knowledge: Breaking the Monopoly with Participatory Action-Research.* London: Intermediate Technology Publicationsand New York: Apex Press.

Feldstein, Hilary Sims and Susan V. Poats. 1989. *Working Together*. West Hartford: Kumarian Press.

Fernandez, Maria. 1989. 'Participatory Technology Validation in Highland Communities of Peru' in Robert Chambers (ed.) *Farmer First: Farmer innovation and agricultural research.* London: Intermediate Technology Publications.

Finnegan, Ruth. 1992. *Oral Traditions and the Verbal Arts*. London: Routledge.

Fisher, Roger. 1994. *Beyond Machiavelli: Tools for Coping with Conflict.* Cambridge, MA: Harvard University Press.

Fisher, Robert and Joseph Kling (eds). 1993. *Mobilizing the Community: local politics in the era of the global city.* London: Sage Publications.

Fisher, Roger and William Ury. 1991. *Getting to YES*. New York: Penguin Books.

Fisher, Stephen (ed.). 1993. *Fighting Back in Appalachia: traditions of resistance and change.* Philadelphia: Temple University Press.

Flora, Cornelia. 1994. 'Using Focus Groups with Rural Women' in Hilary Sims Feldstein and Janice Jiggins (eds). *Tools for the Field.* West Hartford, CT: Kumarian Press and London: Intermediate Technology Publications. pp.63-64.

Ford, Richard, Hussein Adam, Adan Yusuf Abubaker, Ahmed Farah and Osman Hirad Barre. 1994. *PRA with Somali Pastoralists: Building Community Institutions for Africa's Twenty-First Century*. Worcester, MA: Clark University.

Ford, Richard, Francis Lelo, Chandida Monyadzwe, and Richard Kashweeka. 1993. *Managing Resources with PRA Partnerships: A Case Study of Lesoma, Botswana*. Worcester, MA: Clark University.

Ford, Richard, Charity Kabutha, Nicholas Mageto and Karafa Manneh. 1992. *Sustaining Development through Community Mobilization: A Case Study of Participatory Rural Appraisal in the Gambia*. Worcester, MA: Clark University.

Fortmann, Louise. 1993. 'Learning from People, Learning With People, Empowering People with Research'. A paper presented to the Annual Meeting of the Rural Sociological Society. August 9, Orlando, Florida.

Fortmann, Louise and Dianne Rocheleau. 1985. 'Women and Agroforestry: Four Myths and Three Case Studies'. *Agroforestry Systems*. 2: 253-272.

Fowler, Alan. 1995. *State, NGOs and People's Organizations in Service Provision in East Africa*. Unpublished manuscript.

Fowler, Alan. 1993. 'Democracy, Development and NGOs in Sub-Saharan Africa: Where Are We?' *Democracy and Development*. 7 November. p. 1-19.

Fowler, Alan. 1992. 'Building Partnerships Between Northern and Southern Development NGOs: Issues for the 90s.' *Development*, Journal of the Society for International Development: 1 p. 16-23.

Francis, Elizabeth. 1992. 'Qualitative Research: Collecting Life Histories.' in Stephen Devereux and John Hoddinott (eds). *Fieldwork in Developing Countries*. Boulder: Lynne Rienner Publishers.

Freire, Paulo. 1970. *The Pedagogy of the Oppressed*. New York: Herder and Herder.

Ghai, Dharam, 1989. 'Participatory Development: Some Perspectives from Grass-Roots Experiences,' *Journal of Development Planning*. 19.

Ghai, Dharam, and Jessica Vivian. 1992. *Grassroots Environmental Action: People's Participation in Sustainable Development*. London: Routledge.

Grandin, Barbara E. 1988. *Wealth Ranking in Smallholder Communities*. London: Intermediate Technology Publications.

Grandin, Barbara E. 1994. 'Wealth Ranking' in Hilary Sims Feldstein and Janice Jiggins (eds). *Tools for the Field*. West Hartford: Kumarian Press and London: Intermediate Technology Publications.

GTZ/WID Project. Cairo, Egypt. *Tool Book: Gender Analysis and Training*. (forthcoming).

Harries-Jones, Peter (ed.). 1991. *Making Knowledge Count: Advocacy and Social Science*. Montreal: McGill Queens University Press.

Hope, Anne and Sally Timmel. 1984. *Training for Transformation: A Handbook for Community Workers*. Gweru, Zimbabawe: Mambo Press.

ILO Co-operative Project. 1993. *Gender Awareness Manual*. Jakarta, Indonesia.

Kabeer, Naila. 1991. 'Gender Dimensions of Rural Poverty: Analysis from Bangaladesh.' *The Journal of Peasant Studies* 18(21):241-261.

Kapur, Ratna. 1992. 'From Theory to Practice: Reflections on Legal Literacy Work with Women in India.' in Schuler, Margaret and Sakuntala Kadirgamar-Rajasingham (eds). *Legal Literacy: A Tool for Women's Empowerment*. New York: UNIFEM. pp. 93-111.

Kindervatter, Suzanne. 1987. *Women Working Together for Personal, Economic and Community Development*. 2nd ed. Washington, DC: Overseas Education Fund (OEF International).

Kindon, Sara Louise. 1993. 'From Tea Makers to Decision Makers: Applying Participatory Rural Appraisal to Gender and Development in Rural Bali, Indonesia'. University Consortium on the Environment Publication Series. Student Paper 16.

Korten, David. 1989. *Getting to the 21st century*. West Hartford: Kumarian Press.

Korten, David. 1980. 'Community Organization and Rural Development: A Learning Process Approach,' *Public Administration Review*, September-October, 1980. pp. 480-510.

Korten, David, and R. Klass. 1984. *People-Centered Development: Contributions Toward Theory and Planning Development*. West Hartford: Kumarian Press.

Kreidler, William. 1993. 'Creating Peaceable Classrooms: Conflict Resolution in Schools.' Cambridge, MA: Boston Area Educators for Social Responsibility.

Leach, Melissa. 1994. *Rainforest Relations: Gender and Resource Use among the Mende of Gola, Sierra Leone.* Washington, D.C.: Smithsonian Institution Press.

Lecomte, Bernard. 1986. *Project Aid – Limits and Alternatives*. Paris: OECD.

Lisk, Franklyn (ed.). 1985. *Popular Participation in Planning for Basic Needs.* New York: St. Martin's Press.

Manning-Miller, Don. 1993. 'Racism and Organizing in Appalachia,' in Stephen Fisher (ed.). *Fighting Back in Appalachia: Traditions of Resistance and Change.* Philadelphia: Temple University Press.

Mda, Zakes. 1993. *When People Play People: Development Communication Through Theatre*. Johannesburg:Witwatersrand University Press and London: Zed Books.

Mohanty, Chandra, Ann Russo and Lourdes Torres. (eds). 1991. *Third World Women and the Politics of Feminism.* Bloomington: Indiana University Press.

Mohanty, Chandra. 1991. 'Cartographies of Struggle, Third World Women and the Politics of Feminism' in Chandra Mohanty, Ann Russo and Lourdes Torres. (eds). *Third World Women and the Politics of Feminism.* Bloomington: Indiana University Press.

Morehouse, Ward (ed.) 1989. *Building Sustainable Communities*. New York: Intermediate Technology Group of North America.

Morgan, David L. 1988. *Focus Groups as Qualitative Research.* Newbury Park, CA: Sage Publications.

Moser, Caroline. 1993. *Gender Planning and Development, Theory, Practice and Training.* London: Routledge.

Moser, Caroline. 1989. 'Gender Planning in the Third World: Meeting Practical and Strategic Gender Needs.' *World Development*, 17 (11).

Mosse, Julia Cleves. 1993. *Half the World, Half a Chance.* Oxford, UK: Oxfam.
MYRADA. August 7 and 8, 1990 "A Review Workshop on Participatory Learning Methods". Bangalore: PRA-PALM Series No. 4, report on the workshop. p. 27.

MYRADA. No date. 'Sharing our Limited Experience: Participatory Rural Appraisal or Participatory Learning Methods'. Bangalore: PRA/PALM Series, No. 5, p.8.

National Environment Secretariat, Egerton University, Clark University, and Center for International Development and Environment of the World Resources Institute, 1988. *Participatory Rural Appraisal Handbook: Conducting PRAs in Kenya.* Washington, D.C.: World Resources Institute.

National Seminar for Post-Literacy. March 22-27, 1992. 'Community Publishing and Post-Literacy.' Nakuru, Kenya.

Odour-Noah, Elizabeth, Isabella Asamba, Richard Ford, Lori Wichhart and Francis Lelo. 1992. *Implementing PRA: A Handbook to Facilitate Participatory Rural Appraisal.* Worcester, MA: Clark University.

Ostrom, Elinor. 1990. *Governing the Commons: The Evolution of Institutions for Collective Action.* Cambridge: Cambridge University Press.

Overholt, Catherine, Mary B. Anderson, Kathleen Cloud and James E. Austin (eds). 1985. *Gender Roles in Development Projects.* West Hartford, CT: Kumarian Press.

Parajuli, Pramod. 1991. 'Power, Knowledge and Development Discourse: New Social Movements and the State in India'. *International Conflict Research*, 127, February 1991: 173-190.

Participatory Rural Appraisal Handbook. December 1992. National Environment Secretariat, Government of Kenya, Clark University, USA; Egerton Univeristy, Kenya; The Center for International Development and Environment of the World Resources Institute, USA.

Philippine Partnership for the Development of Human Resources in Rural Areas (PhilDHRRA). 1993. *A Manual on the Estate/Barangay-level Productivity Systems Assessment and Planning (PSAP) Methodology.* p.3.

Poats, Susan, Hilary Feldstein and Dianne Rocheleau. 1989. 'Gender and Intra-household analysis in On-Farm Research and Experimentation'. in Richard Wilk (ed.). *The Household Economy: Reconsidering the Domestic Mode of Production.* Boulder: Westview Press.

Poffenberger, Mark. 1993. *Communities and Forest Management in East Kalimantan.* Research Report Network, Number 3, August. Figure 12, p. 41.
Polestico, Rachel. 1988. *Framework and Operation of CIPS* Manila: Philippine Partnership for the Development of Human Resources in Rural Areas (PhilDHRRA).

Polestico, Rachel, Lose Cortez, Rosalina Enciso and the participants of the social awareness workshop, *Manual for Participatory Planning* for the Westy Program of the Archdiocese of Nueva Caceres. Unpublished.

Pradervand, Pierre. 1989. *Listening to Africa*. New York: Praeger.

Pretty, J. A. and I. Scoones (eds). 1989. Rapid Rural Appraisal for Economics: Exploring Incentives for Tree Management in Sudan. London: IIED.

Protz, Maria and Eleanora Cebotarev. 1993. 'Seeing and Showing Ourselves in Print'. Training Module for the CIDA Project, Regional Rural Women's Training, University of Guelph, Canada (p.109).

Puerta, Ivette and Robert L. Bruce. April 1972. 'Data Collection with Low-Income Respondents'. Paper presented at the Adult Education Research Conference, Chicago.

Rahman, Muhammad Anisur. 1991. 'The Theoretical Standpoint of PAR' in Fals-Borda and Rahman. *Action and Knowledge: Breaking the Monopoly with Participatory Action Research*. London: Intermediate Technology Publications and New York: Apex Press. p. 13.

Rahman, Muhammad Anisur. 1984. 'The Small Farmer Development Program of Nepal'. in Rahman (ed.) Grassroots Participation and Self-Reliance: Experience in South and East Asia. New Delhi: OUP. pp. 121-151.

Riano, Pilar (ed.) 1994. *Women in Grassroots Communication: Furthering Social Change*. Thousand Oaks, CA: Sage.

Rocheleau, Dianne. 1994. 'Participatory Research and the Race to Save the Planet: Questions, Critique, and Lessons from the Field.' *Agriculture and Human Values*: 11 (2,3) pp.4-25.

Rocheleau, Dianne. 1991. 'Gender, Ecology and the Science of Survival: Stories and Lessons from Kenya'. *Agriculture and Human Values*. 8 (1): 156-165.

Rocheleau, Dianne. 1987. 'The User Perspective and the Agroforestry Research and Action Agenda' in H. Gholz (ed.). *Agroforestry: Realities, Possibilities and Potentials*. Kluwer Dordrecht, the Netherlands: Academic Publishers.

Rocheleau, Dianne. 1988 'Gender, Resource Management and the Rural Landscape: Implications for Agroforestry and Farming Systems Research'. In S. Poats, M., Schmink, and A. Spring (eds). *Gender Issues in Farming Systems Research and Extension*,149-169. Boulder: Westview Press.

Rocheleau, Dianne. 1984. 'An Ecological Analysis of Soil and Water Conservation in Hillslope Farming Systems: Plan Sierra, Dominican Republic'. Ph.D. Dissertation. Department of Geography, University of Florida-Gainsville.

Rocheleau, Dianne, F. Weber and Alison Field-Juma. 1988. *Agroforestry in Dryland Africa.* Nairobi: International Council for Research in Agroforestry.

Rocheleau, Dianne and Laurie Ross. 1995. *Farming the Forests, Gardening with Trees: Landscapes and Livelihoods in Zambrana-Chacuey, Dominican Republic.* An ECOGEN/ SARSA Case Study. Worcester, MA: Clark University.

Rocheleau, Dianne, Karen L. Schofield and Njoki Mbuthi. 1991. *People, Property, Poverty and Parks: A Story of Men, Women, Water and Trees at Pwani.* An ECOGEN/SARSA Case Study. Worcester, MA: Clark University.

Rocheleau, Dianne, and Luis Malaret. 1987. 'Use of Ethnoecology in Agroforestry Systems Research'. in *How Systems Work: Selected proceedings of the Farming Systems Research Symposium.* Fayetteville and Morrillton: University of Arkansas and Winrock International.

Sabatier, Paul and Hank Jenkins-Smith (eds). 1993. *Policy Change and Learning: An Advocacy Coalition Approach.* Boulder: Westview Press.

Sachs, Wolfgang (ed.). 1992. *The Development Dictionary.* London: Zed Books.

Sachs, Ignacy. 1976. *The Discovery of the Third World.* Cambridge, MA: MIT Press.

Schuler, Margaret and Sakuntala Kadirgamar-Rajasingham. 1992. *Legal Literacy: A Tool for Women's Empowerment.* New York: UNIFEM.

Schumacher, E. F. 1973. *Small is Beautiful: Economics as if People Mattered.* New York: Perennial Library and London: Abacus.

Scoones, Ian, and John Thompson (eds). 1994. *Beyond Farmer First: Rural People's Knowledge, Agricultural Research and Extension Practice.* London: Intermediate Technology Publications.

Sharp, Gene. 1973 *The Politics of Nonviolent Action.* Boston: Porter Sargent.

Sharp, Robin. 1992. 'Organizing for Change: People-Power and the Role of Institutions' in Johan Holmberg (ed.) *Making Development Sustainable.* Washington, D. C.: Island Press.

Shields, Dale and Barbara P. Thomas-Slayter. 1993. *Gender, Class, Ecological Decline and Livelihood Strategies: A Case Study of Siquijor Island, The Philippines.* An ECOGEN/ SARSA Case Study. Worcester: Clark University.

Shields, Katrina. 1994. *In the Tiger's Mouth: An Empowerment Guide for Social Action.* Philadelphia, PA: New Society Publishers.

Shiva, Vandana. 1994. *Monocultures of the Mind: Understanding the Threats to Biological and Cultural Diversity.* Guelph, Ontario: Centre for International Programs, University of Guelph.

Shiva, Vandana. 1988. *Staying Alive.* London: Zed Books.

Stamp, Patricia. 1989. *Technology, Gender, and Power in Africa.* Ottawa: International Development Research Centre.

Stuart, Martha. 1990. *Video SEWA: A People's Alternative.* New York: Martha Stuart Communications.

Sumberg, J.E. and Christine Okali. 1989. 'Farmers, on-farm research and new technology' in Robert Chambers, A. Pacey, and Lori Ann Thrupp (eds). *Farmer First: Farmer Innovation and Agricultural Research.* London: Intermediate Technology Publications.

Svendsen Dian Sesler and Sujatha Wijetilleke. 1983. *Navamaga: Training Activities for Group Building, Health, and Income Generation.* Women's Bureau of Sri Lanka and OEF.

Thomas, Gwen. 1994. 'Central American NGOs: Their Role in the Environmental Policy Arena: Case Studies from Costa Rica, Guatemala, and Belize.' Report prepared for CARE, International. San Jose, Costa Rica.

Thomas, Gwen. 1994. 'Initiating Policy Change at the Grassroots: FUNDEMABV's Approach to Dialogue and Negotiation with the Timber Industry, Salama, Baja Verapaz, Guatemala' in *Central American NGOs: Their Role in the Environmental Policy Arena.* CARE: Proyecto Ambiental Para Centro America.

Thomas-Slayter, Barbara. 1989. 'Politics, Class and Gender in African Resource Management: The Case of Rural Kenya'. Boston University African Studies Center, Working Paper, and 1992 *Economic Development and Cultural Change* 40 (4):809-828.

Thomas-Slayter, Barbara, Rachel Polestico, Andrea Lee Esser, Octavia Tayler and Elvina Mutua. 1995. *The SEGA Manual: Responding to the Development Challenge.* ECOGEN/ SARSA: Clark University. Unpublished manuscript.

Thomas-Slayter, Barbara, Charity Kabutha and Richard Ford. 1993. 'Participatory Rural Appraisal: A Case Study from Kenya' in K. Kumar (ed.) *Rapid Appraisal Methods*. Washington DC: The World Bank. pp.176-211.

Thomas-Slayter, Barbara and Dianne Rocheleau. 1994. 'Essential Connections: Linking Gender to Effective Natural Resource Management and Sustainable Development'. Michigan State University. Women in Development Working Paper Series, 242, April 1994.

Thomas-Slayter, Barbara, Andrea Lee Esser, and M. Dale Shields. 1993. *Tools of Gender Analysis: A Guide to Field Methods for Bringing Gender into Sustainable Resource Management*. ECOGEN Research Project, International Development Program. Worcester, MA: Clark University.

Tripartite Partnership for Agrarian Reform and Rural Development. 1993. *A Manual on the Estate/Barangay-level Productivity Systems Assessment and Planning (PSAP) Methodology*. Quezon City: Philippine Partnership for the Development of Human Resources in Rural Areas (PhilDHRRA).

Uphoff, Norman. 1986. *Local Institutional Development: An Analytical Sourcebook with Cases*. West Hartford, Connecticut: Kumarian Press.

Uphoff, Norman, J. Cohen and Arthur Goldsmith. 1979. 'Feasibility and Application of Rural Development Participation: A State of the Art Paper'. Rural Development Committee, Center for International Studies: Cornell University.

Uphoff, Norman and Milton Esman. 1974. 'Local Organization for Rural Development: Analysis of Asian Experience'. Rural Development Committee, Center for International Studies: Cornell University.

Urban, Anne-Marie and Mary Rojas. 1993. *Shifting Boundaries: Gender, Migration, and Community Resources in the Foothills of Choluteca, Honduras*. An ECOGEN Case Study. Worcester, MA: Clark University.

Van der Hombergh, Heleen. 1993. *Gender, Environment and Development, A guide to the Literature*. Utrecht, the Netherlands: International Books.

Vincent, Fernand and Piers Campbell. 'Alternative Financing Strategies for NGOs in Critical Choices for the NGO Community: African Development in the 1990s'. Seminar Proceedings 30. University of Edinburgh, Scotland: Centre of African Studies.

Woodhill, James, Anne-Marie Wilson, and John McKenzie. 'Land Conservation and Social Change: Extension to Community Development – A Necessary Shift in Thinking.' Paper presented to the Seventh International Soil Conservation Conference, Sydney, Australia, September 27-30, 1992.

Young, Kate. 1993. *Planning Development with Women, Making a World of Difference.* London: Macmillan.